A LIVING CONSTITUTION
OR FUNDAMENTAL LAW?

A LIVING CONSTITUTION OR FUNDAMENTAL LAW?

American Constitutionalism in Historical Perspective

Herman Belz

ROWMAN & LITTLEFIELD PUBLISHERS, INC.
Lanham • Boulder • New York • Oxford

ROWMAN & LITTLEFIELD PUBLISHERS, INC.

Published in the United States of America
by Rowman & Littlefield Publishers, Inc.
4720 Boston Way, Lanham, Maryland 20706

12 Hid's Copse Road
Cumnor Hill, Oxford OX2 9JJ, England

British Library Cataloguing in Publication Information Available

Library of Congress Cataloging-in-Publication Data

Belz, Herman.
    A living constitution or fundamental law? : American constitutionalism
in historical perspective / Herman Belz.
        p.   cm.
    Includes bibliographical references and index.
    ISBN 0-8476-8642-6 (cloth : alk. paper). — ISBN 0-8476-8643-4
(pbk. : alk. paper)
    1. Constitutional history—United States.   I. Title.
KF4541.B44   1998
342.73'029—dc21   98-11843
                                                            CIP

Printed in the United States of America

⊚ ™ The paper used in this publication meets the minimum requirements of
American National Standard for Information Sciences—Permanence of Paper
for Printed Library Materials, ANSI Z39.48—1984.

Contents

Acknowledgments

I gratefully acknowledge permission to reprint the following chapters.

Chapter 1, "Constitutionalism and the American Founding," previously appeared in *The Framing and Ratification of the Constitution*, edited by Leonard W. Levy and Dennis J. Mahoney, © 1987 Macmillan. Reprinted by permission of the editor.

Chapter 2, "Constitutional Realism in the Gilded Age," originally appeared as "The Constitution in the Gilded Age: The Beginnings of Constitutional Realism in American Scholarship" in the *American Journal of Legal History* 13 (1969): 110–25. Reprinted by permission of the publisher.

Chapter 3, "The Critique of Constitutionalism in the Progressive Era," originally appeared as "The Realist Critique of Constitutionalism in the Era of Reform" in the *American Journal of Legal History* 15 (1971): 288–306. Reprinted by permission of the publisher.

Chapter 4, "Andrew C. McLaughlin and the Defense of Constitutionalism," originally appeared as "In Retrospect: Andrew C. McLaughlin and Liberal Democracy: Scientific History in Support of the Best Regime" in *Reviews in American History* 19 (1991): 445–61. Reprinted by permission of the Johns Hopkins University Press.

Chapter 5, "Changing Conceptions of Constitutionalism in the Era of World War II and the Cold War," previously appeared in the *Journal of American History* 59 (Dec. 1972): 640–69. Reprinted by permission of the publisher.

Chapter 6, "The New Left Attack on Constitutionalism," originally appeared as "New Left Reverberations in the Academy: The Antipluralist Critique of Constitutionalism" in the *Review of Politics* 36, no. 2 (Apr. 1974): 265–83. Reprinted by permission of the publisher.

Chapter 7, "Bureaucracy and Constitutionalism," originally appeared as "Constitutionalism and Bureaucracy in the 1980s: Some Bicentennial Reflections" in *News for Teachers of Political Science* (1984): 16–19.

Chapter 8, "Constitutional and Legal History in the 1980s: Reflections on American Constitutionalism," previously appeared in *Benchmark* 4 (1990): 243–64. Reprinted by permission of the Center for Judicial Studies.

Chapter 9, "History, Theory, and the Constitution," previously appeared in *Constitutional Commentary* 11, no. 1 (Winter 1994): 45–64. Reprinted by permission of the publisher.

Introduction

Written Constitutionalism as the American Project

A constitution is an account of the ways in which a people establish and limit the power by which they govern themselves, in accordance with the ends and purposes that define their existence as a political community. To the extent that a constitution identifies the first principles and ultimate ends of political life, it implicates questions of political and moral philosophy. Considered in this light, a constitution is normative, intended to prescribe what ought to be done by individuals and by the community they constitute for their mutual benefit. A constitution also has a practical and descriptive function: it indicates or discloses the institutional structures, forms, and procedures by which governmental power in a community is organized and the laws and rules of action that regulate the conduct of government. Tension between these dimensions of constitutional meaning—between normative standards and practical political reality—is reflected in controversy that often occurs in the life of a people over how they are constituted, or—what is the same thing—what their constitution is.

Conceived of as the problem of how to organize the political life of a people, constitutionalism is as old as political theory itself. Considered in historical terms, however, with reference to the language and discourse that are recognized as distinctive to the subject, constitutionalism is more a modern than an ancient phenomenon. Constitutionalism is synonymous with the rule of law, the idea that good government exists when a body of stable political rules and rights is applied impartially and equitably to all citizens. The rule of law is an ancient idea, but the discovery or invention of means to give it practical effect and institutional permanence, in ways that limit the power of the sovereign, is a development of modern times. The making of agreements between political leaders, such as occurred in the Glorious Revolution in En-

1

gland in 1689, and the writing of constitutions expressing the willingness of constituent groups in the community to accept a set of political
rules, such as occurred in the American Revolution, were the decisive
steps marking the emergence of limited constitutional government.[1]
Since the eighteenth century the adoption of a written constitution,
replacing government based on customary and traditional authority,
has been considered a necessary condition for limited government and
the rule of law.

The broad significance and range of meanings associated with the
concept of a constitution in modern political thought did not obtain in
ancient and medieval usage. In Roman law, *constitutio* referred to a
special law or ordinance of the emperor. Not until seventeenth-century
England was the word "constitution" used to describe the structure
and composition of the body politic, acquiring in the world of politics
an implicitly normative connotation analogous to its use in accounts of
the natural world.[2] Reinforcing this association was the use of "constitution" to refer to fundamental law, meaning immemorial custom and
the principles of reason, justice, and equity that constituted natural
law.[3]

In the American colonies in the eighteenth century, "constitution"
signified the design, structure, and composition of government.
Colonial usage gave the word a normative connotation, proscribing or
limiting the exercise of government power for certain purposes, and
prescribing forms and procedures for the exercise of government
power. Although in England many legal and political documents possessed constitutional significance, the constitution was the structure of
political and governmental institutions, including the principles and
practices that defined and regulated the relationship between institutions. It was customary and traditional, and thus it was prescriptive
or normative by virtue of its customary character. By contrast, in the
American colonies, owing in part to their settlement by means of charters granted by the crown and covenants formed by religious communities, a constitution came to be seen as a written document or text.

In an American constitution were collected the ends and purposes
that defined a political community, as well as the institutional structure and procedures through which government was required to act.
In the American Revolution, constitutions were authoritative because
they were based on the consent of the people and because they were
believed to embody fundamental law. As the people assumed sovereignty or had it claimed by revolutionary leaders on their behalf, constitutional historian William G. Andrews explains, "it became useful
to inscribe on parchment the limits and procedures believed by them
to be imposed by natural law on the governors. . . . The people wanted

to have before them that which they were to interpret." Documentary constitutions eased the task of popular interpretation, making "the directions of the governed to the governors concrete and explicit, on the basic natural law questions." Constitutions provided standards for measuring the performance of governors by the governed.[4]

In the nineteenth century, acceptance of the idea of a written constitution as the fundamental law and framework of government led scholars to seek the origin of constitutionalism in premodern political thought. The closest equivalent was found in the notion of the "regime." This concept referred to the structure and distribution of government power in a manner reflective of the social composition of the community, including standards of reason, virtue, and justice that were the final cause of political life. The difference between premodern and modern constitutionalism was that the former was mainly customary and only incidentally documentary, while the latter was mainly documentary and incidentally customary. The great benefit of having a documentary constitution, it was believed, was to make practicable the enforcement of principles, norms, and rules limiting government. A customary or unwritten constitution, consisting of convention, practice, and usage, was thought to be not a real constitution because it was not enforceable against government.

But was it really possible to impose substantive limitations and procedural rules of action on government, in the same way a government imposes rules of action on individuals? This basic issue in modern constitutionalism is a problem of political theory. It can be understood, however, only in the light of historical inquiry into the practical consequences of conducting government and politics based on written constitutions.

That it would be difficult to limit government through written fundamental law was recognized at the outset. Facing Anti-Federalist opposition to the proposed constitution, James Madison in *The Federalist*, No. 37, discussed the problem of using ordinary language to organize and regulate political life. "[N]o skill in the science of government has yet been able to discriminate and define, with sufficient certainty, its three great provinces—the legislative, executive, and judiciary," Madison wrote. The most enlightened legislators and jurists were equally unsuccessful in delineating the several objects and limits of different codes of laws and tribunals of justice. "The use of words is to express ideas," he said, but there was obscurity and equivocality in all new laws, notwithstanding the deliberation and technical craft with which they were written. Even the meaning intended by God himself, Madison observed, when he "condescends to address mankind in their own language," was rendered "dim and doubtful by the cloudy medium though which it is communicated."[5]

Madison, in the idiom of his time, did not believe that "words are things." He was not a postmodernist ahead of his time who held that language constitutes reality. His remarks on language and politics came in a discussion of the difficulties faced by the Federal Convention and were influenced by the rhetorical strategy adopted to defend the Constitution in the ratification controversy. If Madison's comment is to be taken seriously as a reflection on the feasibility of the written constitutionalist project, his opinion on how the authors of the Constitution overcame the difficulties facing them should also be remembered. Observing the unanimity that finally prevailed in the convention, he wrote: "It is impossible for the man of pious reflection not to perceive in it a finger of that Almighty hand which has been so frequently and signally extended to our relief in the critical stages of the revolution."[6]

How to apply the Constitution so that it is an effective limitation on government has been the continuing challenge of American constitutionalism. In the new type of republican politics that followed adoption of the Constitution, political action was conceived of in relation to provisions of the constitutional text. If the principles of republican government were embodied in the document, fidelity to the text was the measure of fidelity to republicanism as the political creed of the nation. Yet partisanship, ideology, and political exigency threatened to transform textualism into pretextualism, making fidelity to the written constitution a ceremonial gesture. Invoking the constitutional document might serve as a justification for political action divorced from the principles and values of limited republican government.

What raises constitutionalism above the level of a naive trust in the power of written words to control political action is moral and philosophical conviction. Belief that the Constitution is good in itself, that its value is not merely instrumental, is necessary to its maintenance and preservation. Yet to the extent that this belief points beyond the documentary character of the Constitution it tends, paradoxically, to call into question the literal significance of the text. In the ratification controversy Alexander Hamilton acknowledged this feature of constitutionalism. Discussing the necessary and proper and supremacy clauses, he wrote: "it may be affirmed with perfect confidence that the constitutional operation of the intended government would be precisely the same if these clauses were entirely obliterated as if they were repeated in every article. They are only declaratory of a truth which would have resulted by necessary and unavoidable implication from the very act of constituting a federal government and vesting it with certain specified powers."[7]

The documentary text is an instantiation, a sign or symbol, of fundamental law. It expresses in modern form the view of classical philosophy that the "endurance of 'writings' provides the possibility of meeting the variability of human things by preserving wisdom in however diluted a form beyond the demise of the wise founder."[8] In written constitutionalism the text is essential, but it is not, in itself, a generator of constitutionalism.[9]

If the text of a constitution is declaratory of the truths of political science or political philosophy, in what sense is it essential? Hamilton believed it was required by practical reason. Referring to the necessary and proper clause, he said it was written into the Constitution as a precaution, "to guard against all cavilling refinements in those [state government officials] who might hereafter feel a disposition to curtail and evade the legitimate authorities of the Union." On this and other cardinal points, Hamilton observed, the convention thought it best "to leave nothing to construction."[10]

It is possible that the social consensus supporting a written constitution will be so broad as to preclude controversy over its meaning, in which case the value of the document would be symbolic. This has not been true of the American Constitution. On the most essential matters, the meaning of the document has been subject to dispute. A premium has been placed on construction and interpretation of the text, and the outcome of public policy disputes has depended on the meaning of specific constitutional principles and provisions. Although acceptance of the Constitution expresses a consensus that peaceful constitutional controversy is better than violent dispute resolution, interpretation of the text has been a source of conflict that at times has tested the depth of the public's attachment to the Constitution as fundamental law.

That the introduction of textual constitutionalism into American politics would make the rule of law an operational reality, substituting peaceful constitutional change for violent revolutionary upheaval, was perhaps a reasonable inference to be drawn from republican political experience. That it would eliminate conflict over the scope and purpose of government in the American Union was an unrealistic expectation that the practice of constitutional politics showed to be false.

The problem was that basic constitutional principles were indeterminate, or appeared so, because their meaning depended on interpretation of the text in which they were embodied. Yet, while the imperfection and ambiguity of language were recognized, this was not viewed as a fundamental defect in the constitutional order. Even when controversy over the meaning of the Constitution broke the bonds of union during the Civil War, the practice of written constitutionalism was not abandoned. The crisis of the Union meant that the deepest political questions—in this case, nation making and state building— are constitutional problems that demand the prudence of the states- man rather than the jurisprudence of lawyers.

It was after the settlement of war issues in the Reconstruction amendments—a settlement that confirmed the importance of written constitutionalism—that the founders' project came under attack. Crit- ics complained that constitutional formalism and ritualistic devotion to the document prevented the country from coming to grips with the realities of modern society. To structure political controversy on the basis of arguments from the written Constitution, it was said, intro- duced ambiguity, inconsistency, and legalistic sophistry into public life. In the twentieth century, as the essays in this book show, these arguments developed into a practical and theoretical challenge to writ- ten constitutionalism.

This tradition of criticism finds expression in a recent study of cul- tural constitutionalism that presents a wealth of data describing public ignorance and lack of understanding of the Constitution. Historian Mi- chael Kammen attributes this condition to the willingness of public officials, including judges, to change their constitutional arguments for the sake of political expediency. Such behavior opens them to charges of hypocrisy and permits their words to be manipulated for partisan purposes, resulting in legal uncertainty and often outright confusion.[11] The people's lack of constitutional knowledge exists, however, within a framework of constitutional consensus. This is a political good and is directly related to written constitutionalism. Kammen states that "the basic pattern of American constitutionalism" is "one of *conflict within consensus.*"[12] This agreement is manifested in "respect for the Constitution and the system of government it created," which is de- pendent on written constitutionalism. The tradition restrains the be- havior of most citizens, especially public officials. We may not like the constraints that respect for the written Constitution imposes, Kammen observes, but we accept them.[13]

Although expressing doubts and reservations, critics like Kammen are in the end forced to recognize the practical value of the written Constitution. Nevertheless, the argument that cultural constitutional- ism is the basis of the American polity is the most recent expression of the tendency toward "realist" criticism that may be said to be inherent in the project of written constitutionalism. As has been true from the outset, the question can always be asked whether the application of the text Constitution to public policy making and the actions of gov- ernment is consistent with the principles and norms of republican government. This is an essentially political question. If the judgment is negative, the authority of the written Constitution is called into question and is subject to being superseded by an alternative constitutional model. In twentieth-century American politics, this alternative is the idea that beneath forms of government there exists an unwritten constitution that is a true description of the ends, purposes, and values of the political community.

Although written constitutionalism emerged as a reaction against the unwritten English constitution, there is a sense in which the notion of an unwritten constitution is not necessarily incompatible with a written fundamental law. Constructions of the written constitution in the form of statutes, executive orders, and judicial decisions elaborate the meaning of the document. Assuming consistency with the text, they might be thought of as an unwritten, in the sense of uncollected, expression of the written fundamental law as applied. As constructions and interpretations proliferate and become more far-reaching, however, their connection to the text may become tenuous, until the point is reached where they warrant a different description. In contradistinction to the written constitution, they can be understood as an unwritten constitution, similar to judicially evolved common law in English constitutional history.

The concept of the unwritten constitution has generally been appealed to in times of political crisis as a means of challenging the established interpretation of the written Constitution. In 1860 the controversy over the nature of the Union was at one level a dispute over the meaning of the constitutional text: was state secession a valid construction of the document? At a deeper level the controversy reflected uncertainty and ambiguity about how the American people were constituted as a political community. One could formulate the problem by asking what the real constitution of the country was, and it is noteworthy that the first systematic accounts of American republicanism based on the idea of an unwritten constitution were offered at this time.[14] During the Civil War and Reconstruction, moreover, judicially supervised textual constitutionalism was subordinated to political-branch construction of the principles of republican government and the rule of law.

From the 1880s to the 1930s the concept of the unwritten constitution acquired prominence in American political science. As discussed in this book, it was employed by progressive and liberal reformers to attack conservative legal doctrines predicated on written constitutionalist orthodoxy. Criticism of laissez-faire constitutionalism as mechanical and formalistic rested on legal-realist assumptions, referred to as constitutional realism, that culminated in Franklin Delano Roosevelt's plan of 1937 to pack the Supreme Court. Thereafter, the axioms of liberal jurisprudence were known as "living Constitutionalism," a concept derived from Oliver Wendell Holmes's famous assertion that the life of the law is experience, not logic. The rhetoric of living constitutionalism was compatible with the notion of "process jurisprudence," the middle ground that New Deal lawyers staked out between conservative declaratory jurisprudence based on orthodox written constitutionalism and radical legal realism that dismissed constitutional textualism as irrelevant to modern government.[15] In the long run, however, the logic of living constitutionalism was fundamentally antagonistic to the founding project of written constitutionalism.

Claiming for their generation the right to shape constitutional law in accordance with contemporary needs, New Deal lawyers at first justified federal regulatory schemes under doctrines of national authority derived from Marshall Court decisions. When Roosevelt attempted to increase the size of the Supreme Court and consolidate administrative authority in the executive branch, however, he scorned the written constitutionalism of the founding.[16] Regarding the Constitution as "a stumbling block to be circumvented," Roosevelt treated constitutional arguments as a pretext for advancing partisan and ideological ends.[17]

The long-term result of the New Deal was to replace limited-government written constitutionalism with unlimited-government living constitutionalism. As a public philosophy, New Deal liberalism held that in modern industrial society it was necessary to limit economic liberty and property rights in order to promote the public interest. Old doctrines of constitutional law were thrown out and new ones were adopted by the Supreme Court that reinterpreted republican government in statist terms of social welfare and security. Statist liberalism was rationalized in the metaphor of the living Constitution, defining the fundamental law as an adaptive, growing social organism. Superficially and formally a written document, the Constitution was really statutes, executive and administrative orders, judicial decisions, cultural attitudes and values, and public opinion and beliefs, all evolving in response to social forces and political events.

Living constitutionalism appealed to the idea of the unwritten constitution. The real constitution of the American people was a sovereign national government, centered in a chief executive with authority to take any action necessary to promote the public interest, provide social welfare, and protect national security. While rejecting laissez-faire judicial doctrines, living constitutionalism retained judicial supervision of constitutional law, ostensibly as an interpretation and affirmation of the text Constitution. Living constitutionalists used the forms and texts of the written Constitution rhetorically to legitimate the regulatory-welfare state.

From 1937 to 1960 living constitutionalism provided the doctrinal framework of statist liberalism. The famous *Carolene Products* footnote of 1938 was later held up as a prophetic indication of the course of living constitutionalist jurisprudence after World War II.[18] The outstanding example of judicial policy making in the service of living constitutionalism in this period was the school desegregation decision, *Brown v. Board of Education* (1954). Deeply controversial at the time, it was later eulogized as a profoundly moral decision that changed the course of race relations in the United States. The most significant result of the case may have been to encourage judicial activism. As the civil rights revolution proceeded, many lawyers, judges, and government officials concluded that courts should be a major institution for reforming American society.

Supreme Court decisions in the 1960s enacted policies in the areas of race relations, criminal procedure, religion and education, speech and press freedom, legislative apportionment, and welfare rights. The decisions were viewed by the justices as the logical outcome of interpretation of the written Constitution, the traditional means by which the fundamental law was adapted to the changing needs of society. When conservative justices who were expected to show more judicial restraint continued the practice of judicial activism in the 1970s, judicial decision making was more readily acknowledged as legislative in nature. Evidence of this realist view of the judicial function was *Roe v. Wade* (1973), the abortion rights case. The decision was criticized even by liberal scholars as an exercise of judicial fiat not based on any principle found in the text of the Constitution.[19]

The legitimacy of judicial review rested on the assumption that the decisions of the Supreme Court were applications and interpretations of the written Constitution. In *Cooper v. Aaron* (1958), the Court went so far as to say that it was "supreme in the exposition of the law of the Constitution" and that its interpretation was "the supreme law of the land." Always subject to questioning, the presumed identity between Court and Constitution began to break down in the aftermath of *Roe v. Wade*. With increasing candor, constitutional law was described as distinct from, perhaps not remotely related to, the text of the Constitution. To use a legal realist analysis, living constitutionalism manipulated the document as a pretext for policy making based on the ideology and subjective will of Supreme Court justices.

Judicial activist policy making by the Court under Chief Justice Warren Burger provoked a conservative reaction in constitutional theory. It took the form of a demand for a jurisprudence of original intent, based on the text of the Constitution and the original understanding of its framers and ratifiers. The reassertion of written constitutionalism led defenders of living constitutionalism to appeal explicitly to the idea of the unwritten constitution as a justification of judicial activist policy making.[20] Invoking moral philosophy as a source of authority, liberal commentators advocated "noninterpretivism" as a method of adjudication that dispensed with the text of the Constitution. In this theory of judicial review the text Constitution was a rhetorical symbol used to persuade the public of the legitimacy of judicial policy making.

Despite conservative warnings that an excess of judicial activism would destroy the Court's legitimacy, judicial legislation expanded. It was protected by the idea, accorded virtually dogmatic status in the legal culture, that the Court had exclusive authority over constitutional meaning. Seeing themselves as assisting the Court, "noninterpretivist" scholars fashioned constitutional law doctrines that by their own admission were unrelated to the text of the Constitution. The result was judicially managed policy making divorced from the Constitution.

Judicial activism was seen as inherent in the development of constitutional law based on a written Constitution consisting of abstract concepts, a "thing of wax" to be shaped by judicial interpreters for partisan and ideological ends.[21] This perception of constitutional law was given a more up-to-date theoretical justification in postmodernist epistemology, which assumed that language has no intrinsic meaning and words do not correspond to real things. Postmodernist legal theory rejected the distinction between what was in the Constitution and what was not.[22] On this theory, criticism of judicial activism as a rejection of written constitutionalism could be dismissed as a partisan attack on an independent judiciary, as in the controversy over Judge Robert Bork's nomination to the Supreme Court in 1987.

Liberal attacks on originalist jurisprudence express at once intellectual disdain for written constitutionalism and fear that originalism will win popular backing and political support. This ambivalent attitude reflects the fact that the text Constitution, contrary to postmodernist legal theory, has real meaning and practical import. It exacts costs from political and governmental actors, limits government, and shapes and directs political action.

The configurative effect of the Constitution depends in part on the document's symbolic value. Not sharing postmodernist philosophical assumptions, citizens believe that words have meaning and that the written Constitution embodies principles, forms, and procedures that define republican government. Citizens regard the Constitution as paramount and binding law. Treating it as a textual instantiation of fundamental law, they accord it preeminent status as the proximate ground of legitimacy in American government. Citizens, the people as constituent power, believe that the principles and forms of the Constitution are both practically useful and intrinsically valuable in the conduct of political life. From this standpoint, constitutional construction is a basic feature of political life that affirms the value of the text Constitution.[23]

Whether the American people in the late twentieth century have the same constitution as when they assumed their existence as an independent nation is a question of practical as well as historical value. It is surely significant that the written Constitution of 1787, as amended, continues to be the object of discussion, analysis, and argument in American government and politics. Precisely what this fact signifies, however—whether it means that the written Constitution is a normative fundamental law that limits government—is controversial. As the essays in this book indicate, this question can be approached analytically under the concepts of written and unwritten constitutionalism. More perhaps than at any time in the twentieth century, constitutional law is characterized by tension between these theoretical models.

The principal features of American national government in the 1990s are a presidential establishment and judicial hierarchy that claim authority to decide any issue that arises in political and social life, no matter how local it might appear. As a practical matter, the question is whether the executive and judicial authority can be limited to the ends, principles, and forms of constitutional government.

To place this problem in the framework of the unwritten, living constitution raises what appear to be insuperable difficulties. Under this doctrine any arrangement of the parts and powers of government that may exist—anything government does—although politically controversial, is by definition constitutionally legitimate. The idea of a constitution as a standard of legitimacy and limitation on government loses its meaning. Conceived of in this way, a constitution is at best an exercise in prudence, at worst an acquiescence in government power.

Historically and practically, the founding project of written constitutionalism better meets the republican requirement for a fundamental law that limits government. The written Constitution provides an account of the ends, principles, and forms of government that is as relevant to contemporary political life as it was to politics in the founding period. The power of the modern presidency, for example, is a threat to republican government. Under the principles of written constitutionalism, however, the executive power can be construed to impose limits on presidential government.[24] The same can be said of government by judiciary. No warrant for the kind of judicial legislation and policy making that exists today can be found in the written constitutionalism of the republican founding.

Presidential and judicial authority, or any other concentration of power that might threaten limited republican government, can be described as the real constitution of American government produced by twentieth-century historical forces. Under the theory of the unwritten living Constitution, description becomes prescription, conferring legitimacy and normative sanction. Considered from the standpoint of the citizen or government official, however, legitimacy claimed in the name of the unwritten constitution is a counterfeit authority. The better approach to the problem of limited government is critically to make an account of existing institutions and practices in the light of the written Constitution.

Constitutionalism, in the acceptation of the term required by the internal perspective of the citizen, insists on fidelity to the constitutional text. It does so not because the citizen believes that invoking the words of the Constitution, as a shibboleth, will by itself control political and governmental action. What the citizen-constitutionalist knows, rather, is that, supported by republican conviction about the value of self-government, the written Constitution of 1787 supplies the rule of law that is indispensable to the maintenance of free, popular, limited government.

Notes

1. Barry R. Weingast, "The Political Foundations of Democracy and the Rule of Law," *American Political Science Review* 91 (1997), 245–63. See also Charles Howard McIlwain, *Constitutionalism: Ancient and Modern*, rev. ed. (Ithaca, N.Y.: Cornell University Press, 1947).

2. Gerald Stourzh, "*Constitution*: Changing Meanings of the Term from the Early Seventeenth to the Late Eighteenth Century," in *Conceptual Change and the Constitution*, ed. Terrence Ball and J. G. A. Pocock (Lawrence: University Press of Kansas, 1988), pp. 37–38.

3. J. G. A. Pocock, *The Ancient Constitution and the Feudal Law: English Historical Thought in the Seventeenth Century* (New York: W. W. Norton, 1967), pp. 48–51; J. W. Gough, *Fundamental Law in English Constitutional History* (Oxford: Oxford University Press, 1955).

4. William G. Andrews, *Constitutions and Constitutionalism*, 3d ed. (Princeton, N.J.: D. Van Nostrand, 1968), p. 21.

5. *The Federalist Papers*, intro. by Clinton Rossiter (New York: New American Library, 1961), pp. 28–29.

6. Ibid., pp. 230–31.

7. Ibid., No. 33, p. 202.

8. Paul Stern, "The Rule of Wisdom and the Rule of Law in Plato's *Statesman*," *American Political Science Review*, Vol. 91 (1997), 271.

9. Andrews, *Constitutionalism*, p. 26.

10. *The Federalist*, p. 203.

11. Michael Kammen, *A Machine That Would Go of Itself: The Constitution in American Culture* (New York: Random House, 1986), p. 12.

12. Ibid., p. 29. Italics in original.

13. Ibid., p. 123.

14. Sidney George Fisher, *The Trial of the Constitution* (Philadelphia, 1862); Orestes Brownson, *The American Republic: Its Constitution, Tendencies and Destiny* (New Haven, Conn.: College and University Press, 1972; orig. pub. 1866); John C. Hurd, *The Theory of Our National Existence* (Boston: Little, Brown, 1881).

15. G. Edward White, *The American Judicial Tradition: Profiles of Leading American Judges*, expanded edition (New York: Oxford University Press, 1988), pp. 292–316.

16. John A. Rohr, *To Run a Constitution: The Legitimacy of the Administrative State* (Lawrence: University Press of Kansas, 1986), pp. 111–70; Sidney M. Milkis, *The President and the Parties* (New York: Oxford University Press, 1993).

17. David E. Kyvig, *Explicit and Authentic Acts: Amending the U.S. Constitution 1776–1995* (Lawrence: University Press of Kansas, 1996), p. 306.

18. In footnote 4 of *U.S. v. Carolene Products Co.* (1938), Justice Harlan Fiske Stone proposed a judicial policy of deference to legislative policy making in social and economic matters, as well as critical judicial scrutiny of legislative policy making in the area of civil liberties, with a view toward protecting the rights and interests of minority groups. In the 1960s the concept of civil rights was expanded and transformed into a policy of social and economic redistribution in the name of affirmative action.

19. John Hart Ely, "The Wages of Crying Wolf: A Comment on *Roe v. Wade*," *Yale Law Journal* 82 (1973), 947.

20. Thomas C. Grey, "Do We Have An Unwritten Constitution?" *Stanford Law Review* 27 (1975), 703–18.

21. Leonard W. Levy, *Original Intent and the Framers' Constitution* (New York: Macmillan, 1988), pp. 54, 342.

22. J. M. Balkin, "The Rule of Law as a Source of Constitutional Change," *Constitutional Commentary* 6 (1989), 21–27. A general work of constitutional commentary illustrating the postmodernist approach is Sanford Levinson, *Constitutional Faith* (Princeton, N.J.: Princeton University Press, 1988).

23. Standing in sharp contrast to citizens' respect and reverence for the Constitution is a cynical academic attitude, seen in a recent discussion, "Constitutional Stupidities Symposium," *Constitutional Commentary* 12 (1995), 139–225. The symposiasts express irreverence, impatience, and disdain for the Constitution. Focusing attention on "the primary imperfections of our current constitutional scheme," they state that the symposium "is not meant to be the last word on the topic of constitutional stupidity," but is intended as "the initiation of a continuing conversation." Ibid., pp.140–41.

24. Louis Fisher, *Presidential War Power* (Lawrence: University Press of Kansas, 1995).

1

Constitutionalism and the American Founding

Between 1776 and 1789 the American people constituted themselves a nation by creating republican governments in the thirteen former English colonies and then, in the Constitutional Convention, by transforming the Union of confederated states into a genuine law-giving government. The novelty of this achievement was epitomized in the seal of the new nation, "Novus Ordo Seclorum," which announced "a new order of the ages." Yet in founding political societies Americans pursued a goal that had occupied Western man since antiquity: the establishment of government power capable of maintaining the stability and order necessary to realize the purposes of community, yet so defined and structured as to prevent tyranny. This age-old quest for the forms, procedures, and institutional arrangements most suitable for limiting power and implementing a community's conception of political right and justice, we know as constitutionalism. It remains to consider American constitution-making in the perspective of Western and specifically English constitutionalism, and to reflect on its significance in shaping political life in the United States.

Constitutionalism takes as its purpose resolution of the conflict that characterizes political life and makes government necessary, through procedures and institutions that seek to limit government and create spheres of individual and community freedom. Based on the paradoxical idea that the power to make law and to rule can be at once sovereign and effective, yet also defined, reasonable, and responsible, constitutionalism contains an inherent tension that sets it against utopianism and anarchism, which deny the reality of power, and absolutism and totalitarianism, which tolerate no limitations on power. Nevertheless, although constitutionalists can in retrospect be seen as sharing common assumptions, differences among them have sometimes led to irreconcilable conflict. One such division occurred in the eighteenth century when the American people separated from the English nation and adopted a new type of constitutional theory and practice for the conduct of their political life.

Perhaps the most obvious feature of American constitutionalism was its apparent dependence upon legally binding written instruments prescribing the organization of government and fixing primary principles and rules to guide its operation. Texts had of course long been used in law, government, and politics, and the English constitution comprised written elements. Americans' resort to documentary, positive-law techniques of government was more systematic and complete than any previous undertaking, however, so much so as to amount to constitutional innovation. Following the American example, peoples everywhere in the modern world have adopted the practice of forming governments by writing constitutions. But Americans in the founding era did more than invent a new approach to the old problem of limited government. Their constitution-making was informed with a new purpose—the liberal purpose of protecting the natural rights of individuals. American charters of fundamental law were not simply ordinances of government; they were also constitutions of liberty. The meaning of liberty, especially the relation between the individual and the community that was central to any practical definition of it, was a deeply controversial issue that divided Americans in state and national constitution-making. The adoption of the federal Constitution in 1787, however, marked a decisive shift toward protection of individuals in the pursuit of their interests, and away from enforcement of community consensus aimed at making citizens virtuous and moral, as the central purpose of constitutional government in America.

American constitutionalism is thus concerned with organizational and procedural matters, on the one hand, and with substantive questions of political purpose, on the other. Most of the time constitutional politics in the United States deals with the former concern, as groups and individuals assert or deny the existence of proper governmental power or challenge methods used to employ it. Nevertheless, constitutionalism is ultimately normative and purposive. Every state may be said to have a constitution, in the sense of an institutional structure and established procedures for conducting political affairs. But not every state is a constitutional state. In the Western political tradition constitutional government is defined by forms and procedures that limit the exercise of power. American constitutionalism goes farther by pursuing not only the negative goal of preventing tyranny but also the positive end of promoting individual liberty, both in the passive sense of protection against government power and in the active sense of participation in the decisions of the political community. Viewed in this light, American constitutionalism raises basic questions of political value and purpose that connect it with the mainstream of Western political philosophy.

In the history of constitutionalism the great problem has not been to create power but to define and limit it. The Western constitutional tradition has employed two methods toward this end. The first is the theory and practice of arranging the internal structure of government so that power is distributed and balanced. In Greek political thought the purpose of politics was to promote virtue or moral excellence in men, and the founder of a political community was advised to balance the classes of society—kingship, aristocracy, and democracy—in a structure of mixed government which permitted each element to contribute to this end. The pursuit by each class of its special aptitude or interest prevented the others from seeking merely private ends, transforming the polity into despotism, oligarchy, or mob rule depending on which part of society dominated. A second method of constitutionalism has been to subject government to legal limitations, or the rule of law. Roman juristic writing, which regarded natural law as a standard of reason and equity for judging the validity and legitimacy of government enactments, is usually considered the source of the rule-of-law idea. Significant practical steps toward achieving it were taken in medieval England as common law courts created a sphere of law and legal right protecting individual property and liberties against government and constituting a limitation on royal discretionary authority. Further contributing to the rule-of-law tradition was the tendency of courts to regard basic principles of common law adjudication as embodying reason and justice, and hence as a kind of fundamental law limiting the acts of government.

English constitutionalism in the period of American colonization comprised both strands of the constitutional tradition. The common law courts in the early seventeenth century insisted on the superiority of law over the royal prerogative. Sir Edward Coke gave famous expression to the idea of a higher law controlling government in asserting that " 'sovereign power' is no parliamentary word. . . . Magna Charta is such a fellow, that he will have no sovereign." Coke also said that "when an act of Parliament is against common right and reason, or repugnant, or impossible to be performed, the common law will controul it and adjudge such act to be void."[1] Parliament itself, however, subsequently claimed supremacy in lawmaking, and vindication of its authority in the Revolution of 1688 effectively precluded development of the rule of law into a politically relevant form of higher-law constitutionalism. An internally balanced institutional structure, expressed in the revised and revitalized theory of mixed government in the eighteenth century, became the principal model of constitutional government in England.

Essentially descriptive in its connotation, the English constitution was the structure of institutions, laws, conventions, and practices through which political issues were brought to resolution and carried out in acts of government. Yet the constitution was also prescriptive or normative, or at least it was supposed to be. Lord Bolingbroke's well-known definition pointed to this quality: "By constitution we mean . . . that assemblage of laws, institutions and customs, derived from certain fixed principles of reason, directed to certain fixed objects of public good, that compose the general system, according to which the community hath agreed to be governed."[2] More specifically, as Montesquieu, Blackstone, and other eighteenth-century writers affirmed, the purpose or end of the English constitution was civil and political liberty.[3] From the standpoint of modern constitutionalism the legislative supremacy that contemporaries regarded as the foundation of English liberty was incompatible with effective restraints on government. Nevertheless, Parliament was believed to be under a moral obligation to protect the rights and liberties of Englishmen, and the sanctions of natural law were still seen as effective restraints. Moreover, political accountability to public opinion through elections operated as a limitation on government. Englishmen thus continued to see their constitution as fixed and fundamental, notwithstanding legislative sovereignty.[4]

American constitutionalism began in the seventeenth century when English settlers founded political societies and institutions of government in North America. Two things stand out in this early constitutional experience. First, the formation of government was to a considerable extent based on written instruments. In corporate and proprietary colonies the founding documents were charters granted by the crown conferring enumerated powers on a particular person or group within a designated geographical area for specific purposes. Under these charters the colonists adopted further agreements, organic acts, ordinances, combinations, and frames of government giving more precise form to political institutions. In religiously motivated colonies government was more clearly the result of mutual pledging and association under civil-religious covenants. American colonists thus used constitutionlike instruments to create political community, define fundamental values and interests, specify basic rights, and organize governmental institutions.[5]

The second outstanding fact in early American constitutional history was substantial community control over local affairs. To be sure, the colonies employed the forms and practices of English government and generally emulated the metropolitan political culture. Their institutions at the provincial and local levels were patterned after English models, and the theory of mixed government and the balanced constitution was accepted as valid. Yet discordant tendencies pointed to a distinctive course of constitutional development. The fact that in most colonies the power of the governor depended on royal authority while the power of the assembly rested on a popular base, as well as frequent conflict of interest between them, made separation and division of power a political reality discrepant with the theory of mixed government. Furthermore, popularly elected assemblies responsive to growing constituencies and enjoying de facto local sovereignty under written charters introduced a republican element into American politics.

As English subjects, Americans believed they lived under a free— and fixed—English constitution. Long before the American Revolution they expressed this view in the course of conflicts with imperial officials. Numerous writers asserted that the constitution was a contract between the people and their rulers; that the legislature could not alter the fundamental laws from which government derived its form, powers, and very existence; that government must exercise power within limits prescribed by a civil compact with the people. Moreover, the compact chosen to organize and direct government, as a colonial sermon of 1768 put it, must coincide with "the moral fitness of things, by which alone the natural rights of mankind can be secured."[6] Disputing the descriptive English constitution that included parliamentary sovereignty, Americans were coming to think of a constitution as normative rules limiting the exercise of power for the purpose of protecting the people's liberty, property, and happiness.

In declaring their independence from England, Americans in a sense reenacted the founding experience of the seventeenth century. They took what their history and political circumstances determined to be the logical step of writing constitutions to organize their political communities. Before issuing the Declaration of Independence, Congress recommended that the colonies adopt governments that "in the opinion of representatives of the people, best conduce to the happiness and safety of their constituents in particular, and America in general."[7] Although some argued that the people acting in convention should form the government, political exigencies and Whig political theory conferred legitimacy on legislatures, which in all but two instances were responsible for writing or adopting the first state constitutions.

The most distinctive feature of the state constitutions—their documentary or positive character—followed the decision to form new governments as a matter of course. Given the long tradition of founding documents in America, it seemed obvious that the purposes of political community and limitations on government could be achieved better by writing a constitution than by relying on an unstipulated, imprecise constitution like England's, which did not limit government and was not really a constitution after all. Though consisting in part of written documents, the latter was too subjective, ultimately existing in men's minds and premised on the idea that "thinking makes it so."[8] Americans insisted in contrast that the principles and rules essential to organizing power and preserving liberty be separated from the government and objectively fixed in positive form. Old in the tendency it reflected though new in its comprehensive application, American constitutionalism rested on the idea that "saying makes it so," or at least the hope that putting something in writing so it can be authoritatively consulted makes it easier to achieve specified ends.[9]

Professor Lutz's illuminating research has shown that the state constitutions stand in direct line of descent from colonial founding documents which created political communities and established institutions of government. One type of founding document (compact, covenant, combination, agreement) signified mutual promise and consent by which individuals formed a political community and identified basic values, rights, and interests. A second type of document (enactment, ordinance, frame, constitution) specified governmental institutions.[10] Half the state constitutions written between 1776 and 1789 were described as compacts and contained bills of rights that defined basic community values. In the other constitutions the design of government received principal attention. All the constitutions reflected tendencies of previous political development; none created institutions on a completely clean slate. This fact appeared more clearly in documents that were concerned mainly with establishing a framework of government. In these more modern documents, which anticipated the course of American constitutional development, community consensus yielded in importance to protection of individual rights as the main purpose of constitution-making.

In a formal sense American constitutionalism consisted in the stipulation of principles, institutions, and rules of government by the people or their representatives in the state legislatures. As constitutions are distinguished and ultimately justified by their political purpose and effect, however, the political character of the revolutionary founding documents requires consideration.

Historical scholarship in the past two decades has firmly established republicanism as the political philosophy of the American Revolution. Although lacking in precise meaning, the concept is most accurately defined as government resting on the consent of the people and directed by the public will expressed through representative institutions. In the perspective of Western political thought republican philosophy was formulated in the seventeenth century to defend liberty against absolutism. The state constitutions were republican and liberal insofar as they limited government by prescribing public decision-making procedures that prevented government officials from aggrandizing power for private benefit rather than the public good. The constitutions were liberal in yet another sense in confirming and extending the right of political participation that according to republican philosophy constituted true liberty for individuals. In many respects, however, state constitutionalism in the revolutionary era was a doctrine of community power and control that restricted individual rights in a way that would now be seen as illiberal.

Under the state constitutions the most important power in modern government—the power to make law and compel obedience—was lodged in the legislature. Unimpeded by internal governmental checks under the extreme version of the separation of powers that prevailed in the first phase of state-making, and sustained by presumptive identity with popular sovereignty as the source of political authority before the rejection of monarchy, legislatures acted forcefully to promote public virtue and the common good. Requirements of public virtue frequently took the form of restrictions on individual liberty through sumptuary laws and statutes regulating the transfer and use of property. Bills of rights that were part of state constitutions had little effect in curbing legislative power because they were treated as hortatory rather than legally binding. In the name of popular sovereignty and patriotism, state legislatures fashioned a constitutionalism of unity and power in government.

The concentrated power of republican virtue acting through institutions of community control was a useful and perhaps necessary expedient in the wartime emergency. In the doctrines of state sovereignty and the police power, revolutionary republicanism entered into the American constitutional tradition, and it has offered a compelling model of constitutional government throughout our history to reformers and radicals on both the left and the right. However, the actions of the state legislatures too plainly contradicted the constitutional meaning of the Revolution to become accepted as the principal or exclusive expression of American constitutionalism. That meaning was nowhere better stated than by the Massachusetts General Court in its Circular

Letter of 1768, which declared: ". . . in all free States the Constitution is fixed; & as the supreme Legislative derives its Power & Authority from the Constitution, it cannot overleap the Bounds of it, without destroying its own foundation."[11] Yet this was precisely what was happening in the American republics.

The state constitutions may have been fundamental law in the sense of ordaining a framework of government, but they were not fundamental in the sense of controlling legislative power. In all but two states the constitution was written by the legislature and could be altered or abolished by that body if it so chose. More than language of urging and admonition, contained in many of the constitutions, was needed to transform them into effective restraints on the actual exercise of power. Nor was the technique of internal institutional balance effectively employed to limit the state legislatures. In 1784 South Carolinian Thomas Tucker echoed the complaint increasingly heard in other states when he criticized the people of his state for deriving their ideas of government too much from the British constitution, and giving the legislature powers formerly exercised or claimed under a monarchical government. Tucker argued that the South Carolina constitution, written and adopted by the legislature, was not founded on proper authority. He recommended a popular convention to amend the constitution, "fixing it on the firm and proper foundation of the express consent of the people, unalterable by the legislative, or any other authority but that by which it is to be framed."[12]

Attempts to restrict state legislative power in the 1780s broadened and reformed American constitutionalism. As Tucker suggested, writing and amending constitutions by popularly elected conventions clarified the distinction between legislative law and fundamental or paramount law. Massachusetts in 1780 and New Hampshire in 1784 wrote their constitutions in conventions and required them to be ratified by the people in special elections. In theory this was the most effective way to make the constitution an antecedent higher law secure against legislative alteration. Further restriction of legislative power resulted from changes in the internal structure of government. Executive officers were given greater powers as checks and balances—that is, a partial and limited sharing or mixing of functional powers among the departments—were introduced in some states as modification of the separation of powers. Bicameralism, a carry-over from colonial government, was recognized as a means of making legislative action more deliberate. And courts began to play a more prominent political role by treating constitutions as higher law in relation to legislative enactments.

So strong was the tradition of community self-government under legislative sovereignty, however, that it could not easily be dislodged as the main reliance of constitutionalism. Certainly little could be done to alter it by isolated efforts in the several states. Effective reform, if that was needed, could come only from an interstate collaboration working through the state system created by the colonies when they declared their independence. Heretofore peripheral to republican political development, the union of the states in the Confederation became the focus of constitutional change.

The Continental Congress was formed by the colonies in 1774 as a coordinating and advisory body to protect American interests and eventually to pursue the cause of national independence. Exigencies of war and common concerns among the states gave Congress political power, which it exercised through informal rules and practices that were codified in the Articles of Confederation. Considered from a constitutional perspective as a limiting grant of power, the Articles were inadequate because, while they gave Congress ostensible power to do many things, they did not confer the lawmaking authority that is essential to government. Congress could at best make resolutions and recommendations, which in practice amounted to requests that the states could ignore. The Articles were unconstitutionlike in consequence of having been written by Congress and ratified by the states, rather than based in any direct way on popular authority. They were also unconstitutionlike with respect to institutional structure. Whether considered analogous to a legislative or executive body, Congress was the sole governmentlike organ, and only an evolving departmental system saved it from complete incompetence.

As an alliance or league of friendship (the description used in the document), the Articles were a more successful founding instrument. Yet in the form given it in the Articles, the Confederation was incapable of addressing in a constructive manner the defects in American government revealed in the actions of the states. The confederacy provided a field of political action, however, on which the reform of republican constitutionalism could take place. The practical impossibility of amending the Articles in order to strengthen Congress having been demonstrated, and insecurity of liberty and property in the states apparently increasing, proponents of constitutional reform turned a last-ditch desperation move—the calling of a convention of the states at Philadelphia in May 1787—into an enduring achievement of statesmanship and constitutional invention.

Perhaps most significant, the Framers gave institutional expression to the idea that a constitution, in order to function as a limiting grant of power, must be higher as well as fundamental law. In addition to originating or organizing power, it must be maintained separate from and paramount to government. In a formal sense the Constitution as a founding document was superficially similar to the state constitutions. A preamble explained the reasons for the document, proclaimed the existence of a people and political community, defined specific purposes, and ordained a framework of government. In reality, however, the Framers departed from the model of the state constitutions. It was unnecessary to return to the fundamentals of the social compact and the purposes of republican government, as state constitution writers to varying degrees were inclined to do. The authors of the Constitution observed that they were not addressing the natural rights of man not yet gathered in society, but natural rights modified by society and interwoven with the rights of the states.[13] They knew that the nation they were creating—or, to be more precise, whose existence they were recognizing—was amorphous, loosely related in its constituent parts, and united by few principles and interests. It was far from being the kind of cohesive, integrated community that the states by contrast seemed to be, and most unlike the nation-state communities of Europe. Hence the Framers briefly addressed in the Preamble those few basic unifying purposes and values—liberty, justice, domestic peace, military defense, the general welfare—and gave virtually the entire document to stipulating the institutions and procedures of government. As fundamental law the Constitution thus was less a social compact for a coherent, like-minded community, and more a contractlike specification of the powers, duties, rights, and responsibilities among the diverse polities and peoples that constituted the American Union.

Far more effectively than writers of earlier founding instruments, the Framers made the Constitution a paramount, controlling law. In a practical sense this boiled down to a question of law enforcement. Creating a real government to operate directly on individuals throughout a vast jurisdiction raised a new and potentially difficult compliance issue, but this received little attention at the convention. It was the old compliance problem of the states that stood in the way of making the Constitution binding and effective. At first the delegates considered a congressional veto on state legislation to deal with this issue. Rejected as impracticable, the veto was replaced by the supremacy clause (Article VI, section 2), stating that the Constitution, laws made in pursuance of it, and treaties made under U.S. authority "shall be the supreme Law of the Land; and the Judges in every State shall be bound thereby, any Thing in the Constitution or Laws of any State to the Contrary notwithstanding." This language expressed the paramountcy of the federal constitution over the states, and by inference over national legislative law as well. Not explicitly stated but implied in the judicial article was the idea that the superior force of the Constitution depended on its application and interpretation by the courts.

The higher-law character of the Constitution was further affirmed and institutionalized in the method of its drafting and in provisions for its ratification and amendment. Although delegates to the Philadelphia Convention were appointed by the state legislatures rather than elected by the people, the Constitution was a more genuine expression of the will of the people than were the Articles of Confederation, which were written by Congress. It has always been difficult for historians convinced of the democratic character of the Articles to admit this fact, but the Framers' acknowledged apprehension about unlimited popular rule does not gainsay their commitment to the republican idea that government derives its just powers from the consent of the governed. Consistent with this commitment, institutions of direct popular consent that were still exceptional at the state level were incorporated into the national constitution. Ratification would be decided by conventions in the states, presumably popularly elected. Amendment of the Constitution could occur through popular approval, in state legislatures or special conventions, of proposals recommended by Congress or by a convention to be called by Congress on the application of two-thirds of the state legislatures. The superiority of the Constitution to legislative law was enhanced by this provision for its amendment, since an utterly fixed and inflexible political law would become irrelevant to the task of governing an expanding society. If the Constitution required change, however, the people must amend it. Thus were popular sovereignty and the higher-law tradition incorporated into American constitutionalism.

To make the Constitution paramount law in operational fact, however, it was not enough to assert its supremacy and assume that the people's innate law-abidingness would give it effect. This was to rely on "paper barriers," concerning the efficacy of which there was much skepticism among the Framers. It was necessary also to structure the organs of government so that power would be internally checked and limited.

A persistent theme in constitutional theory since the late nineteenth century has been that power should be concentrated and unified—the more so the better, in order to deal with social problems—provided only that government be kept responsible through institutions of political accountability and the rule of law. Although the Framers' objective was to create coercive authority where none existed, they rejected concentrated sovereign power as a proper constitutional principle. Delegated, divided, reciprocally limiting power formed the motif of their institutional design.

Unlike the state constitutions, which organized the inherent plenary power of the community, the Constitution delegated specific powers to the general government. The contrast was most significant in the plan of the legislative department, to which the state constitutions assigned "the legislative power" and which the federal constitutions defined by the enumeration of congressional powers. Stable and energetic government seeming to require a strong executive and an independent judiciary, the Constitution made grants of power of a more general nature to these branches, which under the separation of powers were a counterweight to the lawmaking department. The separation principle by itself, however, as the state experience showed, was not a sufficient limitation on legislative power. Accordingly, checks and balances, by which each branch was given a partial and limited agency in the others' power, as in executive participation in legislation through the veto or legislative judging in the impeachment process, built further restraints into the Constitution.

The structure of the Union of course presented the most urgent question of institutional arrangements affecting the constitutional reality of a supreme political law. A division of power was already evident in the plan of the Articles of Confederation; what was needed was to transform the Union's political authority into the genuine power to impose lawful requirements on its constituent parts. This was achieved by reconstituting the Confederation as a compound republic, based on both the people and the states. Once this was accomplished, the pertinent fact for the paramountcy of the Constitution was the division of sovereignty. By giving the central government power over objects of general concern and allowing the states to retain almost all of their authority over local matters, the Framers divided sovereignty, thereby effectively eliminating it from the constitutional order. Arguments were certain to arise about the nature and extent of the powers of the several governments in the American state system, but the effect of such controversy would be to focus attention on the Constitution as the authoritative source of answers to questions about the rights of constituent members.

The Constitution was both fundamental and higher law because it expressed the will of the people, the ultimate source of authority in America. But it would truly limit power only if it was superior to the people themselves as a political entity, as well as to the legislative law. At the time some theorists of popular sovereignty argued that the people could alter their government at will, exercising the right of peaceful revolution and disregarding legalities of form and procedure, even as the Framers did in drafting and securing ratification of the Constitution against the express requirements of the Articles of Confederation.

However we view their action—as illegal, unconstitutional, revolutionary, or merely statesmanlike—the authors of the Constitution rejected the notion of unlimited popular sovereignty. They provided restraints on the people in the form of a limited number of offices, long terms of office, indirect elections, large electoral districts, and separated and balanced departments of government. Although these provisions have often been viewed as antidemocratic and in conflict with republican theory, they are more accurately seen as modifying the popular form of government adopted during the Revolution. The Framers' intent, as James Madison wrote in *The Federalist* #10, was to supply "a republican remedy for the diseases most incident to republican government."[14] And one should not forget that despite careful distribution and balancing of authority, Congress remained potentially the most powerful branch of the government, most responsive to the people and possessed of the lawmaking power.

Making the Constitution effective as a permanent higher law involved matters of form, procedure, and institutional structure. Yet as procedural issues carry substantive implications, and means sometimes become ends in themselves, it is also necessary to ask what a constitution is for. To prevent tyranny, the constitutionalist goal, is to create a space in which differences among people become manifest, in which politics can appear and questions of purpose arise. If running a constitution always reflects political concerns, making a constitution is all the more a form of political action that derives from or partakes of political philosophy. We thus consider the purposes and ends of the Framers' constitutionalism.

If the end of the English constitution was acknowledged to be political freedom, Americans were all the more emphatic in declaring liberty to be the purpose of their constitutions. Moreover, if the purpose of politics in modern times, as the history of political thought teaches us, is to protect men's natural rights rather than to make them virtuous and good as the ancients thought, then American constitutions were liberal in purpose. Yet the concept of liberty, universally embraced as a political good, can obviously be defined in different ways. And while recognition of natural rights gave modern politics a new purpose, it is equally true that virtue and moral excellence did not disappear from political discourse. In light of these considerations we may discern two conceptions of political freedom in the constitutionalism of the founding period. The first refers to the liberty of self-governing political communities, which were still thought to have an obligation to make men virtuous and on which individuals depended for their happiness and well-being. The second conception of freedom rests on the primacy of natural rights and generally asserts individual liberty over community consensus as the purpose of government.

Although these conceptions of liberty stand in theoretical opposition to each other, they coexisted in the Revolutionary era. After protesting imperial policies in the language of English constitutional rights, Americans justified national independence by appealing to universal natural rights. Wartime exigencies required decisive political action, however, which was based on the right of local communities to control individuals for the sake of the common good. States interfered with the liberty and property of individuals by controlling markets, restricting personal consumption, awarding monopoly privileges, and limiting imports and exports. They also regulated the speech and press freedoms of persons suspected of disloyalty to the patriot cause. In many ways Revolutionary republicanism subordinated the rights of individual citizens to the community, defining true liberty as the pursuit of public happiness through political action.

Reacting against state encroachments on liberty and property, the Constitution makers of 1787 emphasized protection of individual rights rather than promotion of virtue and community consensus as the purpose of government. Rather than an unattainable ideal of public virtue in ordinary citizens, they appealed to enlightened self-interest as the social reality on which the Constitution would rest. The Framers recognized factional conflict as a limiting condition for creating a constitution, yet also as an opportunity for broadening and redefining republican government. Alongside the communitarian idea, which remained strong in many states, they created a new constitutional model in the complex and powerful government of the extended republic, based partly on the people yet so structured and limited that individual liberty, property, and pursuit of personal interests would be substantially protected against local legislative interference. This is not to say that mere private enrichment at the expense of the community good or general welfare was the end of the Constitution. The concepts of virtue and the public interest remained integral to political thought and discourse. But virtue assumed a new meaning as the prudent and rational pursuit of private commercial activity. Instead of telling people how to live in accordance with a particular conception of political right or religious truth, the Framers promoted ends believed beneficial to all of society—peace, economic growth, intellectual advancement—by accommodating social competition and upholding citizens' natural rights against invasion by the organized power of the community, whether local, state, or national.

The Founding Fathers are often seen as antidemocratic because they created a strong central government, removed from direct popular and local community control, which they expected to be managed by an aristocratic elite. Notwithstanding its foundation in popular sovereignty and protection of individual liberty and rights, the Constitution in this view contradicted the real meaning of the Revolution, defined as rule by local communities guided by republican civic virtue. Yet while the Revolution stood for government by consent, there is no sound reason for regarding Revolutionary state-making as the single true expression of the republican principle. It was an essential part of that principle that government should operate through law to which all were subordinate, both citizens and government officials, and further that legislative law should be controlled by the higher law of the Constitution. This was the meaning of the rule of law in the United States, and its more complete realization in the Constitution of 1787 signified climax and fulfillment of the Revolution.

The Framers' purpose must also be considered in relation to the threat of national disintegration, either from internal discord or foreign encroachment, that has traditionally characterized accounts of the "critical period" in American history. The weakness of Congress in discharging its responsibilities was surely an impediment to protecting American interests and an embarrassment to patriotic men. Yet the belief that national disintegration was imminent perhaps depends too much on the idea, born of subsequent crises, that American nationality must be expressed through a strong central government or else it cannot exist. Some degree of formal cooperation among the states was necessary, but America could have existed as a plural nation, as it did in the Confederation period (and to an important extent continued to do under the Constitution). The problem in 1787 was not the threat of total rupture of the Union attended by actual warfare among the states. The problem was the character of American politics and government, or the nature and tendency of republican government. Republicanism was the defining idea of the nation, and without it we may say that America would no longer exist. The country was growing in the 1780s as population expanded, economic development occurred, westward settlement continued. Yet the state system of 1776 was incapable of adequately accommodating and guiding this development. The states were too strong for the good of republican principles, the Union not strong enough. By restructuring the state system, by reconstituting the Union on a republican constitution that crystallized tendencies in congressional–state relations in the 1780s, the Framers sought to reform American government to the end of securing the republican ideals of the Revolution.

We are so accustomed to thinking of constitutions as a reflection of, and hence determined by, social forces that we tend not to consider that the historical significance of the Constitution really was to demonstrate, as Alexander Hamilton wrote in *The Federalist* #1, that men are "capable . . . of establishing good government from reflection and choice."[15] Historical analysis may lead to the conclusion, for example, that the idea of a constitution as a higher, fixed law appealed to colonial Americans as an effective means of protesting imperial policy. Not so readily do we entertain the view that the constitutionalism of 1787 was based on a sound understanding of human nature, that it propounded valid principles of government, that it possessed intrinsic and not merely instrumental value. These are normative reflections more appropriate to political science, and an older political science at that, than to history. In writing about constitutionalism, however, it is hard categorically to deny a normative dimension, because the basic questions—the effectiveness of limitations on government, abuses of power, the nature of liberty—defy objective measurement.[16]

Yet, while historical analysis need not judge whether the Framers formulated a valid science of politics, it can employ as an evaluative criterion the requirement that a constitution must recognize and conform to a people's principal characteristics and nature. Considered from this point of view the achievement of the Founding Fathers is undeniable. They created a complex government of delegated and dispersed, yet articulated and balanced powers based on the principle of consent. Confirmation of that principle was in turn required by the Constitution in the cooperation and concurrence among the branches of government that was necessary for the conduct of public business. Made for an open, acquisitive, individualistic, competitive, and pluralistic society, the Constitution ordered the diverse constituent elements of American politics. More than merely a neutral procedural instrument for registering the play of social forces, it was a statement of ends and means for maintaining the principles that defined Americans as a national people. The Framers made a liberal constitution for a liberal society.

That the nation has marked the bicentennial of the Constitution is perhaps evidence enough of the Framers' success in establishing a new kind of constitutional government. Yet formal continuity may conceal substantive alterations. We need to ask how the higher-law and limited-power constitutionalism expressed in the document of 1787 actually worked in practice.

It is a striking fact, considering the unhappy outcome of most revolutions and the high rate of failure of constitution makers in the twentieth century, that the Constitution was not only formally ratified but quickly accorded full political legitimacy. The state constitutions, while not merely pretextual or façade documents, were not invoked and applied in the actual conduct of government as the United States Constitution was. And the new federal instrument was more than accepted: it rapidly became an object of veneration. This "cult of the Constitution," as it has unappreciatively been described by many students of American government, requires explanation.

Historians have offered a number of reasons for constitution worship, including popular identification of the document with economic prosperity; the Federalists' propagandizing to create an instant tradition of the Constitution and inculcate public commitment to it; the people's need for a unifying social myth and object of loyalty to replace monarchy as a course of authority. It has further been argued that anti-Federalist critics of the document in the ratification debate became its most vigorous supporters because of ideological conditioning that led them to treat it as an ancient constitution requiring literalistic defense to prevent political corruption. More broadly we may say that the Constitution took deep and abiding hold on the American political mind because it reflected a sober regard for the propensities of ordinary human nature and the realities of republican society; created powerful institutions capable of attracting men of talent, ambition, and enlarged civic outlook; and introduced changes in the conduct of public affairs that most people saw as improvements and that caused them to form an interest in the government it created.

The Constitution stipulated institutions, rules, and procedures embodying and symbolizing the principles of republican liberty, national unity, and balance and limitation of power. It was a fixed, objective document that could be consulted and applied, not a formless assemblage of principles, statutes, and decisions carried about in men's minds and dependent on social internalization for its effect. Yet the Constitution's principles and provisions were general and ambiguous enough to allow of varying interpretations. Liberty, union, and reciprocally limiting power meant different things to different people, as did the rules and institutional arrangements expressing and embodying them. At a superficial level this circumstance produced conflict, but at a deeper level the effect was unifying. For groups and individuals were encouraged to pursue political goals within the framework of rules and requirements established by the Constitution. Thus the document became permanent and binding. In the language of social science it was an integrative mechanism. Only the most extreme groups in our history—radical abolitionists and slaveholders in the nineteenth century, totalitarian parties in the twentieth—have repudiated the Constitution as a framework for political action.

The Constitution possessed force and effect because it was useful and relevant to political life. Responsive to the social environment, it had instrumental value. At the same time, repeated reference to the document as the source and symbol of legitimate authority confirmed its intrinsic value, apart from the practical results of specific controversies. People believed, in other words, that it was important to follow the Constitution for its own sake or for the common good, rather than for a particular political reason. The intrinsic value of the Constitution lay not only in the wisdom and reasonableness of its principles in relation to the nature of American society but also in the form those principles were given in a written instrument. The effect of the Constitution as binding political law has much to do with its textual character.

The Framers addressed this issue in discussing "parchment barriers." The state constitutions were evidence that written stipulations were no guarantee of performance, especially when it came to limiting legislative power. Madison in particular said it was not enough to erect parchment barriers in the form of constitutional provisions stating that the legislative department must confine itself to lawmaking. It was further necessary to arrange the interior structure of government so that the constituent parts would limit each other. Personal motives of ambition and interest, Madison reasoned, when linked with a constitutional office would lead men to resist encroachments from other departments. These were the "auxiliary precautions" (supplementing accountability to the people) that would oblige government to control itself.[17] Madison was saying that pluralistic differences in opinion and interest are necessary to make the prescriptions of the text function effectively.

Nevertheless, American constitutionalism insists that the text of the fundamental law be given its due. Madison's auxiliary precautions are in fact rules written into the document. We may agree with an early writer who said political legitimacy consisted "not in the words and letters of the Constitution; but in the temper, habits, and the practices of the people."[18] But it is equally true that while the written text may not be sufficient, it is necessary to achieve the purposes of constitutionalism, or so it has seemed most of the time to Americans. In the Constitutional Convention Rufus King said he was aware that an express guarantee of states' rights, which he favored, would be regarded as "a mere paper security." But "if fundamental articles of compact are no sufficient defence against physical power," King declared, "neither will there be any safety against it if there be no compact."[19] The observation of Carl J. Friedrich is in point: "The 'constitution' tends to become a symbol, and its provisions become so many symbols in turn. It is this symbolic function of *words* which makes the constitution a political *force*."[20]

Reference to the constitutional text has been a fixed feature of American politics. Its significance and effect have been variously estimated. A long tradition of criticism holds that the document has failed to limit government, especially the federal government in relation to the states. Others argue that constant invoking of the Constitution has trivialized politics by translating policy debate into legalistic squabbles that discourage dealing with issues on their merits. Reformers seeking a more programmatic politics have lamented that the Constitution by fragmenting power prevents responsible party government. And still others contend that the Constitution has worked precisely as intended: to eliminate genuine political action and make citizens passive subjects interested in private economic pursuits rather than public happiness and civic virtue.

These criticisms misunderstand the nature of constitutional politics and hence the binding and configurative effect of the Constitution. If politics is concerned with the end or purpose of political community, the proper role of government, the relationship between the individual and society, then it is difficult to see how the Constitution can be said to have brought an end to politics or prevented political action. As an expression of modern liberalism, however, the Constitution did signify a change in the nature of politics. To elevate natural rights into constitutionally protected civil rights, as the Framers did, was to discourage an older politics based on the pursuit of glory, honor, conquest, and political or religious truth, as well as a newer ideological politics born of modern revolution. The Framers' constitutionalism was a way of organizing political life that paradoxically placed certain principles, rules, and procedures beyond politics, according them the status of fundamental and paramount law. Premised on the idea that citizens could pursue private interests while preserving community, it was intended to limit the scope and intensity of politics, preventing a total absorption of society that would impose tyranny in the name of ruler, party, people, or community.

Starting in the 1790s and continuing with remarkable continuity to the present day, public policy advocates have charted courses of action with reference to the Constitution. Using constitutional language firmly embedded in political rhetoric, such as due process of law, equal protection of the law, and the separation of powers, et cetera, they invoke its principles and values to justify their goals, argue over the meaning of its requirements, and align themselves with its manifest tenor as explicated in constitutional law and legislation. Political leaders do this not because they are unwaveringly committed to a specific constitutional principle; in different circumstances they may advocate a different principle. The decisive fact is the high public status accorded the Constitution: policy makers and political actors know that the people take the Constitution seriously, regard it as supreme law, believe it is powerful because embodying sound principles of government and society's basic values, and, indeed, venerate it. Aware of this popular prejudice in favor of the Constitution, and seeking the approval of public opinion, political groups and individuals are constrained to act in conformity with its provisions. Thus the Constitution as binding political law shapes the form and content of policies and events.

The constraining effect of the Constitution might nevertheless be questioned, for it will appear obvious that while some requirements are unequivocally clear (for example, the minimum age of the president), many provisions are ambiguous and imprecise in meaning. Facing this fact, many scholars have concluded that there is no single true meaning of the Constitution, rather several possible readings none of which possesses exclusive legitimacy. Some contend there is no real Constitution against which arguments about it can be evaluated, only different assertions as to what the Constitution is at any given time, or what we want it to be. Expressed in the oft-cited statement that the Constitution is what the Supreme Court says it is, this view, carried to its logical conclusion, would mean that the American Constitution is a developing, evolving, growing thing that is changed by the actions of judges, lawmakers, and executive officers. In that case the Constitution ceases to be a fixed, prescriptive, paramount law.

Politically and historically realistic as this analysis appears, it has never been accepted as legitimate in constitutional theory or in the conduct of constitutional politics. From the standpoint of the people and their representatives, the Constitution, in both its procedural requirements and essential principles, has a true, fixed, ascertainable meaning. This popular understanding has existed from the beginning of constitutional politics in the debate over ratification, and it will probably continue until the popular belief that the Constitution as a document says what it means and means what it says is eroded or superseded by a more sophisticated view of the nature of texts and political language. There is still a strong tendency in public opinion to think that written constitutions, in Jefferson's words, "furnish a text to which those who are watchful may again rally and recall the people: they fix too for the people principles for their political creed."[21]

The importance of the constitutional text in American government has been raised anew in recent years in the controversy over original-intent jurisprudence. Many legal scholars have expressed doubt about the wisdom and legitimacy of consulting the original intent of the Constitution or its authors in settling constitutional disputes. The words of the text, it is argued, apart from anything that its authors may have written or said about its meaning, must be considered as expressing the original intent. And the text must be read and understood according to the accepted meaning of words in the interpreter's own time, place, and historical situation.[22] Some dispose of original intent more directly by asserting that constitutional interpretation need not be bound by the constitutional text, but may be based on fundamental social values and conceptions of justice and moral progress that judges are specially qualified to understand and apply. Either way, the Constitution is assured of its status as a "living document" adaptable to changing social conditions.

Although there may be sound reasons for disconnecting constitutional politics from original intent, from a historical standpoint it seems clear that neither the Framers nor the people over 200 years have taken so narrow a view of the meaning and relevance of original intent. The purpose of making a fixed, objective constitution was to decide the most important basic questions about politics and government once and for all—or until the people changed their mind and amended the document. The idea was to bind future generations in fundamental ways. This purpose would be defeated if those who later ran the Constitution were free to substitute their own definitions of its key terms. Yet the fact remains that constitutional principles and rules have been reinterpreted and redefined, in apparent contradiction of the Framers' intent, in decisions and statutes that have been accepted as politically legitimate. The Supreme Court has in a sense acted as a continuing constitutional convention.

Although the Founding Fathers intended the Constitution to be permanent and binding, the language of the document cannot realistically or reasonably, in a categorical sense, be frozen in its eighteenth-century meaning. It is the Constitution's essential purposes, its fundamental principles and procedures that were not intended to change. The question to be asked is whether fundamental principles and values—the values of individual liberty, national union, distributed and balanced power, the consent of the people—can be defined in an authoritative text and thereby realized in public law and policy to the satisfaction of the political community. American political history generally provides an affirmative answer to this question. But it is important to remember that an overriding imperative in American politics, law, and government has been to reconcile public policy with constitutional principles and rules as embodied in the text and in accordance with the Framers' intentions. Moreover, original intent has not been viewed in the narrowly positivistic manner urged by current critics of original-intent jurisprudence. The text was thought to have a definite and lasting meaning, and speeches, writings, and letters of the authors of the Constitution have always been thought pertinent to the task of elucidating its meaning. Whatever the practical effect of dismissal of the text and repudiation of original intent would be, such a step would alter the historic character of American constitutionalism.

The issue of original intent is pertinent to the larger question of the purpose of the Constitutional bicentennial. What is it that we seek in study and commemoration of the Constitution? In a sense the purpose is the same that informs all historical investigation, namely, the desire to learn how things came to be as they are. Yet commemoration of the founding has implications different from other historical celebrations and remembrances because the Constitution is peculiarly and directly relevant to public life. Historical knowledge about it therefore acquires special political significance. Of course any number of politically interested purposes may be served by facts about the founding, including defense of the original-intent position in the contemporary debate over constitutional adjudication. Broadly conceived, however, the bicentennial may be viewed as having the fundamental purpose of clarifying and confirming the meaning of American nationality.

Diverse in ethnic, religious, cultural, and social characteristics, Americans were united in 1776 by the political principles set forth in the Declaration of Independence. Inchoate though it was, the new nation was defined by these principles—liberty, equality, government by consent, the pursuit of happiness as an individual right—which in various ways were written into the state constitutions. By establishing a republican government for the nation, the Framers of the Constitution confirmed these principles, completing the Revolution and making it permanent. Since then American politics has derived from and been shaped by the Constitution and has periodically been renewed by popular movements resulting in electoral realignments that have included a return to the first principles of the founding as an essential element. After more than 200 years the United States may be old enough and sufficiently secure in its national identity to exist apart from the political principles that marked its appearance in the world. On the other hand, it may not be, in which case the nation still depends for its existence on preserving the principles of the founding. And when one reflects that a great deal of writing about the Constitution has been shaped by attitudes hostile to the Framers, such as those of the Beardian school, the possibility of gaining useful insight into the nature of our fundamental law through historical investigation warrants serious consideration.

Bicentennial activities focused attention on the text of the Constitution, and this as a matter of course. (The American Political Science

Association and the American Historical Association, in describing their conjoint Project '87 for commemorating the Constitution, stated that its purpose was to promote "public understanding and appraisal of this unique document.") From a social science point of view the documentary character of the Constitution is easily exaggerated; the internalization of principles and values in officials and citizens is seen as the essential thing in achieving constitutionalist purposes. Looked at in this light, the American Constitution is not and never has been simply the text of the Constitution, but consists in addition in concepts not expressly written in the document, such as the rule of law or the presumption of innocence, as well as institutions and practices that derive from political sources, such as the party system. From the standpoint of public opinion, however, legitimacy in American government still appears dependent upon or derived from direct reference to or necessary inference from the text of the Constitution. Perhaps the text-based constitutional order, in a society as open, pluralistic, and dynamic as the United States, has been an obstacle to the kind of internalization of values that characterizes English political life. After 200 years Americans still seem to be constitutional fundamentalists in regarding the text and original intent as conclusive of legitimate authority. Or perhaps we should say that while a narrow, legalistic textualism has not been the dominant characteristic of constitutional government in America, when an issue is made of the constitutional text the people will insist on the indispensable documentary foundation of constitutionalism.

Understanding this attachment to the constitutional text has often been difficult for scholars and intellectuals, who tend to disparage it as Constitution worship. Perhaps reverence for the Constitution expresses not so much a naive literalism, however, as an awareness of the act of foundation as a source of authority. Considered in this perspective the constitutional text stands for the founding, and the principles written into the document symbolically represent values evident in the actions of the Framers. The founding required rational discussion, deliberation, compromise, and choice; consent, concurrence, and mutual pledging. These procedural values are embodied in constitutional provisions which require government under a fixed institutional structure and by deliberative processes that depend on compromise and concurrence, in accordance with substantive principles of natural rights, consent, and limited and balanced power.

We study the making of the Constitution for the same reason Americans have always turned to the founders: to strengthen and preserve our character as a free people, to continue on a course that has brought us prosperity as a nation. In a world in which governments that impose tyranny on their people are described by some as democracies, we study the founding in an effort to achieve the substance of liberty and natural rights that we believe it is the purpose of government to secure. Ultimately, commemoration of the Constitution expresses the belief that the principles, institutions, and procedures of free government cannot be maintained if divorced from the purpose, intention, and spirit of the Framers of our fundamental law.

Notes

1. Quoted in Charles H. McIlwain, *Constitutionalism: Ancient and Modern* (Ithaca, 1940; rev. ed., 1947), pp. 126–127, and Edward S. Corwin, *The "Higher Law" Background of American Constitutional Law* (New York, 1955), p. 44.

2. Quoted in McIlwain, *Constitutionalism*, p. 3.

3. Daniel J. Boorstin, *The Mysterious Science of the Law* (Boston, 1958), pp. 155–159.

4. J. W. Gough, *Fundamental Law in English Constitutional History* (Oxford, 1955), pp. 174–191.

5. Donald S. Lutz, "From Covenant to Constitution in American Political Thought," *Publius*, 10 (Fall 1980): 101–133.

6. Daniel Shute, *An Election Sermon* (1768), in Charles S. Hyneman and Donald S. Lutz, eds., *American Political Writings during the Founding Era, 1760–1805*, 2 vols. (Indianapolis, 1983), vol. I, p. 117.

7. Quoted in Fletcher M. Green, *Constitutional Development in the South Atlantic States, 1776–1860* (New York, 1966), p. 54.

8. Benjamin Fletcher Wright, *Consensus and Continuity, 1776–1787* (Boston, 1958), p. 10.

9. Walton H. Hamilton, "Constitutionalism," *Encyclopedia of the Social Sciences* (New York, 1937), vol. III, p. 255; Aaron Wildavsky, "Why Amending the Constitution Is Essential to Achieving Self-Control Through Self-Limitation of Expenditure," *The Bureaucrat*, 9 (Spring 1980): 53.

10. Lutz, "From Covenant to Constitution"; Lutz, "The Purposes of American State Constitutions," *Publius*, 12 (Winter 1982): 27–44.

11. Henry Steele Commager, ed., *Documents of American History* (New York, 1963), p. 66.

12. Thomas Tucker, *Conciliatory Hints, Attempting by a Fair State of Matters, to Remove Party Prejudice*, in Hyneman and Lutz, eds., *American Political Writings*, vol. I, p. 620.

13. Max Farrand, ed., *The Records of the Federal Convention of 1787*, 4 vols. (New Haven, 1911–1937), vol. II, p. 137.

14. *The Federalist*, ed. Edward Mead Earle (New York, 1938), p. 62.

15. Ibid., p. 3.

16. Observing that the purpose of constitutional government is to prevent tyranny, and that the exact definition of where tyranny begins is difficult to establish, M. J. C. Vile writes: "There are inescapable value-judgments here,

and we must accept that a discussion of constitutionalism can only begin by pointing to certain specific examples of societies which are asserted to be non-tyrannical, and to attempt to elucidate their major characteristics," *Constitutionalism and the Separation of Powers* (New York, 1967), p. 308.

17. *The Federalist*, p. 337.

18. Samuel Miller, Sermon (1795), quoted in Michael Lienesch, "The Constitutional Tradition: History, Political Action and Progress in American Political Thought," *Journal of Politics*, 42 (1980): 7.

19. Farrand, ed., *Records of the Federal Convention*, vol. I, p. 493.

20. Carl J. Friedrich, *Constitutional Government and Democracy*, 4th ed. (Waltham, Mass., 1968), p. 169; emphasis in original.

21. Quoted in Charles A. Miller, *The Supreme Court and the Uses of History* (Cambridge, Mass., 1969), p. 184.

22. H. Jefferson Powell, "The Original Understanding of Original Intent," *Harvard Law Review*, 98 (1985): 855–947.

2

Constitutional Realism in
the Gilded Age

Constitutional history was one of the first distinct fields to emerge when the writing of history became professionalized toward the end of the nineteenth century. Throughout the century the constitutional dimension was a natural focus for the analysis of political affairs, and the earliest academic historians and political scientists often wrote from that point of view. Because they began the modern study of history and politics, scholars in the constitutional field such as John W. Burgess and Herman Eduard von Holst have figured in accounts of general American historiography and political science.[1] They have not, however, been studied in a comprehensive way from the perspective of constitutional history.[2] One result has been the common assumption that modern constitutional studies began only during the progressive movement of the twentieth century, with scholars such as Charles A. Beard, and that in the previous era students of the Constitution, in the words of professor Paul Murphy, wrote " 'revealed' history to underwrite the virtue of established institutions."[3] While it is true that many constitutional writers reflected a reverential, uncritical attitude, the more important fact is that in the years after Reconstruction American scholars began the realistic study of the Constitution, preparing the way for the more critical, reform-oriented scholarship of the early twentieth century.

The conception of the Constitution as a formal legal instrument or code giving existence to government and prescribing and limiting the exercise of its powers, rather than as the basic structure of the polity, not consciously constructed but growing organically through history, was one of the distinctive achievements of the American Revolution. It oriented constitutional description and analysis in the early republic toward a legalistic approach. For most students of American government in the first half of the nineteenth century the chief fact about the American Constitution was, in the words of Francis Lieber, that "It was the positive enactment of the whole at one time, and by distinct authority." This quality of being an "enacted or written constitution," said Lieber, "distinguishes it especially from the English polity with its accumulative constitution" consisting in "usages and branches of the common law, in decisions of fundamental importance, in self-grown and in enacted institutions, in compacts, and in statutes embodying principles of political magnitude." Writers in the antebellum period also generally held that America's Constitution was a decisive guarantee of liberty because it effectively limited government. Without a written constitution, wrote Frederick Grimke, parties would do what the exigencies of the moment dictated, "for how would it be possible to argue upon the constitutionality of any measure, when there was no constitution in existence." The written constitution was furthermore regarded as definite and clear in its meaning. "Some of its provisions may be subject to dispute," Grimke said, "but in the great majority of instances, it will be a clear and most important guide in judging the actions of all the public functionaries." Generally to discuss the meaning of the Constitution at this time meant to discuss the problem of the nature of the Union—whether it was a compact that could be withdrawn from or a binding political obligation. But however they answered this question, according to Alfred H. Kelly, almost all writers and commentators on constitutional matters maintained "the assumption of an ahistorical, static constitution."[4]

Yet there is evidence that at least some students of the Constitution disagreed with the prevailing formalistic, static approach. As example, the *American Review* in 1847 carried an article, inspired by opposition to President Polk's actions in the Mexican War, which argued that the government's practical construction of its own powers effectively altered the Constitution and enlarged the scope of its "real authority." Observing in English history how "an unwritten or historical Constitution" could develop, the writer warned, "We, in this country, deceive ourselves egregiously if we suppose that, because we began with a written instrument, we are therefore secure against any changes in its features or provisions, except such as may be made according to the forms prescribed in the terms of the written instrument itself, and plainly written down, like the rest, as a part of it."[5] During the Civil War, Sidney George Fisher criticized the conventional wisdom about the American Constitution from a similarly realistic point of view. Fisher attacked the "received theory" that the Constitution was alterable only by the people and not by the government. If Congress in an emergency exceeded its usual powers and its action went unchallenged, he asked, "What power has the Constitution to protect itself?" The answer was, none. In time such governmental action would become custom and organic law, he reasoned, so that "we get at last to the English doctrine, that Parliament is omnipotent, that is to say, it cannot be legally restrained." Rejecting the idea that the Constitution was "to be interpreted only by itself, and [that] a thousand years hence it will be still the Constitution, unaltered and supreme," Fisher asserted that in actuality "the construction put on the Constitution by the practice of the Government and by judicial decisions [was] the supreme law."[6]

In the last quarter of the nineteenth century the writing of constitutional history took its place alongside, indeed, began to supersede in importance, the traditional legal commentary as an established part of constitutional studies. What is more, much general history was written from a constitutional perspective, a fact which has struck some modern historians as strange or ironic, since both federal and state governments had little direct contact with the average citizen in his everyday life.[7] Yet against the background of nationalism and constitution-making that characterized the nineteenth century, and in view of the great war fought to determine the nature of the American Union, it was perfectly understandable that constitutional history should become a popular field of study. The typical work in constitutional history, in any event, usually described the formation of the Constitution in 1787 and the growth of the nation through the crisis of civil war in the mid-nineteenth century. This was the pattern in the works of George Bancroft, George Ticknor Curtis, Herman E. von Holst, John W. Burgess, and James Schouler, written from a Unionist point of view, and the works of Alexander Stephens and Jefferson Davis, written from a Southern view. More interesting than the theme of support for or opposition to nationalism, however, are the ideas about law, politics, government, and constitutions that informed these and other works in the constitutional field.

The central themes or concerns in historical and analytical writing about the Constitution in the period 1875 to 1900 were the historical origins of the American Constitution, the role or place or usefulness of the Constitution in the conduct of public affairs, and the nature of the Constitution. Traditional formalistic concepts of law and politics of course were present in this constitutional writing, as was idealism as represented by the old Jacksonian Democrat, George Bancroft, or the younger German-trained scholar John Burgess. But prominent also were attempts to define and describe the American Constitution according to standards of critical historical realism which anticipated the point of view of progressive historiography of the twentieth century.

In the years when historical study was being transformed into a professional discipline which its practitioners likened to science, and in a conservative era which valued stability in its political institutions rather than precipitous change, it was natural that historians, in dealing with the first of these problems, should be concerned to repudiate the theory of the Constitution as either a divinely inspired or creative act of the Founding Fathers themselves, or the sudden product of revolutionary upheaval. It seemed to von Holst, writing in 1876, that Americans overlooked the struggle waged over the Constitution and preferred to see instead evidence of "the 'divine inspiration' which guided the 'fathers' at Philadelphia." This was fine for Fourth-of-July addresses, he said, but it had nothing to do with history. The American Constitution, wrote von Holst, like every constitution, was "a result of actual circumstances of the past and present, and not a product of abstract political theorizing."[8] Even George Bancroft, whose quotation of William Gladstone's statement that the American Constitution was the most wonderful work ever struck off at one time by the brain and purpose of man incurred criticism from a professional historian a short while later, held that the Framers "followed the lead of no theoretical writer" and made "the least possible reference . . . to abstract doctrines."[9] A few years later Brooks Adams wrote an article to disprove the belief that Americans had suddenly invented the written constitution. Explaining that the charters of English trading companies were the embryo of American constitutions, Adams concluded, "Americans are subject to the same general laws that regulate the rest of mankind; and accordingly . . . they have worked out their destiny slowly and painfully, . . . and . . . far from cutting the knot of their difficulties by a stroke of inventive genius, they earned their success by clinging tenaciously to what they had."[10]

Around 1890, as though in response to the outpouring of uncritical patriotic sentiment a few years earlier on the centennial of the Constitution, several of the emerging class of professional historians turned their attention to the problem of the origins of the Constitution. J. Franklin Jameson, in the preface to a book of essays dealing with constitutional developments in the Confederation period, stated that many educated persons "think of our Constitution as having sprung full-armed from the heads of Olympian conventioners." With the progress of historical science, however, he explained, great national acts of settlement were being found to have been preceded by numerous tentative steps or by a long course of gradual development in the nation.[11] To refute the unhistorical implications of Gladstone's famous dictum about the Constitution, Alexander Johnston, James Harvey Robinson, and W. C. Morey described the historical roots of the organic charter written in 1787. Writing in a frame of mind that is difficult to appreciate, so obvious does the matter appear to us today, Johnston, a professor of history at Princeton, argued that it was not possible to create *de novo* a scheme of government such as the Philadelphia convention produced. According to Johnston, the Framers selected from provisions of state constitutions that had been tested by experience, so that the Constitution "was no empty product of political theory," but rather "a growth, or . . . a selection from a great number of growths then before the Convention."[12] James Harvey Robinson, a young instructor at the University of Pennsylvania, raised the same issue in asking: "Did they [the Founding Fathers], left without guide or precedent, by a simple effort of the intellect, draw up a form of government hitherto unknown, . . . Or did they rely on the experience of others, and find in the history of government . . . materials for the new structure?" Of course they did the latter, said Robinson, and their chief model was "their home experience" in the several state constitutions and governments.[13] A third scholar, William C. Morey of the University of Rochester, seeking to prove that the laws of historical development applied as well to a written as to an unwritten constitution, insisted that the American Constitution was "not a fiat-constitution projected from the brain of the Fathers, nor a copy of the contemporary constitution of England." Morey stressed as the historical basis of the American Constitution the royal charters to English trading companies, which became the first written constitutions.[14] Thus constitutional historians disposed of the creative- or divine-inspiration as well as the revolutionary theory of the origins of the Constitution. By 1897 James Schouler could fairly disregard the problem as a serious matter for investigation in writing, almost as afterthought following an account of the formation of the Union, "Any notion that our Federal constitution of 1787 was a spontaneous birth must be a false and fanciful one. . . . Our brief exposition of the facts has shown that it was a gradual conception; . . . that it ripened as the matured fruit of political experience."[15]

The attitudes of constitutional historians and other scholars toward the Constitution as an instrument of government and their conceptions of its usefulness and value varied more than did their views of its origins. The prevailing attitude in the conservative years following Reconstruction was, predictably, one of considerable satisfaction with the Constitution as a source of political stability. It is apparent that one of the main conclusions drawn from researches into the origins of the Constitution, and one that was not reached reluctantly, was that American political institutions were conservative. Brooks Adams drew the moral with unmistakable clarity: "Their [the American people's] political genius did not lie in sudden inspiration, but in the conservative and at the same time flexible habit of mind which enabled them to adapt the institutions they had known and tested as colonists to their new position as an independent people. . . ." American governmental institutions, he added, "are not the ephemeral growth of a moment of revolution, but . . . are the offspring of a history and tradition as ancient as those which have moulded the common law." [16] Similarly Alexander Johnston held that the secret of success in American politics was to allow institutions to develop simply and naturally, then when they reached maturity to fix them permanently in legislation or in Constitutions.[17]

That the Constitution ensured social and political stability and best solved the ancient problem of the conflict between governmental power and individual liberty has been a favored notion throughout American history, but it had a special currency in the last quarter of the nineteenth century. George Bancroft, concluding a long life of scholarship and public service, wrote in 1882 that in America the gates of revolution were bolted down, for the Constitution provided a legal and peaceful way to bring about change. In his best romantic style Bancroft rhapsodized: "The constitution establishes nothing that interferes with equality and individuality. It knows nothing of differences by descent, or opinions, of favored classes, or legalized religion, or the political power of property. . . . Each one of the three departments [of government] proceeded from the people, and each is endowed with all the authority needed for its just activity."[18] Almost equally uncritically Thomas M. Cooley, the prominent jurist and legal commentator, pointed out some of the conservative benefits of America's Constitution. By it the political authority of the national government was conferred and measured exclusively, he said, and could not be enlarged merely by precedent as in other countries. Comparing the value of written and unwritten constitutions, Cooley wrote that in America written constitutions prescribed the extent to which power was exercised and were the "absolute rule of action and decision for all departments and offices of the government."[19] The British writer James Bryce discerned the same conservative effect of the American Constitution. Though it was not a magic tool that of itself could restrain passions and cause reason to prevail, Bryce held that it blocked rash and hasty change and tended "to render the inevitable process of modification gradual and tentative, the result of admitted and growing necessities rather than of restless impatience." Moreover, the Constitution trained Americans "to habits of legality" and strengthened "their conservative instincts, their sense of the value of stability and permanence in political arrangements."[20] Christopher Tiedeman, another leading jurist and constitutional commentator, felt that the operation of democracy had eroded many limitations placed on government officials by written constitutions. Nevertheless, he regarded the written constitution as an important "check upon the popular will in the interest of the minority." Making the same point that progressive critics of American government would emphasize but without any misgivings, Tiedeman wrote: "It [the Constitution] legalizes, and therefore makes possible and successful, the opposition to the popular will," thereby enabling the United States to prevent the development of "democratic absolutism."[21]

Although criticism of the politically conservative nature of the constitutional system did not emerge among constitutional scholars until the early twentieth century, in the years 1875 to 1900 there were some dissenters to the general approval of the Constitution as an instrument of government and its effect on American political life. Von Holst, for example, railed against the veneration of the Constitution among Americans, which prevented them from seeing the realities underlying their government. Thus he called it "a happy sign of progress towards a clearer judgment among thinking people" when a writer in *The Nation* declared that the Constitution, in spite of its supposed precision and subjection to judicial construction, had through the theory of "latent powers" been made to serve party demands "quite as effectively as though congress had the omnipotence of parliament." Here was the same insight that had informed Sidney George Fisher's criticism of the Constitution during the Civil War: the formal legal instrument did not prevent the national government from acting as any other sovereign government would have acted under similar circumstances. Furthermore, it was a "fundamental defect in the constitution itself," von Holst reasoned, that led to the undesirable situation so common in American politics in which discussion of the expediency of a measure was subordinated to discussion of so insubstantial a thing as its constitutionality.[22]

A few years later Woodrow Wilson continued the criticism of "an undiscriminating and almost blind worship" of the Constitution, which on the one hand had not prevented congressional control of the federal government from being established, overriding "all niceties of constitutional restrictions and even many broad principles of constitutional limitation," but on the other hand did prevent a clear and general understanding that the practices of American government were very different from what they ought to be according to the "literary theory" of the Constitution. In seeking reforms along the lines of a strengthened executive branch and new forms of responsibility imposed on Congress, Wilson said he was asking "whether the Constitution [was] still adapted to serve the purposes for which it was intended."[23] Henry Jones Ford, like Wilson a political scientist, also was concerned with the effect of giving excessive attention to the formal Constitution and thus obscuring the realities of the political system. In popular belief, Ford wrote, "The constitutional ideal is noble; but the politicians are vile. If only the checks could be made more effective, if only a just balance of power could be established beyond the strength of the politicians to disarrange,— . . . the constitution would work perfectly." But according to Ford it was precisely the checks and balances of the Constitution and its failure to provide clear and direct responsibility for running the government which was the source of the political troubles symbolized by party machines and boss rule. Political parties, even the party machines, were "a necessary intermediary between the people and their government," Ford concluded. If the Constitution did not operate well in practice the defect lay in the Constitution itself.[24]

The third major concern of constitutional historians and scholars in the last quarter of the nineteenth century, implicit in the criticisms of writers such as Wilson and Ford, was the very problem of defining the American Constitution and the nature of the constitutional process. Here the conflict between law and politics, or legal formalism and political reality, stood out most prominently. The usual view was to regard the Constitution as formal, positive law. As noted earlier, throughout most of the nineteenth century when writers dealt with this issue they referred to the question of the nature of the Union, asking what kind of compact or contract, involving what kind of legal obligations, the Constitution was. This was the approach of George Bancroft, George Ticknor Curtis, John W. Burgess, Jefferson Davis, and others whose thinking was shaped by the Civil War. That such writers conceived of the Constitution in a legalistic way did not, it should be pointed out, mean that they wrote narrow legal history; their works were typically broad, general political histories, as we would describe them today, which gave a prominent place to constitutional disputes and interpretation. They understood, moreover, that answers to legal questions depended on nonlegal ideas and events. George Ticknor Curtis, for example, distinguished constitutional history from constitutional law by pointing out that the former consisted of "those events and that public action which have shaped the text of a written Constitution, or which should be regarded in its interpretation." Constitutional law was the body of jurisprudence which included the text of the Constitution and the constructions it had received from those whose duty it was to interpret its meaning. In the period with which Curtis was concerned, before the era of judicial supremacy, the president and Congress construed the Constitution authoritatively, but the Constitution was always the formal, written legal document or code; it was not legislation and governmental action, as in England, which there determined the powers of government and the rights of individuals.[25]

Typical of the orthodox formalistic conception of the Constitution that prevailed once the question of the nature of the Union was settled was a volume edited and in part written by Thomas M. Cooley, *Constitutional History of the United States as Seen in the Development of American Law* (1889). Henry Wade Rogers, a professor at the University of Michigan Law School, contributed a preface to this volume praising constitutional law as a distinctively American contribution to jurisprudence and calling it "peculiarly the pride and glory" of the country. "Written constitutions," asserted Rogers, "have been the distinguishing feature of American institutions."[26] Constitutional history written under these assumptions concentrated almost entirely on the Supreme Court, which Rogers said was "in reality . . . more powerful in its influence on the character of the government than [were] the President or Congress." The result was the history of constitutional law, but according to Rogers and Cooley, addressing themselves to the student of history, the study of this subject was the best way "to understand the nature of the [American] government."[27]

Other writers, however, especially historians, conceived of the Constitution more in political terms, with emphasis on the actual practices of government, than in formalistic, juristic terms. Simon Sterne, a reformer of the 1870s and 1880s, anticipated this more realistic—as its exponents saw it—point of view in stating that an account of the American Constitution ought to consider, in addition to the formal text and its interpretation by the Supreme Court, the political controversies that led to changes in the instrument as well as the situation of political parties. A constitutional history, he thought, should be tantamount to "a view of the institutional condition" of the United States. Frankly approving of the interaction of law and politics in the American Constitution, Sterne wrote: "There is an unconscious influence exercised by public opinion upon the minds of those who are called upon to decide finally constitutional questions, which is neither corrupt nor sinister, but which causes a written constitution to approximate more closely to an unwritten one."[28] The idea of the Constitution as political institution was more naturally conceivable to an Englishman and in part informed Bryce's *The American Commonwealth*. Disavowing concern with the legal aspects of the Constitution and seeking to explain the "framework and constitutional machinery," Bryce described the system of electing presidents, the powers of Congress, the spoils system, and other political institutions and practices which had "sprung up round the Constitution and profoundly affected its working." Similarly, legislation of Congress had "become practically incorporated" with the original text of the Constitution and had given to its working a decisive character and direction.[29]

Around the time Bryce offered to the American public his study of the Constitution seen partly as institutional rather than legal development, three young American scholars—J. Franklin Jameson, Woodrow Wilson, and Henry Jones Ford—produced works subscribing to and encouraging a similar broad, political, and to their way of thinking more realistic conception of the American Constitution. Jameson, introducing a series of essays dealing with the development of executive and judicial institutions under the Articles of Confederation as well as with constitution-making in American churches and the status of slaves, said that people who lived under a written constitution were inclined to take too narrow a view of constitutional history, confining their interest alone to the document and its formation, adoption, amendment, and interpretation. The chief purpose of the volume, therefore, he explained, was to broaden the conception of constitutional history. The American Constitution included elements not embodied in the written document, such as the "systems of party organization . . . , democracy, . . . the Speaker of the House, [and] . . . its committees, . . . federal statutes, . . . the constitutions and laws of the states, and . . . the practices and usages of the government and the people." Jameson believed that his view of constitutional history was not simply a difference of opinion in the use of terms, and that too narrow a conception of the field would lead to the neglect of the history of aspects of American political life which went as far toward determining "our form of government as anything set down in the Federal Constitution itself."[30]

What was necessary in Jameson's point of view was to understand that as law and politics are constantly interacting, the study of the Constitution must go beyond merely formal, legal elements to include things political. This idea informed the work of Woodrow Wilson and Henry Jones Ford, who described essential elements of the constitutional system in terms similar to those of Jameson. The Civil War and Reconstruction according to Wilson had made clear "that there has been a vast alteration in the conditions of government; . . . and that we are really living under a constitution essentially different from that which we have been so long worshiping as our peculiar and incomparable possession." The Constitution of 1787 was "now our *form of government* rather in name than in reality"; it was a "tap-root," he explained, and "the chief fact . . . of our national history is that from [it] has grown a vast constitutional system,—a system branching and expanding in statutes and judicial decisions, as well in unwritten precedent." Stressing the need in describing this system to "escape from theories and attach himself to facts," Wilson said the main inquiry must concern "the real depositories and the essential machinery of power." He concluded from a study of the "actual practices of the Constitution" that the balance inherent in the formal written instrument, or in what Wilson called the "literary theory" of the Constitution, was ideal only, and that congressional government was "the real government of the Union."[31] Henry Jones Ford, whom Wilson brought to a teaching position at Princeton, studied political parties as an element in the American Constitution. Ford's conception of the Constitution was evident in the title of his great work, *The Rise and Growth of American Politics: A Sketch of Constitutional Development,* and in the fact that nowhere in it did he discuss John Marshall and the Supreme Court. His purpose was to describe the "political structure" or "the actual constitution of the government." Relying in large part on historical analysis, Ford said that party organization in the early nineteenth century stimulated democratic tendencies which made the electoral college a party agency and transformed the presidency into an instrument of popular control. By the end of Jackson's second term, Ford wrote, this transformation had marked a "profound change in the nature of the constitution." As politics became democratized, party organization took the place of class interests and social connections in providing unity of control between the legislative and executive branches, and became "virtually a part of the apparatus of government itself."[32]

By the start of the twentieth century this realistic approach to constitutional studies, defining the Constitution in essentially political terms and positing an unwritten constitution, was fairly established, at least in academic circles. The historian and political scientist Albert Bushnell Hart epitomized the new learning in his well-known college textbook, *Actual Government as Applied under American Conditions,* first published in 1903. Asserting that the formal Constitution and statutes were merely an enveloping husk and that "the real kernel [was] that personal interest and personal action which vitalizes [sic] government," Hart took as his task to describe "the purpose, extent, division, exercise, and limitations of governing power." In an encyclopedic survey of American legal and political institutions that was historical in scope though not in organization, he attempted to explain how government operated "not simply by what constitutions and statutes say ought to be done, but by the experience of what is done."[33] The constitutional historian Francis Newton Thorpe, though inclined to see the genius of American political science in written constitutions, nevertheless recognized the existence of an unwritten constitution in governmental actions, political parties, and, in general, "the manner of doing the public business." The constitutional historian must explain as his foremost

duty the nature and growth of the principles or "civil notions" underlying the governmental system, Thorpe said, reflecting an older idealism; but he conceded that "whatsoever in the history of the unwritten
constitution will make clearer the origin and development of civil notions has a just demand on the historian." In a practical sense Thorpe
defined the Constitution broadly and politically, including in his two-
volume constitutional history, which he described as a record of the
evolution of government in America, accounts of democracy in the
eighteenth century, the organization of state governments, suffrage requirements, westward migration, slavery and the free Negro, legislative apportionment, banking and finance, and the judicial system.[34]

Though lawyers naturally were critical of the definition of the Constitution in terms of "actual government" and the conception of an
unwritten constitution, some were attracted to the new realistic approach.[35] Christopher Tiedeman, for example, defined the Constitution
as "the order and structure of the body politic" and, anticipating the
point of view of progressive historians such as Charles Beard, saw constitutional law as "the resultant of all the social and other forces which
. . . make up the civilization of the people." He described among other
things the electoral college, the two-term tradition concerning the presidency, and corporation and charter rights as aspects of the unwritten
constitution. Expressing a kind of conservative sociological jurisprudence and asserting that judges make law rather than declare it, Tiedeman reserved his praise for what he considered the most important
element in the unwritten constitution: "the disposition of the courts to
seize hold of these general declarations of rights as an authority for
them to lay their interdict upon all legislative acts which interfere with
the individual's natural rights, even though these acts do not violate
any specific or special provision of the Constitution."[36]

In the late nineteenth century, then, an attitude of critical realism
became an important attribute of constitutional scholarship. Research
into the origins of the Constitution, refuting the divine-inspiration theory about the Founding Fathers and showing that the laws of historical
development applied as well to Americans as to any other people, reflected this attitude in part, as historians tried to establish the credentials of their discipline as a true science. The critical evaluation of the
constitutional system and the attempt to go beyond the façade of the
formal written document in describing the Constitution were a clearer
manifestation of this realistic approach. The evidence is insufficient as
to a correlation between this constitutional realism and the advocacy
of political reform, but it is at least suggestive that Wilson's and Ford's
realistic studies were related to specific reformist purposes. A conservative, reverential attitude relying on the traditional legalistic or juris-

tic approach to the Constitution persisted alongside this politically oriented constitutional realism. But the more important fact was that several constitutional scholars conceived of their subject in realistic, political terms, thus preparing the way for the broader, more vigorous reformist campaigns of constitutional history and political science in the twentieth century, and raising fundamental issues about politics, law, and the Constitution which have remained central to the present day.

Notes

1. For example, in John Higham *et al.*, *History* (Englewood Cliffs, N.J., 1965); Anna Hadow, *Political Science in American Colleges and Universities, 1636–1900* (New York, 1939); Bernard Crick, *The American Science of Politics: Its Origins and Conditions* (Berkeley, 1959).

2. Paul L. Murphy has adverted in a general way to the constitutional historians of the late nineteenth century, but without attempting to document his highly critical assertions about their accomplishments and methodology, which he described as "one of philosophic metaphysical analysis." See "Time to Reclaim: The Current Challenge to American Constitutional History," *American Historical Review*, vol. LXIX (Oct. 1963), 64–79. The quoted words are at p. 66.

3. *Ibid.*, 66.

4. Francis Lieber, *On Civil Liberty and Self-Government* (London, 1853), 131, 221; Joseph Story, *Commentaries on the Constitution of the United States*, second ed. (2 vols.; Boston, 1851), ix; Frederick Grimke, *Considerations upon the Nature and Tendency of Free Institutions* (Cincinnati, 1848), 123, 131; Alfred H. Kelly, "Clio and the Court," *The Supreme Court Review*, 1965 (Chicago, 1965), 122.

5. "The Constitution: Written and Unwritten," *The American Review: A Whig Journal of Politics, Literature, Art, and Science*, vol. VI (July, 1847), 1–3.

6. Sidney George Fisher, *The Trial of the Constitution* (Philadelphia, 1862), 41, 56. Fisher's relationship to English political thought is discussed in William Riker, "Sidney George Fisher and the Separation of Powers," *Journal of the History of Ideas* vol. XV (June, 1954), 397–412.

7. Cf. William T. Hutchinson, "The Significance of the Constitution of the United States in the Teaching of American History," *The Historian*, vol. 13 (Autumn, 1950), 7, and Murphy, "Time to Reclaim," 65.

8. Herman Eduard von Holst, *The Constitutional and Political History of the United States*, transl. by J. J. Lalor and A. B. Mason (7 vols.; Chicago, 1877–1892), I, 62–63; *The Constitutional Law of the United States of America*, transl. by A. B. Mason (Chicago, 1887), 2.

9. George Bancroft, *History of the Constitution of the United States*, 6th ed. (2 vols.; New York, 1900), II, 322. The criticism of Bancroft was made by William C. Morey, "The Genesis of a Written Constitution," *The Annals of the American Academy of Political and Social Science*, vol. I (April, 1891), 530.

10. Brooks Adams, "The Embryo of a Commonwealth," *The Atlantic Monthly*, vol. LIV (Nov. 1884), 610.

11. J. Franklin Jameson, ed., *Essays in the Constitutional History of the United States in the Formative Period, 1775–1789* (Boston, 1889), viii.

12. Alexander Johnston, "The First Century of the Constitution," *New Princeton Review*, vol. IV (Sept. 1887), 176–178, 186–187.

13. James Harvey Robinson, "Original and Derived Features of the Constitution," *The Annals of the American Academy of Political and Social Science*, vol. I (Oct. 1890), 203–207.

14. William C. Morey, "The Genesis of a Written Constitution," *ibid.*, (April, 1891), 530, 533–535.

15. James Schouler, *Constitutional Studies* (New York, 1897), 95–96.

16. Adams, "Embryo of a Commonwealth," 619.

17. Johnston, "First Century of the Constitution," 187.

18. Bancroft, *History of the Formation of the Constitution*, II, 334, 324, 327.

19. Thomas M. Cooley, ed., *Constitutional History of the United States as Seen in the Development of American Law* (New York, 1889), 31; T. M. Cooley, *The General Principles of Constitutional Law in the United States of America*, 3d ed. (Boston, 1898), 22.

20. James Bryce, *The American Commonwealth* (3 vols.; London, 1888), I, 536–538.

21. Christopher Tiedeman, *The Unwritten Constitution of the United States* (New York, 1890), 163–165.

22. von Holst, *Constitutional and Political History*, I, 71, 78–79.

23. Woodrow Wilson, *Congressional Government: A Study in American Politics*, Meridian Books ed. (New York, 1956), 31, 27.

24. Henry Jones Ford, *The Rise and Growth of American Politics: A Sketch of Constitutional Development* (New York, 1898), 334–335, 352–353.

25. George Ticknor Curtis, *Constitutional History of the United States* (2 vols.; New York, 1903), I, iv. This work was first published in 1889.

26. Cooley, ed., *Constitutional History of the United States*, 5–6.

27. *Ibid.*, 13, 23–24. By the 1890s a body of literature on the Supreme Court and judicial review was beginning to develop which assumed the proportions of a major political as well as scholarly controversy during the early twentieth century. Generally the focus of such studies were the questions of when judicial review began and whether the Framers of the Constitution supported it, and the issue of its legitimate scope and place in American politics. Whether for or against judicial review, students of this problem tended to think in terms of the juristic conception of the Constitution at this time. For a discussion of this literature see Alan F. Westin's essay, "Charles Beard and American Debate over Judicial Review, 1790–1961," in Charles A. Beard, *The Supreme Court and the Constitution*, Spectrum ed. (Englewood Cliffs, N.J., 1960), 1–34.

28. Simon Sterne, *Constitutional History and Political Development of the United States* (New York, 1882), iii, 145–146.

29. Bryce, *The American Commonwealth*, I, 6–7, 521–522, 517–518. When discussing judicial interpretation of the constitutional document, however, Bryce

was very formalistic, subscribing to the view that judges had no will of their own and simply discovered and declared the law, rather than shaped or made it themselves.

30. Jameson, ed., *Essays in the Constitutional History of the United States,* ix–xi.

31. Wilson, *Congressional Government,* 28–30, 53.

32. Ford, *The Rise and Growth of American Politics,* v, 217–220.

33. Albert Bushnell Hart, *Actual Government as Applied under American Conditions* (New York, 1908), vii, ix. Other textbooks employing the new realistic approach to constitutional studies were B. A. Hinsdale, *The American Government: National and State* (Chicago, 1891), and Roscoe J. Ashley, *The American Federal State* (New York, 1902).

34. Francis Newton Thorpe, "What Is a Constitutional History of the United States?" *The Annals of the American Academy of Political and Social Science,* vol. XIX (March, 1902), 96–97; *A Constitutional History of the American People, 1776–1850* (2 vols.; New York, 1898).

35. For a critique of the idea of an unwritten American constitution see Emlin McClain, "Unwritten Constitutions in the United States," *Harvard Law Review,* vol. XV (March, 1902), 531–540. McClain begged the question of whether there was an unwritten constitution by asserting that institutions, practices, traditions are not part of the law, and since the Constitution was "a part of the positive law," there could be no unwritten constitution in the United States.

36. Tiedeman, *The Unwritten Constitution of the United States,* 16, 40, 44, 81.

3

The Critique of Constitutionalism in the Progressive Era

Constitutional realism as a basic approach to the study of public law and government in the United States had its origin in the rejection of static, legalistic conceptions of the nature and function of the Constitution in the last quarter of the nineteenth century. Seizing upon the ancient distinction between law and fact, and operating on the assumption that the first step toward effective reform was to describe things as they are, scholars such as Woodrow Wilson, J. Franklin Jameson, and Henry Jones Ford dissented from the reverential approval usually accorded the American Constitution. Rather than blaming bad men for preventing theoretically sound institutions from working properly, they laid to the constitutional system many of the political and governmental difficulties of the Gilded Age. In their very conception of the nature of the Constitution, moreover, realist critics abandoned the formalistic, juristic view of traditional constitutional theory. Instead of defining the Constitution in static terms as a code of law, they viewed it in political institutional terms. The changing relationships between the branches or parts of government, the role and influence of political parties, legislation of an organic character which altered the structure of actual government or the exercise of governmental power in derogation of written law—these were the kinds of problems that concerned constitutional realists. Employing an evolutionary rather than a mechanistic model, they described the constitution of government as the effective distribution and actual exercise of power—a shifting complex of laws, formal and informal rules, governmental processes, and political philosophical understandings. America had an unwritten constitution, and it was this rather than the documentary charter which demanded more careful and scientific study if political progress were to be realized.[1]

Realist insights into the function and effect of constitutions and laws in the conduct of politics were of course not altogether new. The attempt to construct a polity on the basis of a written fundamental law had for a century stimulated lawmakers and statesmen to consider the relationship between constitutionalism and political action. The worthlessness of paper guarantees, given certain circumstances, was well understood. The significance of constitutional realism as a mode of interpretation was not only that it broadened the forum within which these questions were raised. In the nature of their work as scholars, teachers, publicists, and intellectuals constitutional realists also offered a different kind of public forum from the more narrowly political one in which these matters had previously been dealt with. This is to call attention to the fact that the realists were leaders in the attempt to establish history and political science as professional scholarly disciplines in the late nineteenth century. Though obviously and intentionally not divorced from political concern, they sought to bring objective and scientific knowledge to bear in their efforts to effect change. It is not necessary to credit their use of the scientific method with a high degree of success in order to appreciate the importance that constitutional realists had in the development of a modern way of looking at politics. Their inductive, empirical, pragmatic, and melioristic approach, with emphasis on the actual functioning of the political system, remains one of the major methodological alternatives in the study of politics.[2]

Constitutional realism in the latter years of the nineteenth century formed the basis for and was continuous with a more far-reaching and critical attack on constitutional law and institutions in the era of reform. In the 1890s the transformation of limited judicial review into judicial supremacy gave courts a seemingly decisive position in the governmental system. Accordingly, as legislative and party institutions were the main concern of the early realists, judicial power absorbed the attention of realist critics in the progressive period. Insight into the political and social dimension of court actions that had always been available was made into a theory of judicial decision making by proponents of a sociological jurisprudence. Consideration of the judiciary as the linchpin of traditional constitutionalism in turn led to a more conscious exploration of the motivating forces behind constitutional and legal change in general. What most impressed realist critics in their analysis of this question was of course the seemingly pervasive influence of economic interests. This discovery became the basis of criticism of the very idea of constitutionalism itself. The traditional constitutionalist's belief in the value of limited government seemed hopelessly out of place in the face of social and economic needs requiring decisive governmental action. Constitutionalism appeared to be essentially a defense of existing property rights and economic power which prevented effective political action. Events of the 1920s tended to confirm this judgment and led constitutional realists to adopt an increasingly cynical attitude toward a system of politics theoretically based on the rule of law. Rejecting the conservative constitutional ideal, they stressed the sense in which governmental affairs turned upon the political will and action of men rather than the automatic operation of impartial law. In thus emphasizing the need for political action and governmental energy constitutional realists helped prepare the way for the renewal of the reform movement in the 1930s.

As early as the 1880s scholarly interest in the courts had begun to increase as the traditional practice of judicial review was expanded past all previous limits into the broad instrument of social and political control known as judicial supremacy.[3] Although the judiciary in the progressive era lent its support to certain aspects of the reform movement, its great potential power as well as its demonstrated power in the service of egregiously conservative causes, as in the *Lochner, Adair,* and *Dagenhart* decisions, invited attack. The burden of the constitutional realist critique was that courts usurped the power of popularly elected legislatures in their irresponsible exercise of the review function.

Appreciation of the uniquely political character of the American judiciary was fundamental to the constitutional realist outlook. In English law, Charles Grove Haines explained in an early essay, courts traditionally decided controversies between persons and administered relief or punishment. In the United States, however, the existence of written constitutions as the basic governmental law and the legalistic tendencies they encouraged led the judiciary to depart from this limited role and become involved in politics. Written constitutions being regarded as a means of preventing governmental tyranny, it seemed reasonable that courts should maintain and apply them as though they were ordinary law. And yet, Haines pointed out, prescriptive constitutions were much more than instruments of ordinary private law: they were primarily a form of political law, interpretation and application of which led judges to consider problems of political theory. The upshot was that American courts were "continually called upon to deal with questions that [were] purely political and governmental; to enter partially at least into the realm of legislation; and to discuss questions of political, economic, and social theory."[4]

Within the political context outlined by Haines the legislative character of judicial action was a common theme in constitutional realist analysis. In a highly critical assessment, Brooks Adams viewed constitutional interpretation as an essentially political function. It brought about a fusion of law and politics, he observed, but this tended "to lower the courts toward the political level" rather than elevate politics. Adverting to the enormous growth of judicial power in the 1890s, Adams distinguished between acceptable judicial review in which a court might declare a legislative act to be beyond the scope of its granted powers, and judicial supremacy by which it might declare an act to be unreasonable.[5] The political scientist Walter F. Dodd similarly stressed the recent tendency of courts to usurp legislative power by judging the reasonableness of legislation. One of the most important developments in the nation's unwritten constitution, Dodd observed, was the courts' invasion of the field of public policy and their quickness to declare unconstitutional almost any law of which they disapproved. The traditional presumption of the constitutionality of legislation had thus become meaningless, especially in the field of social and industrial regulation. And the law itself became more uncertain as results depended not on fixed rules, but on individual opinions of judges on political and economic questions. Dodd urged courts to leave the determination of policy to the legislature while themselves construing constitutional provisions broadly and liberally.[6]

While criticism of the conservative political character of constitutional interpretation was implicit in these discussions of the judicial process, other realists took a more direct approach. In *The Spirit of American Government* (1907) J. Allen Smith attacked the judiciary as the most antidemocratic part of the constitutional system. Professing to be the guardians of the fundamental law, the Supreme Court actually controlled and shaped that law by its power to annul the legislative acts of the people. Although Smith was chiefly critical of the lack of political democracy in the system, he also pointed out that protection of economic interests had been the central purpose of the Constitution from its very origin. In particular judicial review was intended to secure the political power of conservative property-holding classes.[7] The class character of Supreme Court decisions provided the focus for Gustavus Myers's realist account of constitutional development. Seeking to clear away the mystery enshrouding the Court, Myers called it "the one all-potent institution automatically responding to . . . and enforcing" the demands of the dominant capitalist class.[8]

Though centering on the judiciary, these assessments added up to an indictment of the constitutional system as a whole. In the late nineteenth century constitutional realists had decried the lack of efficient and responsible administration; in the era of reform they charged further that the Constitution was being made to serve the economic and political purposes of an exclusive minority rule. J. Allen Smith's entire book was an attack on the reactionary Constitution. In part Smith referred to antidemocratic and irresponsible tendencies produced by such obstacles to majority rule as the amending process, judicial review, and the system of checks and balances. But he also had in mind the economic self-interest of the wealthier classes who supported the movement for a new government in 1787 and had determined so much of its operation since. The liberty that the Framers were concerned with had mainly to do with property rights, he wrote, and "the American scheme of government was planned and set up to perpetuate the ascendancy of the property-holding class in a society leavened with democratic ideas."[9]

A few years later Charles A. Beard presented seemingly irrefutable proof of the antidemocratic and conservative foundations of American national government in *An Economic Interpretation of the Constitution*. Beard's thesis was that the politics of the 1780s were dominated by a deep-seated conflict between a popular party based on paper money and agrarian interests, and a conservative party centered in the towns and resting on financial, mercantile, and personalty interests. He held that the latter, suffering under the Confederation government and failing to achieve reforms through the prescribed channels in Congress, went outside the existing legal framework to adopt "a revolutionary programme"—the Constitution of 1787.[10] Through the critical studies of Smith and Beard, to name only the most prominent examples, property interests in general were identified with defense of the existing Constitution as the basis of political conservatism.

The intellectual basis of constitutional realist criticism was a revolt against legalism and juridical formalism. The late nineteenth century had seen a beginning of this critical reaction in analysis of the Constitution centering on the actual operations of political and economic institutions. Continuing to view the Constitution as a dynamic political process, realist critics after 1900 studied the interaction between law and politics with special reference to the forces that motivated constitutional change. This search ultimately led them to consider the nature and effect of constitutionalism itself. Given their disposition to reform, they viewed existing constitutional arrangements as the result of men responding to specific political pressures and concrete economic forces, rather than the necessary outcome of reliance on right principles of political science.

Frank J. Goodnow's *Politics and Administration* (1900) illustrated constitutional realism at the descriptive, institutional level. A colleague of Beard's on Columbia's faculty of law and political science, Goodnow argued that customs, political forces, and especially the administrative system shaped government far more decisively than did the formal Constitution. In his attempt to describe "the real political life of the people," he pointed out, for example, that the ideal of a separation of powers did not accord with the constitutional reality. The people, the legislature, and the executive all shared the function of expressing the will of the state in legislation, while courts, executive departments, and administrative agencies executed the will of the state.[11] Goodnow also rejected the favored juridical conception of a static political system resting on natural rights principles. Social progress, he believed, depended on getting courts and other agencies of government to view the Constitution not as fixed, immutable rules, but as set of general principles whose application should take into account changing social conditions.[12]

Goodnow extended the realist approach begun in the years after Reconstruction. The more distinctive contribution of twentieth-century constitutional realists was to illuminate the motivating forces behind the political law by which the nation was governed. Beard's was of course the most famous exploration of this theme, having an impact such that Robert L. Schuyler could write in 1916 that while the economic interpretation was occasionally overworked, "its claim has been securely established and must be recognized by all sober-minded students of the past."[13] Important also were studies which pointed the direction that Beard would take. In 1907 J. Allen Smith wrote that while the political system and economic organization were interrelated and interacting, "constitutional forms are always largely the product and expression of economic conditions." "The Constitution was in form a political document," Smith asserted, "but its significance was mainly economic."[14] In legal scholarship Brooks Adams and Melville Bigelow illustrated the drift toward a sociological jurisprudence which rejected the notion that principles of right and justice were the basis of the law. Legal principles, Bigelow wrote in 1906, were "only the resultant of conflicting forces in society" that were mainly economic.[15] A particularly significant realist contribution, which Beard acknowledged as an influence on his own work, was made by the philosopher Arthur F. Bentley. "I am engaged simply in showing," Bentley explained in 1908, "that the use of specific forms of soul-stuff gives us absolutely no help in interpreting the doings of social men." Political and constitutional principles were precisely the "soul-stuff" which most needed demolishing in this view. Pressures and interests were the causes of social change, not abstract ideals, and law itself was not a resultant of government, "it *is* government," Bentley concluded. Law was an activity, a group process, a struggle, an adaptation of group interests just as government was.[16]

Beard regarded *An Economic Interpretation of the Constitution* as especially important for introducing into American historiography, and into the constitutional and legal field in particular, an "analysis of determining forces." Critical of traditional constitutionalists for neglecting economic elements, he wrote: "It is necessary to realize at the outset that law is not an abstract thing. . . . So far as it becomes of any consequence to the observer it must take on real form; it must govern actions; . . . Separated from the social and economic fabric by which it is, in part, conditioned and which, in turn, it helps to condition, it has no reality." Constitutional law had seemed to be a special branch of law, Beard noted, because of its concern with the control of government. In reality, however, the main business of government was to make rules determining property relations in society. In this context Beard went so far as to define the Constitution as "the social structure by which one type of legislation [was] secured and another prevented." Yet even then the Constitution was "a secondary or derivative feature arising from the nature of the economic groups seeking positive action and negative restraint." It was against this theoretical and historiographical background that Beard went on to argue that the Founding Fathers represented distinct economic interest groups and were not operating "merely under the guidance of abstract principles of political science."[17] According to this point of view, then, the ultimate reality in constitutional affairs was economic forces, and the Constitution, however broadly defined, was no longer a primary datum in understanding political and governmental history.

This insertion of social and economic forces into the foreground of historical analysis was the principal development in constitutional studies during the era of reform. The change can be seen in the assessments of constitutional history presented to the American Historical Association by William MacDonald in 1907 and James G. Randall in 1929. Certainly MacDonald took a broad view of his subject. Recognizing the interaction between law and social forces, he pointed out that Supreme Court decisions were more than technical expositions of legal doctrine; they registered stages of social progress and were points of departure for subsequent governmental action. MacDonald also saw, however, an antagonism between the constitutional or legal element and other factors in history. Thus he expressed concern that social and economic aspects were being overemphasized "to the neglect of the part which law has played in determining the course of our development." Despite a certain breadth of view MacDonald still considered constitutional history essentially the history of constitutional law decisions, a position which other historians criticized on the ground that in many instances such decisions were merely formal.[18]

The antiformalist attitude found full expression in James G. Randall's 1929 analysis of constitutional history. Defining his field as the

study of civil processes based on critical examination of civil and governmental data, he distinguished it from the history of constitutional
law. It was no subject for a legalist whose concern for the forms of law
blinded him to the essential forces that worked through the law. In
Randall's view constitutional history had significance insofar as it supplied material for the social historian. "It is well to seek out the social
motives constituting the reality of which constitutional arguments are
but the reflection," he stated in *Constitutional Problems under Lincoln*
(1926). "Only so may we preserve the important study of constitutional
history." Thus whereas MacDonald viewed law as a kind of autonomous and determining, though socially conditioned, force in history,
Randall saw it as essentially derivative and subordinate. He doubted
that any significant issue could be said to be primarily constitutional.[19]
Harry Elmer Barnes summarized the realist critique of traditional constitutionalist thought: "Political and legal concepts and institutions are
looked upon as either originating in the void anterior to man or society
and gradually setting down and mingling with humanity, . . . or as
developing mysteriously, and independent of any non-political influences in society." As a result conventional histories were in Barnes's
view "devoid of life, reality, and true instructiveness."[20]

In discounting the inherent importance of constitutional issues Randall and Barnes did not speak for all students of public law and government. Although it had received serious challenge, the legalistic,
juridical approach was by no means given up as a lost cause in the era
of reform. Responding in part to the threat presented by the economic
interpretation, traditional constitutionalists reexamined major developments in American constitutionalism.

In the early 1920s Charles H. McIlwain and Randolph G. Adams
reinterpreted the American Revolution along the lines of legal and constitutional theory rather than social and economic analysis. Although
recognizing an intricate network of economic, social, and political
causes of the revolution, McIlwain considered them "non-essentials."
At bottom the revolution resulted from a collision of different conceptions of the constitution of the British Empire. Taking a narrow legalistic view of the matter, McIlwain attempted to show that the American
interpretation of the imperial constitution was the correct one in the
light of legal precedent. This essentially legalistic consideration he
treated as the dynamic force in the minds of revolutionary leaders.[21]
Randolph G. Adams was chiefly concerned with the problem of imperial organization in international law, but his study of *The Political Ideas
of the American Revolution* assumed from the outset that fundamental
constitutional principles were the key to understanding the American
separation from Great Britain. Although Adams did not deny a social

and economic dimension to the revolution, he did not regard it as central. Recognizing the distinctiveness of their society, Americans demanded a reorganization of the empire based upon the facts of the economic world. Englishmen, however, could not grasp the Americans' ideas that authority must be distributed and that law must be sovereign. "When a given political form can not be made to respond to the demands of an economic situation," Adams wrote underscoring the primacy of the constitutional question, "it is not always the economic situation which is at fault, or which will be changed. . . . [T]he empire was broken by its own rigidity."[22]

A focal point for traditional constitutionalism was the problem of the Founding Fathers. In 1905 Andrew C. McLaughlin presented the classic statement of the conservative nationalist view of the constitution-making period. According to McLaughlin, the new constitution was the work of men who with "a reckless disregard of political obligations" appreciated the national danger existing in 1785 and were able to settle the problem of imperial or continental political organization inherited from the British.[23] In 1913 Max Farrand, after editing three volumes of the records of the Federal Convention, treated the formation of the Constitution as an attempt to deal with the problem of a confederated republic, in particular the defect of excessive power and independence in the states.[24] And after the publication of Beard's researches, Charles Warren asserted flatly that historians who left out political and nationalistic factors, contending that the Framers were moved mainly by economic considerations, utterly failed to interpret their character and acts. According to Warren, the idea of the convention arose from "a patriotic desire for a united Nation," and from a conviction that without a new constitution "a dissolution of the Union and disappearance of republican government were inevitable."[25]

One of the ablest representatives of the constitutionalist position during the progressive era was Edward S. Corwin. A professor of political science, Corwin had received his doctorate in history, and his writing, never that of a mere legalist, combined knowledge of public law with an historical appreciation of the political circumstances surrounding constitutional change. Although critical of reactionary tendencies in Supreme Court decisions and sympathetic to reform, Corwin's most important work before the 1930s supported the traditional view that the exercise of government power must always be subordinated to objective, rational principles. This was the point of his well-known study, *The Higher Law Background of American Constitutional Law* (1927), in which he traced the origins of judicial review as a means of restraining government through fundamental law.[26] Another defendant of constitutionalism was Benjamin F. Wright, who in a study of natural law thinking criticized constitutional realists' tendency to dismiss the importance of political ideas. In order to prove that natural law is an outworn concept, he reasoned, "It is necessary to show that political philosophy has no need of a concept which is expressive of standards of right and justice other than, perhaps higher than, those set forth in the positive laws. . . ." Wright acknowledged the value of knowing the actual workings of political institutions in order to shape their future growth. Yet the most complete analysis of the actual system could not in his view provide "standards or criteria of justice, equity, political right."[27]

In 1932 Andrew C. McLaughlin published *The Foundations of American Constitutionalism,* a series of essays which epitomized the traditionalist constitutionalist outlook. Far from being narrowly legalistic in his writing, McLaughlin reflected the influence of the constitutional realism of the late nineteenth century. He had concluded an earlier work on the relationship between political parties and the Constitution with the judgment that "The development of these associations is the greatest fact in our constitutional history."[28] But, insisting on the primacy of constitutionalism and the rule of law, McLaughlin did not agree with the more advanced position of constitutional realists in the age of reform. The economic interpretation of history he could not accept. In his presidential address of 1914 to the American Historical Association, he noted that "many of us are even now looking out upon the field of constitutional history as a branch and only a branch of economic history." Analysis of economic influences on political institutions was important, he conceded, but he thought that the historian adopting this approach might fail to see "the infinite variety of motive and interest and personal and social character."[29] Reviewing McIlwain's book on the Revolution in 1924, McLaughlin praised it for proving decisively that the Revolution was "essentially a constitutional struggle," not an economic one.[30]

McLaughlin's chief historical interest, as he stated in his AHA presidential address, was the American experiment in self-government.[31] Accordingly his 1932 essays dwelt upon the colonial foundations of American constitutionalism in an attempt to "bring out the relationship between political philosophy and constitutional achievement." Church covenant, colonial corporation, social compact, constitutional convention, the division and separation of power, the right of judicial review—all figured in McLaughlin's account of how Americans in the revolutionary era "made . . . ancient theories, of which they were entirely conscious, into actual institutions." And the quintessential feature of the constitutional settlement achieved was limited governmental authority. This was what the reign of law meant, and it required that a preeminent place be given to the judiciary "to announce the law and to decide controversies according to law." McLaughlin further asserted that in exercising the right of review courts were not acting as umpires superior to legislatures and dictating to them; they were merely fulfilling their duty "to find and declare the law."[32]

McLaughlin's impressive achievement notwithstanding, the ideas of traditional constitutionalism had lost their intellectual power and appeal for a growing number of public law scholars. In consequence a defensive attitude often characterized the constitutionalist position. It can be seen, for example, in the *Constitutional Review*, a journal edited throughout the 1920s by Henry Campbell Black and dedicated to the affirmation of orthodox legal values.[33] Shortly before suspending publication in 1929 the *Constitutional Review* featured an essay by Alpheus T. Mason which tried to mediate between traditional constitutionalism and the realist critique. Mason, who later gained renown as a liberal constitutionalist, acknowledged that judicial decisions were influenced by training, education, and economic and social backgrounds of individual judges. Constitutional interpretation, he observed, was "determined not so much by the document itself as by the influences which society brings to bear on the judicial mind." Yet it was quite as true that this did not mean that American government was not a government of laws. "The Constitution does provide the rules of the game," Mason continued, "and the judges can never proceed to lay down whatever decision seems best to them on the grounds of reason alone." Although the notion of a government of laws could not be accepted uncritically, Mason believed it to be an accurate description of the American constitutional system.[34]

Other students of public law and government voiced emphatic disagreement as they questioned the very concept of constitutionalism. Unable to see that the idea of a government of laws and not of men had ever worked in America, they ceased to define the Constitution as a legal code the main purpose of which was to limit governmental action. The word "constitutional" lost its normative content and became merely descriptive: every country had a constitution, and this was not principally a form of legal restraint, but the arrangement and actual exercise of governmental power. Arthur F. Bentley put the matter succinctly when he wrote: "The constitution is always what is."[35] In explaining human affairs, moreover, realist critics considered constitutional ideas and rules less important and less real than social and economic forces. Many shared the belief of James G. Randall that "laws and constitutions have importance not in themselves, but because of the social purposes which they embody."[36]

Several works written in the 1920s challenged traditional constitutionalism. Typical was Howard L. McBain's *The Living Constitution,* published in 1927 by the Workers Education Bureau Press. A Columbia law professor, McBain attacked the idea of a government of laws on the ground that law had no life of its own, but merely a borrowed life from the actions of men. Though it suggested arbitrariness and instability, a government of men was the inevitable result to which attempts to establish the rule of law tended. Scornful of legal formalism McBain pronounced: "The constitution of the United States was not handed down on Mount Sinai by the Lord God of Hosts. It is not revealed law. . . . It is human means. The system of government which it provides can scarcely be read at all in the stately procession of its simple clauses."[37] Charles E. Merriam, the noted political scientist and reform leader, dismissed political and constitutional theorizing as "more or less thinly veiled propaganda of particular social interests." A nation's constitution, he explained, consisted not of words alone, but of public attitudes and habits; it was a general understanding as to ways of doing things political. And it was delusory to think "that there is magic in the written word, apart from the situations of which it is a part." Yet that was the meaning of constitutionalism to many people.[38]

Conservatives' firm identification with the written fundamental law led realist critics to become cynical toward constitutionalism. When they did so they sometimes seemed to lapse inconsistently into the static, legalistic conceptions of their adversaries. The philosopher A. K. Rogers seemed to do so in defining constitutionalism as the belief in "law as an entity existing apart from the hesitating opinions and wavering wills of men in a higher realm of pure reason." What was so baneful about this outlook was its tendency to stifle the spirit of social experiment. "We have been trying by the constitutional ideal to keep things from changing except within narrow limits," Rogers complained. Skeptical of the central premise of constitutionalism, he questioned whether particular forms of law and legal process were necessary to the guarantee of liberty and other basic values.[39] William Bennett Munro's *The Invisible Government* (1928) also assumed an anticonstitutionalist position. Munro questioned the validity of the separation of powers and checks and balances doctrine as a safeguard for liberty, and the belief that the Constitution guaranteed a government of laws and not of men. Rejecting the idea that constitutions and laws could compare in their importance to social, economic, and personal forces, Munro invoked William Penn's famous dictum: "Governments are like clocks; they go from the motion that men give them." Thus a government of laws and not of men was an impossibility: the rule of law was a mere fiction of political fundamentalism.[40]

Realist disillusionment with constitutionalism was only too apparent in J. Allen Smith's gloomy analysis, *The Growth and Decadence of Constitutional Government* (1930). Originally intended to restrain arbitrary power, constitutionalism, Smith argued, had been made into a doctrine of the supremacy of government over the people. Through the fiction of a government of law bound by constitutional limitations which it was the special duty of courts to enforce, conservatives had kept the people from recognizing this truth. Political apathy was an important further consequence of what Smith called "the prevalent anthropomorphic conception of the Constitution . . . as the guardian and protector of the rights of the people." Constitutionalism resting on the fiction of the rule of law in Smith's view precluded an intelligently critical attitude toward politics; it blinded people to the need for political action.[41] In actuality then the national government had unlimited, irresponsible power, and the rights of individuals who dissented from the social and economic consensus were in jeopardy. Smith called the new conception of the state a doctrine of governmental absolutism.[42]

Cynicism about the rule of law was further evident in the treatment of constitutionalism in *The Encyclopedia of the Social Sciences,* the monument of progressive scholarship that was published in the early 1930s. Constitutionalism was not, as it was for Edward S. Corwin, the limitation of arbitrary government through the rule of law, with roots reaching back to ancient and medieval times. Rather, according to Walton H. Hamilton, "Constitutionalism is the name given to the trust which men repose in the power of words engrossed on parchment to keep a government in order." Not only was this definition extraordinarily truncated, seeming to deny constitutionalism historical actuality or validity, it was based on the simplistic, formalist view of the Constitution that realists criticized in other contexts. Hamilton, professor in the Yale Law School, identified his subject with the attempt to limit irresponsible authority, but dated it only from the first American state constitution of 1776. Although he considered the writing of fundamental law an important political invention, its disadvantages outweighed its benefits. Constitutionalism offered exact language as a test for official conduct, Hamilton noted, yet it did so "at the risk of imposing outworn standards upon current activities." With fine impartiality he pointed out that an unwritten constitution was no more certain to adjust politics to popular needs. Nevertheless, his central conclusion was that "the faith of the fundamentalist" was unfounded; the Constitution "is not a self-regulating mechanism which automatically holds official conduct to conformity with its lines." Even more serious, "constitutionality" in Hamilton's view blocked popular legislation and shackled the present to the past.[43]

In 1932 two great works of constitutional history appeared which summed up the point of view and achievements of three decades of progressive scholarship. Louis B. Boudin's *Government by Judiciary* and Charles Grove Haines's *The American Doctrine of Judicial Supremacy* were to constitutional realism what McLaughlin's *Foundations of American Constitutionalism* was to traditional constitutionalism. Boudin in a long and distinguished career combined the roles of socialist theoretician, labor lawyer, and constitutional historian and commentator.[44] *Government by Judiciary*, an historical account of the Supreme Court's use of judicial review, was a powerful attack on the judiciary as an undemocratic institution committed to the defense of a conservative social and economic order. By no single dramatic step but rather by a gradual and continuous process, Boudin argued, the judiciary encroached upon the legitimate rights of legislature, executive, and people. The result, which Boudin and a good many other progressives had sought to overcome, was "Judicial Despotism": a government "with all powers lodged in an irresponsible judiciary."[45] Boudin also reflected constitutional realists' preoccupation with economic forces. Judicial decisions were not controlled by the Constitution, he insisted, but by the "general outlook on life, chiefly economic life,"of the judges involved. Constitutional disputes were thus decided according to "some economic or political assumption or predilection . . . as to what is desirable or undesirable in legislation." Like other constitutional realists, Boudin also questioned the idea of constitutionalism. Not only was American government a government of men, because of the absence of restraints on the judiciary it was a government of irresponsible men. Professing faith in "old-fashioned democracy," Boudin believed that judicial power rested on popular ignorance of the actual workings of the government. When people learned what was happening to them, learned "the true inwardness of this system," as Boudin put it, they would demand genuine self-government.[46]

Charles Grove Haines's study of judicial supremacy was more moderate in tone, as befitted its academic provenance, but it was equally critical and realistic in its conclusions. First published in 1911, *The American Doctrine of Judicial Supremacy* in the revised and enlarged edition of 1932 summarized the era of constitutional realism. Although Haines recognized limitations on the judiciary which Boudin disregarded, he agreed that the courts exercised every form of governmental power: legislative, executive, administrative, as well as judicial. "What may be termed government by the judiciary, . . . or the supremacy of the judiciary, is unquestionably the most significant principle of the politics and public law of the United States," Haines asserted.[47] Most of the book surveyed in objective, scholarly fashion the growth of judicial power and its conservative political and economic significance. A final chapter, however, attacked fictions about judicial review and the idea of a government of laws.

Rejecting the "mechanical theory" of constitutional interpretation, according to which courts merely discovered and applied legal principles, Haines subscribed to the theory of "free legal decision." This referred to a judicial process influenced by a judge's conscience, training, and experience, as well as by general social conditions. It also included, however, the idea that courts could consciously shape the law in accordance with their perception and evaluation of dominant social trends and needs. Though this appealed to some progressives, its suggestion of social engineering was inconsistent with the democratic and anti-judicial outlook of most constitutional realists, including Haines. His solution, if courts must inevitably perform a legislative function, was to insist on closer scrutiny of the political and economic affiliations and views of judicial nominees. Like Boudin, however, Haines preferred a drastically restricted power of judicial review. Betraying perhaps a naive view of the character of constitutional interpretation, he urged judges to confine themselves to "the normal function of defining and applying the express requirements of written constitutions, concerning which few serious controversies arise." And like most constitutional realists he hoped that trust in the people would bring an end to the system of political arbitration by the judiciary.[48]

Through the first third of the twentieth century constitutional realists thus brought constitutional history and analysis into the mainstream of critical historical and social science scholarship. Ironically, however, the realist point of view that invigorated constitutional studies could become a reason for abandoning the field. Skeptical toward constitutionalism, realists ultimately denied the significance of constitutional principles, theories, and rules as causative forces in history. They concluded, with James G. Randall, that constitutional issues were not real issues.[49] Although Randall claimed that a realist approach was the only way to preserve constitutional history as a worthwhile subject of study, it was more likely that, if viewed in this way, the field would become irrelevant. For if constitutional issues were but a superficial manifestation of economic or social reality, it was understandable that scholars should study this reality at first hand, rather than once removed in its legalistic reflections. Randall himself turned away from constitutional history to general Civil War history, contributing to what one constitutional scholar saw as the growing neglect of the field.[50] Constitutionalism, meanwhile, came to seem a false and trivial issue. The cynicism that could result when the insight of constitutional realism was translated into a general historical account was evident in

Howard K. Beale's view of the coming of the Civil War. "Constitutional discussions," he wrote, "determined nothing. They were pure
sham. . . . For all the heat and bombast of their enunciation, these constitutional arguments were mere justifications of practical ends."[51]

If the Constitution were viewed narrowly as a formal legal code
which only obscured real motives, as Beale in this instance viewed it,
constitutionalism as a field of study might well be judged irrelevant.
Yet not even Beale was able to dismiss constitutional considerations
when seen in broader, more political terms. In describing the history
of Reconstruction, for example, he held that the Radical Republicans
sought to replace the traditional scheme of checks and balances with a
centralized parliamentary system. This, he declared, was not "mere
embroidery for more practical desires," but a "fundamental constitutional issue that in importance outranks the whole reconstruction question."[52] Apparently, then, not all constitutional arguments were sham.
The realists' ambivalence on this point arose from their reform-
inspired criticism of the social and economic reality behind the conservatives' legalistic Constitution, which operated alongside their broad,
political institutional approach to the study of public law. Traditional-
ists like McLaughlin, who accepted the primacy of constitutional issues
in essentially legalistic terms experienced no such ambivalence.

Though taking a cynical view of the conservatives' rule of law, constitutional realists like Smith, Boudin, and Haines did not relinquish
altogether the constitutional symbol. What they did was to try to fill it
with a different content. In general, realist critics were unreconstructed
democrats who in their scholarship sought to provide an intellectual
basis for political action that would revitalize constitutional government. This meant energizing government to make it responsive to social needs and accountable to the popular will. "The real difference
between despotism and constitutional government," Henry Jones Ford
wrote in 1918, "does not lie in limitation of power but in the existence
of means of enforcing responsibility." Ford saw "nothing but deceit
in the notion of maintaining republican institutions and democratic
government by limitation put to the scope of authority." Like most of
the realists he would recognize "the inevitable fulness of power" and
insist on its responsible behavior.[53] Constitutional realists thus hoped
to infuse American constitutionalism with a new content of positive,
responsible government. By the start of the 1930s their critique of traditional constitutionalism helped provide the intellectual framework for
the constitution of powers that the New Deal created.

Notes

1. Herman Belz, "The Constitution in the Gilded Age: The Beginnings of
Constitutional Realism in American Scholarship," 13 *Amer. J. of Legal Hist.*
110–25 (1969).

2. Martin Landau, "The Myth of Hyperfactualism in the Study of American Politics," 83 *Pol. Sci. Q.* 378–99 (1968); Glendon L. Schubert, "The Rhetoric of Constitutional Change," 16 *J. of Public Law*, 16–49 (1967).

3. Arnold M. Paul, *Conservative Crisis and the Rule of Law: Attitudes of Bar and Bench, 1887–1895* (1960).

4. Charles G. Haines, "Political Theories of the Supreme Court from 1789–1835," 2 *Amer. Pol. Sci. Rev.* 221–24 (1908).

5. Brooks Adams, *The Theory of Social Revolutions*, 45–47, 79 (1913).

6. Walter F. Dodd, "The Growth of Judicial Power," 24 *Pol. Sci. Q.* 193–95 (1909).

7. J. Allen Smith, *The Spirit of American Government*, 65–66, 97–98, 298–300 (1907).

8. Gustavus Myers, *History of the Supreme Court of the United States*, 7 (1918).

9. Smith, *op. cit. supra* note 7, at v–vii.

10. Charles A. Beard, *An Economic Interpretation of the Constitution of the United States*, 292, 63 (2nd ed. 1935).

11. Frank J. Goodnow, *Politics and Administration*, 1–5, 17–18 (1900).

12. Frank J. Goodnow, *Social Reform and the Constitution*, 2–4, 6 (1911).

13. Robert L. Schuyler, "Agreement in the Federal Convention," 31 *Pol. Sci. Q.* 290–92 (1916).

14. Smith, *op. cit. supra* note 7, at 299.

15. Melville W. Bigelow, ed., *Centralization and the Law*, 3 (1906).

16. Arthur F. Bentley, *The Process of Government*, 110, 113, 272 (1949).

17. Beard, *op. cit. supra* note 10, at 10, 12–13, 73.

18. Remarks of William MacDonald, quoted in A. C. McLaughlin, "Report of the Conference on American Constitutional History," 1 *Amer. Hist. Assoc. Annual Report 1907*, 79–80 (1908).

19. James G. Randall, "The Interrelation of Social and Constitutional History," 35 *Amer. Hist. Rev.* 1–2, 7 (1929); *Constitutional Problems under Lincoln*, 2–5 (rev. ed. 1951).

20. Harry Elmer Barnes, *The New History and the Social Studies*, 510 (1925).

21. Charles H. McIlwain, *The American Revolution: A Constitutional Interpretation*, x, 5, 16 (1924).

22. Randolph G. Adams, *The Political Ideas of the American Revolution*, 196–97 (3rd ed. 1958). Charles M. Andrews also adopted a constitutional interpretation of the Revolution. The problem that had to be dealt with, he wrote, was not mercantile subordination, but rather "the very constitution of the British empire." The Revolution came when the British were unable to make concessions meeting the Americans' constitutional demands (*The Colonial Background of the American Revolution*, 206, 217 [1924]).

23. Andrew C. McLaughlin, *The Confederate and the Constitution*, 184, xvii (1905).

24. Max Farrand, *The Framing of the Constitution of the United States* 201–02, 43–47 (1913).

25. Charles Warren, *The Making of the Constitution*, 5, 8, 54 (1929).

26. Robert E. Newton, "Edward S. Corwin and American Constitutional Law," 14 *J. of Public Law*, 211 (1965).

27. Benjamin F. Wright, Jr., *American Interpretations of Natural Law* 343–44 (1932).

28. Andrew C. McLaughlin, *The Courts, the Constitution, and Parties: Studies in Constitutional History and Politics*, 113 (1912).

29. Andrew C. McLaughlin, "American History and American Democracy," 20 *Amer. Hist. Rev.* 260 (1915).

30. Book review, 18 *Amer. Pol. Sci. Rev.* 180 (1924).

31. McLaughlin, *op. cit. supra* note 29, at 261.

32. Andrew C. McLaughlin, *The Foundations of American Constitutionalism*, v, 104, 107, 109–110 (1932).

33. Black was the author of *The Relation of the Executive Power to Legislation* (1919), a critique of the enlargement of the presidency under Wilson.

34. Alpheus T. Mason, "Ours—A Government of Laws and Not of Men," 13 *Constitutional Review*, 197–203 (1929).

35. Bentley, *op. cit. supra* note 16, at 295.

36. Randall, *op. cit. supra* note 19 *(Constitutional Problems)*, at 2.

37. Howard L. McBain, *The Living Constitution: A Consideration of the Realities and Legends of Our Fundamental Law*, 3–5, 272 (1927).

38. Charles E. Merriam, *New Aspects of Politics*, 53–54 (1925); *The Written Constitution and the Unwritten Attitude*, 11, 25 (1931).

39. A. K. Rogers, "Constitutionalism," 40 *Inter'l J. of Ethics*, 289, 296 (1930).

40. William Bennett Munro, *The Invisible Government*, 4–5, 20, 113 (1928). See also Munro, *Personality in Politics* (1924).

41. Ironically, the same criticism came from the conservative James M. Beck, who complained that "our very dependence upon a written Constitution and our mistaken belief in its static nature and its self-executing powers has tended to deaden the political consciousness of the American people" ("The Changed Conception of the Constitution," 69 *Proc. of the Amer. Philosophical Soc.* 111 [1930]).

42. J. Allen Smith, *The Growth and Decadence of Constitutional Government*, 149, 160, 185, 277, 285–86 (1930).

43. Walton H. Hamilton, "Constitutionalism," 4 *Encyclopedia of the Social Sciences*, 255–59 (1935).

44. In addition to his activities as a member of the Socialist Party of America Boudin gained recognition for his study, *The Theoretical System of Karl Marx* (1907).

45. In 1911 Boudin argued that the major issue facing the country was the question of the limitations on the judicial power to annul legislation. Referring to the expanded judicial review of the 1890s and after he asked: "Shall we permit this great revolution in our political institutions to take place undisputed?" ("Government by Judiciary," 26 *Pol. Sci. Q.* 238–70.) Although Beard in his *The Supreme Court and the Constitution* (1912) tended to defend judicial review as part of the original constitutional settlement, most progressives criticized it as a departure from the Framers' intentions.

46. Louis B. Boudin, *Government by Judiciary*, v. 1, iv–x (1932).

47. Charles Grove Haines, *The American Doctrine of Judicial Supremacy*, 530–34 (2nd ed. 1932).

48. *Ibid.,* 500–04, 538–40.

49. Randall, *op. cit. supra,* note 19 *(Constitutional Problems),* at 2–3.

50. Remarks of George M. Dutcher, quoted in Henry E. Bourne, "The Fifti-eth Anniversary Meeting," 40 *Amer. Hist. Rev.* 426 (1935).

51. Howard K. Beale, *The Critical Year: A Study of Andrew Johnson and Recon-struction,* 147, 150 (1930).

52. *Ibid.,* 211.

53. Henry Jones Ford, "The Growth of Dictatorship," 121 *Atlantic Monthly,* 634–35 (1918).

4

Andrew C. McLaughlin and the Defense of Constitutionalism

Although we commonly say that each generation writes its own history, we do not carry this idea to its logical conclusion and discard past historical writings. Whether this fact suggests that history is a progressive science capable of accumulating a useful body of knowledge, or merely a form of intellectual socialization within a tradition of discourse, the assumption of continuity that it implies can be applied to American constitutionalism. Choosing to govern themselves under written constitutions, the American people have required knowledge and understanding of these legal instruments to carry on their political life. To a significant extent this knowledge and understanding are historical in nature. Moreover, because the United States as a nation is governed under the fundamental law ordained and established by its founders over two hundred years ago, historical knowledge about the Constitution may be of practical importance.

These reflections warrant reexamining the first general synthesis of American constitutional development written in the era of modern professional scholarship, Andrew C. McLaughlin's *A Constitutional History of the United States* (1935; hereafter *CHUS*). Although the book was awarded the Pulitzer prize for history in 1936—the only history textbook ever to be so honored—it was not long preeminent in its field. McLaughlin appeared to many critics as a defender of the old order who was "more interested in showing how ideas shape institutions than in proving that material interests shape ideas."[1] Asserting that McLaughlin's approach to history lacked realism because it failed to distinguish between "the Constitution in the textbooks . . . and the living Constitution," liberal scholars objected that his book was "not calculated to encourage the average citizen to apply any engines of criticism and verification to constitutional issues."[2] As works more sympathetic to centralized authority and the economic interpretation of history gained favor, McLaughlin's pioneering work was largely ignored.[3] Two generations later, when the historiographical assumptions of the 1930s have lost much of their persuasiveness, the time may be propitious for a fresh evaluation of McLaughlin's account of constitutionalism in America.

Twelve years in preparation, and anticipated by historians of McLaughlin's generation as "a classical publication," *A Constitutional History* climaxed a long and distinguished scholarly career.[4] Born in Illinois in 1861 of Scottish Presbyterian immigrant parents, McLaughlin grew up in Michigan and was graduated from the University of Michigan in 1882. After teaching Latin in high school and reading law for two years, he attended the University of Michigan school of law where he became a student of the noted jurist and constitutional scholar, Thomas M. Cooley. Awarded the LL.B. degree in 1885, he was admitted to the Illinois and Michigan bars and practiced law briefly in Chicago. In 1886 he returned to Michigan as an instructor in classics, and in 1887 took over Judge Cooley's course in constitutional history when Cooley left to become the first chairman of the Interstate Commerce Commission. McLaughlin, who never received the doctoral degree, taught at Michigan until 1906, when he accepted an appointment at the University of Chicago. He remained at Chicago for the rest of his career.[5]

McLaughlin's first published writings were in the fields of western and diplomatic history.[6] The interest in constitutional matters evident in these early works became the principal focus in two seminal articles in the late 1890s that marked his emergence as a leading constitutional historian.[7] In the next two decades a number of major works followed, including *The Confederation and the Constitution 1783–1789* (1905); *The Courts, the Constitution, and Parties: Studies in Constitutional History and Politics* (1912); "American History and American Democracy," *American Historical Review* (1915); "The Background of American Federalism," *American Political Science Review* (1918); and *Steps in the Development of American Democracy* (1920). Prominent in the affairs of the American Historical Association throughout his career, McLaughlin was editor of the *American Historical Review* from 1901 to 1905, during which time he also served as the first director of the Carnegie Institution Department of Historical Research. In 1914 he was president of the American Historical Association. Although not a strong advocate of preparedness, McLaughlin during World War I actively supported the Allied effort, writing for the Committee on Public Information and lecturing in England in defense of democracy and against

German autocracy. In the 1920s he commenced work on *A Constitutional History.*[8]

McLaughlin was a scientific historian whose writings, informed by the insights of law and political science, evinced an abiding concern for the best regime. Although by no means an uncritical defender of existing political arrangements in the United States, McLaughlin's understanding of modern history led him to conclude that liberal democracy under the federal Constitution was the form of government that most closely approximated this ancient standard.

This essay examines McLaughlin's interpretation of the fundamental constitutional issues in American history that formed the basis for this judgment. These issues, which have lost little of their salience in the intervening years, include federalism and the social compact philosophy, limited government and individual rights, democracy and political parties, and the responsibility of the historian as scholar and citizen. McLaughlin in masterly fashion presented a distillation of his views on several of these questions in lectures delivered at New York University in 1932 and published as *The Foundations of American Constitutionalism.* In this work and in the comprehensive account that followed three years later, he continued his life-long endeavor of "teaching constitutional principles historically." Among other things, this involved focusing on the essential matters that "the American citizen, not highly trained in the law, should know familiarly," and showing "the relationship between political philosophy and constitutional achievement."[9]

Federalism was the constitutional principle with which McLaughlin was perhaps most closely identified. He defined federalism as "the distribution of essential powers of sovereign authority among governments" (*CHUS*, p. 5). Involving more than relations among states or the technical question of intergovernmental relations, federalism in McLaughlin's view was the basic form that constitutionalism in the United States assumed. The idea of limited government for the protection of individual liberty was the starting point in his understanding of constitutionalism. This idea was quintessentially expressed in the founding of political communities based on "the doctrine of individual liberty and the process of association of individuals into a new and more vital whole."[10] As individuals by agreement and consent formed political societies based on "compact-or-covenant thinking," so communities of individuals through a social compact could form a political body to which portions of sovereignty were granted. According to McLaughlin, the Constitution of 1787 was a social compact that created a federal state as the political form of constitutionalism in America.[11]

One of McLaughlin's most seminal interpretations was his view of federalism as the product of the British empire. He argued that although in theory the empire was a unitary state, in reality it functioned as a system of divided sovereignty. The colonies managed internal or local affairs through the colonial assembly, while Parliament regulated commerce and other matters of concern to the empire as a whole. The result of "natural forces" and "spontaneous growth," the idea of divided sovereignty was conceptualized by America's leading political thinkers in the 1760s as an answer to the problem of imperial organization—"the central, dominating, irrepressible task of a generation (1750–1788)" (*CHUS*, p. 17).

With the Revolution, the problem of imperial organization crossed the ocean. Recognizing that complete unification was impossible, Americans provided for a distribution of powers between the states and the Confederation Congress that in broad outline resembled the structure of the old empire. The defenders of state power contested the locus of sovereignty as a legal proposition, however, and succeeded in writing the doctrine of state sovereignty into the Articles of Confederation. While acknowledging that a plausible claim to state sovereignty could be made, McLaughlin argued that the states as political communities could only maintain their independent existence by entering into a union that denied their ultimate sovereignty. Although the logic of "self-government and self-control" tended toward separation and autonomy of states, the paradoxical fact was that the "very desire for political self-determination constituted a common quality and made for cooperation when political interests and economic needs were at stake" (*CHUS*, p. 19).

The Constitutional Convention solved the problem of imperial organization by forming "a new kind of body public." Although the states' evasion of their responsibilities was the chief problem of the time, the delegates were determined to create "a strong and infrangible union without destroying the state as integral, and in many respects, autonomous parts of an integral system." Accepting the division of sovereignty that was the legacy of the British empire, the Framers made their "signal contribution . . . to the political life of the modern world" by creating "a real government" at the center: a federal republic that while it was endowed with certain additional powers, above all possessed legitimate authority and the sanction that resulted from being based directly on the people (*CHUS*, p. 154).

As a historian and constitutionalist, McLaughlin held to a conception of federalism known as states' rights nationalism. A contradiction in terms to late-twentieth-century scholars, this constitutional outlook affirmed American nationalism while resisting the tendency of unionism to consolidate state powers in a centralized sovereign government

(*CHUS*, p. 173). McLaughlin began his professional career at a time when the constitutional conflicts that produced the Civil War were being refought in the pages of scholarly publications. His states' rights nationalism staked out a moderate position between the extremes of centralization and state sovereignty.

McLaughlin's states' rights nationalism can be seen in his interpretation of John Marshall's theory of the Union. Orthodox nationalist theory attributed to Marshall in *McCulloch* v. *Maryland* the view that the Constitution was adopted by the people of the United States acting as a single political community. McLaughlin in contrast contended that "Marshall . . . believed that the people of the states adopted the Constitution" (*CHUS*, p. 280n). To support this assertion he relied on Marshall's description, in the *McCulloch* opinion, of popular ratification of the Constitution: "It is true, they assembled in their several states—and where else should they have assembled? No political dreamer was ever wild enough to think of breaking down the lines which separate the states, and of compounding the American people into one common mass. Of consequence, when they act, they act in their states. But the measures they adopt do not, on that account, cease to be measures of the people themselves" (*CHUS*, p. 388). McLaughlin interpreted this passage to mean that Marshall "thought of a supreme law resulting from the action of thirteen bodies of people, a law which when adopted was to be the supreme law of the land."[12] Rejecting thus the centralizing nationalist view, McLaughlin also rejected the state sovereignty theory in arguing that the people of the states acted as part of the people of the United States, not as agents of the states in their sovereign capacity (*CHUS*, p. 388n).[13]

The second fundamental principle that McLaughlin traced in *A Constitutional History* was the idea of legally limited government under a written constitution. An inheritance of the struggle to liberalize government under the Stuarts in the seventeenth century, this concept was developed by the American colonists in the eighteenth century in the light of Lockean social contract theory. The essence of Locke's political philosophy was the idea of government established by consent and bound by law for the protection of the natural rights of individuals to life, liberty, and property. While stressing individual rights, McLaughlin also noted Locke's argument that the good of the society is the object of the laws, and further that it is sometimes necessary for the executive power to transcend or go beyond the law, acting "according to discretion for the public good" (*CHUS*, pp. 94, 96).

Based on Lockean ideas, the Declaration of Independence expressed liberal republicanism as the philosophy of the American Revolution. Among the ideas in the Declaration, McLaughlin called attention to the

principle of natural equality. It meant that all men were equally enti-
tled to "certain great rights," not that each individual was as strong,
virtuous, or competent as every other. It was not an assertion of social,
economic, or political equality. Jefferson's central argument, according
to McLaughlin, was that government has only delegated powers, not
inherent or intrinsic authority. "The most important word in the Declaration," McLaughlin wrote, "is 'deriving' " (*CHUS*, p. 103).

In the most general sense, *A Constitutional History* is the story of a
democratic state founded on the idea of legally limited government for
the protection of individual rights. The two principal institutions for
implementing this idea are constitutional law, depending mainly on
the courts and judicial review, and constitutional politics, consisting of
legislation and policy making by the political branches in the context
of political parties. Having explained the origins of these institutions
in the era of the Revolution and constitution-making, McLaughlin focused on the way in which Americans used them to deal with the two
great social and political problems of the nineteenth century: slavery
and industrialization. His account of these problems provides further
insight into the nature of his constitutionalism.

Throughout most of McLaughlin's career the legitimacy of judicial
review and the role of the courts in American government were deeply
contested issues. Progressive reformers and scholars attacked the
newly developed doctrine of comprehensive and final judicial review
as a usurpation of power by the courts aimed at protecting propertied
interests against regulation by democratically elected legislatures.
Conservatives justified heightened judicial scrutiny of state and national legislation as an exercise of the rightful power of the courts to
determine the meaning of the Constitution in all cases whatsoever,
rather than simply in those of a judiciary nature.[14] In this debate
McLaughlin adopted a moderate position that defended judicial review within the framework of political constitutionalism.

Rejecting the progressive interpretation, McLaughlin said the exercise of judicial review in *Marbury* v. *Madison* was consistent with the
Framers' design. He denied, however, that the judiciary had a general
power to fix the meaning of the Constitution as a rule of political action
for the political branches. McLaughlin differed from many conservative commentators in holding that the power of a court to declare a
legislative act void could not simply be asserted as a formal logical
argument from a written constitution. The practice could only be justified by reference to "historical forces" and "fundamental theories
upon which constitutions and laws must be supposed to rest" (*CHUS*,
p. 309). The relevant history and theory on which *Marbury* rested consisted of the idea, rooted in English history and taken for granted by

the delegates to the Philadelphia Convention, that the Constitution is law, an act against the Constitution is not law and no one is bound to obey it, and the Constitution is enforceable in the courts and is "to be handled as any other law is handled, . . . for the duty of any court is to announce and apply the law." Ultimately McLaughlin concluded that judicial review was based on the philosophy of the American Revolution and was justified as the attempt of a free people to establish and maintain a nonautocratic government (*CHUS*, pp. 184–85, 310).

The separation of powers was an essential basis for judicial review because under it the judiciary is an independent and coordinate branch of government. Reciprocally the separation principle prevented judicial review from developing into judicial supremacy over constitutional interpretation. Denying that it is the peculiar function of the Supreme Court to pronounce legislative acts void, McLaughlin said the Court is "not charged with the special and exclusive duty of upholding the Constitution which is law." It was "the duty of any and every court to announce the law and to apply the law in distributing justice to litigants" (*CHUS*, p. 308). This analysis implied that judicial review was limited to cases of a judiciary nature, and was improper in political questions. The corollary was that the executive was under no obligation to regard the constitutionality of a given policy matter as settled by a Supreme Court decision. Referring to Andrew Jackson's bank veto and his theory of departmental constitutional review, McLaughlin acknowledged the validity of Jackson's assertion that every officer had a right to support the Constitution "as he understands it." McLaughlin further denied, with Lincoln, that the *Dred Scott* decision as a constitutional opinion established a rule binding on voters, lawmakers, and executive officers. "From the acknowledgment of the Court's right and duty to interpret the Constitution," he observed, "to the declaration that the Court by its decision fixes upon the Constitution an interpretation that must last forever and beyond, it is a far cry" (*CHUS*, pp. 414–15, 582).

McLaughlin offered a moderate interpretation of substantive due process and expanded judicial review in the late nineteenth century. He explained that the judiciary was called upon to adapt constitutional law to rapidly changing social conditions at the very time when "there was new need of determining what was the nature or the limits of liberty" (*CHUS*, p. 724). The problem was to balance regulation of property with the protection of individual property rights. McLaughlin criticized *Munn* v. *Illinois* as a solution to the problem. Instead of holding that a business affected with a public interest could be regulated, he said the Court should have declared more broadly that when a business assumed such a character that there was need for legislative control of rates, measures for that purpose would be constitutional (*CHUS*, p. 736).

McLaughlin was sympathetic to the new judicial review, with its concern for the reasonableness of legislation, because it affirmed the principle of limited government and individual rights. At the same time he noted that expanded review, which a later generation would refer to as judicial activism, "allows a modification or an accommodation to new conditions of society and to a changing belief concerning the essence of liberty." This approach was able to accommodate decisions expressing public opinion and the legislature's judgment "as to what constituted justice, and what was reasonable interference with private property and liberty of contract." It was "far better than any rigid definition of right and justice or any highly technical formulas which give no opportunity for development" (*CHUS*, pp. 755, 758).

Although judicial review was an essential feature of limited government, the success of liberal democracy depended mainly on the political branches and the people. The development of constitutional law was accordingly subordinated in *A Constitutional History* to a general survey of political history, with special emphasis on political theories and legal aspects of political controversies.[15] The political party system was a pivotal institution that altered the constitutional order. A means by which citizens could control the formal legal government and direct the working of the constitutional system, parties were intended to accomplish "the two supreme jobs of democracy": electing officers whom the people wanted, and transferring the people's desires into legislation and administration. McLaughlin understood that parties had problematic features insofar as they tended to serve their own interests rather than promote the common good. Reformers therefore faced the constitutional problem of controlling "the government that would control the government" (*CHUS*, p. 403). On balance, however, McLaughlin maintained a positive view of party as a democratic institution that, by reason of its quest for votes, tended toward inclusiveness and promoted national unity and social solidarity against "mere individualism," group factionalism, and "class-selfishness" (*CHUS*, p. 404).

The party system had a major effect on the slavery controversy, which McLaughlin viewed as a conflict between liberalism and autocracy. At issue was the struggle between free rational discussion as a way of conducting government, in order to protect personal liberty and fundamental human rights, and "the right of the strong and those possessed of assumed authority to be served by the many, whether . . . black or white" (*CHUS*, p. 489).

Constitutional questions were of course pertinent to this struggle.

The fight over the gag rule, for example, showed that the essential issue was "the right and the duty of free speech, free discussion, and interchange of opinion" versus the rule of force and enforced silence demanded by slavery. McLaughlin held that although the Constitution recognized the existence of slavery in some of the states, it marked it as a local institution. This could be seen in the fact that while it was not considered necessary to say in the Constitution that if horses should escape from one state into another they would remain the property of the person from whom they fled, it was thought necessary to say this of persons held to service or labor. McLaughlin subordinated technical legal discussion of slavery issues, however, to the political philosophical ideas that guided his analysis. When considered in relation to "the perennial question" of "whether the strong shall inherit the earth and rule it with their strength," he reasoned, "constitutional history in the ordinary sense falls into the background of obscurity" (*CHUS*, pp. 483, 492, 495, 612).

McLaughlin analyzed the slavery issue in relation to the forces of national integration that were transforming American society. He observed that improvements in transportation and communication were often said to have the effect of unifying people and creating one world. In fact they revealed not the unity but the dualism of the world, as the slavery struggle showed. The "dualism of America by the mid-nineteenth century had become more evident because of the integrating forces drawing North and South together," McLaughlin reasoned. "The more nearly North and South came together, the farther they were apart."[16] A striking passage in *A Constitutional History* expressed the division into which the country had fallen as well as the urgent sense of nationalism that was driving it toward a resolution of the slavery conflict. McLaughlin wrote: "Slavery belonged to the south, and the south must be left alone; slavery was a local matter, so local that to discuss it a thousand miles away endangered its existence; so local that it must be national—at least there was national obligation binding Massachusetts and Vermont not to discuss the denial of human rights by South Carolina" (*CHUS*, p. 492). Both sides struggled to define the principle of American nationality in an irrepressible conflict between "the developing forces of occidental civilization" and the South's "worn-out system of economic order" (*CHUS*, p. 475).

McLaughlin's philosophical idealism, concern for the evolution of ideas and institutions, and belief that "the long course of history seems to find its culmination in the establishment of the American constitutional system" are reasons for regarding him as a conservative historian.[17] His substantive view of American history, however, was socially progressive and liberal nationalist in outlook.[18] This can be seen in his interpretation of the antislavery movement and the response to industrialization.

Nineteenth-century humanitarian reform was directed at industrial, social, and labor problems, which McLaughlin said were perceived in the United States as early as the 1830s. Americans could not deal with these issues, however, until slavery—"a system of labor as old as the pyramids"—was eliminated. Agitation against slavery therefore was "one of those movements for liberalism and social righteousness— humanitarianism—which were transforming the modern world." A positive result of the struggle was that it "brought into clear relief the value of freedom." Yet McLaughlin critically observed also that "men were induced to indulge in further glorification of their own freedom and likewise, to suppose that, if the laborer were not *owned* by the capitalist, he was free." He wrote that "one would expect to find men, upon the extirpation of slavery, also anxious, at the first opportune moment, to reach out the hand of helpfulness to the serfs of the machine and the factory." This humanitarian response was long delayed, however, and only after the issues of the war lost their appeal did the movement for the social control of industry begin (*CHUS*, pp. 721–22).

Sympathetic to the social reform purposes that guided American political thought in the early twentieth century, McLaughlin adopted a historical approach to constitutionalism that was grounded in the normative perspective of political science or political philosophy. To be sure, he emphasized obedience to law and viewed the Constitution as law to be applied by ordinary courts. Yet there was nothing of judicial supremacy in his concept of judicial review, and he denied that constitutional interpretation and the preservation of liberal democratic government were primarily a matter of applying "abstract principles of disembodied law, if there be any such thing" (*CHUS*, p. 300). The substance of constitutional history—and the essence of constitutionalism—was not "judicial pronouncements, but great controversies, discussed and rediscussed by statesmen and the common people." In the resolution of these controversies, judgments and decisions about the constitutionality of public measures involved the ends, purposes, and objects of the Constitution in relation to social needs and political philosophy. Government officials did not burn candles "before the altar of a disembodied principle of constitutional interpretation," McLaughlin noted, and consistency in the application of constitutional principle was not honored as a criterion of statesmanship. In the political crisis caused by the Alien and Sedition Acts, for example, the real issue was not whether specific words of the Constitution were violated or given an improper construction, but whether the acts were "contrary to the spirit of the Constitution and . . . at variance with the elementary principles of free and liberal government" (*CHUS*, pp. vii–viii, 233–34, 295, 271).

McLaughlin's conception of constitutionalism was fundamentally political rather than legalistic or juridical in nature. Historically it was best illustrated in the statesmanship of John Marshall and Abraham Lincoln. McLaughlin wrote that Marshall's duties as chief justice "called for the talent and the insight of a statesman capable of looking beyond the confines of legal learning and outward onto the life of a vigorous people entering upon the task of occupying a continent." He suggested that if Marshall had been more of a technical lawyer, steeped in the history and intricacies of the law, he would have been a less effective jurist. Marshall's greatness lay not in any constitutional creativity he possessed, but in his ability to understand and expose the very foundations of the constitutional system (*CHUS*, pp. 300, 383).

McLaughlin's most considered analysis of constitutionalism focused on Lincoln's exercise of executive power during the Civil War. While noting Lincoln's conscientious adherence to the forms and procedures of constitutional government, he said the president acted on the premise that encroachments on constitutional limitations were justified by the necessity of preserving the life of the nation and its fundamental law. "No one would deny Lincoln's moral right to break the Constitution in order to save it," he wrote. Although conceding that from the standpoint of constitutional precedent Lincoln's action at the start of the war "bears an ominous look," McLaughlin declared that "safety from tyranny lies not so much in the technicalities of law as in the constitutional conscience of officials and people and in the intelligence of the voting masses, who, if they use discretion, will seek to place in office men of wisdom and of rectitude rather than greedy graspers for power" (*CHUS*, pp. 615, 619, 627).

McLaughlin believed executive discretion, exercised for the public good and the ends of the political community, is an essential feature of constitutionalism.[19] His study of Lincoln led him to state that the Constitution was "the actual structure of a nation, . . . the common and conventional attitudes of the citizens, the principles which animate them, their substantial concepts of justice, liberty, and safety." Forced to go beyond legal forms, Lincoln "penetrated the foundations of democratic government restrained by law" and acted on the premise that "It is the prime duty of a democratic statesman to maintain the very system on which his power rests." Calling him an "arch-constitutionalist," McLaughlin concluded that the "primal and elemental responsibility of free government" responsive to the people's needs was "the central principle of Lincoln's constitutionalism."[20]

In McLaughlin's writings the constitutionalist's concern for the best regime existed in tension with the obligation of a scientific historian to refrain from moral judgment. Rejecting the notion that the purpose of history was "to garner a few well-phrased precepts . . . whereby virtue may be obtained," he disavowed the idea that the historian was a philosopher or moralist. At the same time, McLaughlin said the problem of teaching American history "was complicated by what may be the need of inculcating Americanism or of building up of national spirit." Concerning this "difficult and distracting subject" he concluded: "We cannot deny a certain amount of obligation" to teach patriotism and develop the spirit of American nationalism.[21]

McLaughlin explained the sense in which the historian had a civic obligation in advice he offered, as editor of the *American Historical Review*, to a high school history teacher. Asserting that "the stress that is laid upon industrial history is in great danger of being overdone," he stated that "with the great majority of students it is of vastly greater importance to give an understanding of the declaration of independence and the constitution of the United States than the discovery of coal or the development of the sewing machine." Economic and social facts could be of value if "treated in a really historical way in order to develop the historical spirit in students," he conceded. "But every boy and girl must be a citizen of the United States whether he will or not." McLaughlin reasoned, "and he must perform his political and social duties whether iron can be made out of pit coal or charcoal alone."[22]

Mutatis mutandis, McLaughlin delivered essentially the same message in his presidential address to the American Historical Association in 1914. Taking "the whole democratic regime" as the paramount subject for the American historian, he declared: "We may well question whether a nation can ever become truly great without intense self-consciousness and self-appreciation, and, however closely the historian may cling to ideals of scientific objectivity, he may well believe that one duty of historical study and writing is to help make a nation conscious of its most real self, by bringing before it its own activity and the evidences of its own psychology."[23] When two years later the United States entered the world war, McLaughlin placed his scholarship more directly in the service of the nation. "In my judgment," he wrote in April 1917, "the value of the historian now is chiefly in pointing out the route into the future which his various experiences have enabled him to see. In other words, it is time for us to dare to use our historical information for purposes of prophecy and actual guidance."[24]

In the broadest sense, *A Constitutional History* embodied the view expressed in McLaughlin's AHA presidential assertion: "The history of a popular state must be no other, at its inmost heart, than the story of the attempt to become and remain a popular state."[25] Approaching his subject from the standpoint of an objective historical observer and a constitutionalist, McLaughlin conceived of the study of constitutional history as "on the very brink of political science and political philosophy." Its essential task was to provide "the proper interpretation of constitutional documents and speeches bearing upon the most significant questions." And this involved showing that the authors of public documents often "were thinking differently from the men of the present day on certain fundamental things, that terms have lost or changed their meaning in the lapse of one hundred and twenty–five years."[26]

The dual perspective of historian and constitutionalist concerned for the regime of liberal democracy are evident at many points in *A Constitutional History*. McLaughlin wrote, for example, that "In an attempt to decide where at a given moment sovereignty resides in any nation, the investigator is engaged in an historical task." Yet "his conclusion is within the field of law," and "though he be a mere historian, he is under no obligation to withhold from his readers his own conclusion which is a necessary product of his historical study" (*CHUS*, p. 132). Tension between constitutionalist and historical perspectives also appears in McLaughlin's practice of evaluating constitutional actions and decisions in the light of subsequent developments in constitutional law. The historian Robert Livingston Schuyler commented that this approach implied "that constitutional liberty is a constant, unaffected by historical developments."[27] The political scientist Robert E. Cushman nevertheless believed McLaughlin satisfied the criterion of historical mindedness. His book expressed the view that "the Constitution for any generation in our national history is what that generation conceives it to be, as disclosed by what it says and does about it."[28] Henry Steele Commager was right when he said that McLaughlin, addressing themes of abiding significance that transcend a single historical period or nation, sought an orderly sequence of facts "not for narrative purposes, but for philosophical."[29]

As a scientific historian and liberal constitutionalist, McLaughlin attached great importance to reason, reflection, deliberation, and debate as critical forces in history. At a time when many historians were adopting the economic interpretation of history, he acknowledged the relevance of the new approach. "There is no reason for denying the influence of economic causes on the Revolution," he wrote. Nevertheless, "men have and had their pride as well as thrift," he argued, "and it is folly not to see the immense significance of the struggle for constitutional liberty" (*CHUS*, p. 62). The Constitution represented the triumph of reason in pursuit of liberty. "Men of mind," "thoughtful men," "those willing to think" were responsible for the Federal Convention, in which "results were reached by debate, by interchange of opinion, by deliberate but earnest consideration of problems." No faction worked its will and no leader dominated. "For once at least in the course of history," McLaughlin wrote, "opinions were formed and changed as the result of argument." In the adoption of the Constitution, as in the making of the state constitutions, "the principles of political philosophy were to be put to the test" (*CHUS*, pp. 142–43, 148, 108).

From the standpoint of late-twentieth-century constitutional history, McLaughlin's contribution can be shown in a variety of ways. As indicated earlier, a number of recent works express intellectual obligation to McLaughlin or employ the concept of liberal republican political philosophy that informed his writings.[30] Moreover general accounts of constitutional history emulate his broad, political-institutional approach to the constitutional system.[31] A more important reason for consulting *A Constitutional History* is that it identifies perennial problems in American history and government. It seems unnecessary to add that federalism, judicial review, limited government and individual rights, and the nature and tendency of liberal democracy continue to be vital issues in American politics. On all of these matters McLaughlin's commentary remains penetrating and perspicacious.

More broadly, McLaughlin's unifying conception of liberal democratic constitutionalism is pertinent at a time when historians are busily engaged in disaggregating the American past into the discrete experiences of racial, ethnic, and gender groups, in effect denying the possibility of a coherent synthesis of our national history. The purpose and motive of this historical deconstruction may be to secure the inclusion of previously excluded groups into the society. The historical conclusion it reaches, however, and the political logic on which it rests deny the existence of a common culture and national political community. In McLaughlin's era comparable pressures, born of industrialization and emphasizing the conflict of social classes, threatened the liberal democratic order that formed the basis of American nationality. McLaughlin warned of a new sectionalism, functional rather than geographic in nature, by which "men and women in the same locality are divided into classes by impervious walls which belie real nationalism and already betoken disintegration." Asserting that "men should have a chance and not be sorted or sifted on any artificial or traditional theory of worth," he declared: "We look with foreboding on stratification and classification which will either benumb personal effort, or by setting up group barriers, prevent free play of common sentiments and motives."[32]

McLaughlin saw the issue as nothing less than the existence of the nation. This involved more than blood and race, or subjection to a government and inclusion in territorial limits. Nationality depended on the common possession of ideals and beliefs, which in the United States were preeminently equality before the law, protection of individual rights, and the responsibility of government to the people. In McLaughlin's view these ideals constituted "the ethical principle of justice," grounded in the Declaration of Independence, that held the American nation together as a living thing.[33]

It is instructive furthermore, at a time when a new normativism is evident in the fields of history and political science, to consider the balance in McLaughlin's scholarship between constitutionalism and objective historical analysis. Over a decade ago Michael Kammen reported that historians have rejected the values of nationalism and detachment and allowed their subjective relationship with their subject to guide the moral judgments to which they are increasingly given.[34] In a recent analysis the political scientist James W. Ceaser describes the complementary role that historians of the republican ideological school play in the effort of political scientists to design a communitarian regime of democratic participation and egalitarian justice.[35] Of this attempt to define the political tradition the historian Gordon S. Wood comments: "the stakes are high: nothing less than the real nature of America."[36]

If it is true that all serious historical writing is ultimately normative, it is all the more important for historians to approach their subject in a disciplined and scientific way. Perhaps the most that can be achieved is a constructive tension or balance between these conflicting pressures. McLaughlin's morally grounded yet judicious and restrained scholarship may serve as an example. Declaring that "History is not written or taught for the purpose of inculcating any particular moral or immoral lesson," he said that "careful, accurate, truthful examination of historical facts and evidences is a virtue itself."[37] The task of the historian was to present the long story of human life as it actually was and the succession of events as they really took place. At the same time the historian was part of "the stream of human energy that was carrying mankind onward and perhaps forward."[38] McLaughlin could therefore acknowledge that while "as a laborer in the field of history, I ought not, I suppose, be pleading for anything, . . . I feel free to suppose that as citizens as well as historians, we are interested in the vicissitudes of democracy and all its connotations."[39] McLaughlin reminds us that rules guiding historical investigation, although necessary, are not sufficient, and that good history, like good government, depends on prudential judgment and practical reason.

Finally, McLaughlin's view of the significance of American democracy in world perspective is probably still valid. "We must remember," he said in his AHA presidential address, "that, if we have in our later days judged ourselves by other standards and lost our sense of what we are and mean, Europe has not ceased for one moment in the last hundred and fifty years to watch us—in war, diplomacy, industrial growth, education, and religion—as a democracy."[40] Now that free institutions appear to have prevailed in eastern Europe over the repressive autocracies that darkened McLaughlin's world, it is perhaps worthwhile to reflect on the development of ordered liberty in the nation that supported the struggle and inspired this transformation. For that purpose McLaughlin's judicious account of the regime of liberal democracy is timely and pertinent.

Notes

1. Homer C. Hockett, Book Review, *Mississippi Valley Historical Review* 22 (March 1936): 610.

2. Sidney Ratner, Book Review, *Political Science Quarterly* 52 (Dec. 1937): 611; Charles A. Beard, "The Constitution in Cotton Wool," *The New Republic* 92 (Sept. 15, 1937): 163.

3. Obituary of Andrew C. McLaughlin, *Proceedings of the American Antiquarian Society* 57, part 2 (1947): 259.

4. Robert E. Cushman, Book Review, *American Political Science Review* 30 (June 1936): 565; J. Franklin Jameson to Andrew C. McLaughlin, Feb. 15, 1926, Box 110, J. Franklin Jameson Papers, Manuscript Division, Library of Congress.

5. *Dictionary of American Biography,* Supplement Four, 1946–1950 (1974), pp. 530–32; *National Cyclopedia of American Biography* (1950), 36: 137; Obituary, *American Historical Review* 53 (Jan. 1948): 432–34; Obituary, *Proceedings of the American Antiquarian Society* 57, part 2 (1947): 258–60; John Higham, *History: Professional Scholarship in America* (1983), p. 23.

6. *A History of Higher Education in Michigan* (1891); *Lewis Cass* (1891); *Elements of Civil Government in the State of Michigan* (1892); "The Western Posts and the British Debts," *American Historical Association Annual Report for 1894* (1895): 413–44.

7. Andrew C. McLaughlin, "James Wilson in the Philadelphia Convention," *Political Science Quarterly* 12 (March 1897): 1–20; and "Social Compact and Constitutional Construction," *American Historical Review* 5 (April 1900): 467–90.

8. Andrew C. McLaughlin to J. Franklin Jameson, June 7, 1916, Box 110, J. Franklin Jameson Papers, Manuscript Division, Library of Congress.

9. Andrew C. McLaughlin, *The Foundations of American Constitutionalism* (1932), pp. xi–xii; *CHUS,* p. vii.

10. McLaughlin, *The Foundations of American Constitutionalism,* p. 21.

11. Ibid., pp. 28, 80. Drawing in part on McLaughlin, Daniel J. Elazar has recently developed the idea of federalism as a new constitutional form for

organizing political life, not simply a structural compromise that permitted unification of separate states into a larger polity. See his *The American Constitutional Tradition* (1988), pp. 13–38.

12. Andrew C. McLaughlin, "Social Compact and Constitutional Construction," *American Historical Review* 5 (April 1900): 480n.

13. McLaughlin distinguished between Marshall's theory of the Union and that of Daniel Webster. He said that in the debate with Robert Y. Hayne of South Carolina in 1830, Webster "took a definite step forward, declaring the Constitution to have been ordained and established by the people of the United States in the aggregate." According to McLaughlin, Webster held that "the Constitution emanated from a single will, the people as a whole" (*CHUS*, p. 438).

Edward S. Corwin disputed this interpretation of Marshall, asserting that McLaughlin's "State Rights Federalist" sympathies led into "positive error." Corwin read *McCulloch* as expressing the purely popular origin of the Constitution, and denied that there was any difference between the views of Marshall and Webster. Book Review, *American Historical Review* 41 (Jan. 1936): 349–50.

14. Robert Lowry Clinton, *Marbury v. Madison and Judicial Review* (1990), pp. 161–91.

15. This characterization of the work was provided by W. W. Willoughby, Book Review, *A.B.A. Journal* 21 (Sept. 1935): 605. Willoughby criticized McLaughlin's conception of constitutional history because it failed to give sufficient attention to the institutional structure, functions, and activities of government.

16. Andrew C. McLaughlin, "Lincoln, the Constitution and Democracy," *International Journal of Ethics* 47 (Oct. 1936): 15–16.

17. McLaughlin, *The Foundations of American Constitutionalism*, p. 156; Higham, *History*, p. 166.

18. Referring to McLaughlin's emphasis on ideas and institutions, Clifford K. Shipton said that "Inevitably he was a conservative in his constitutional views, although much more devoted to social work than are most liberals" (*Proceedings of the American Antiquarian Society* 57 part 2, 1947: 259).

19. For an extended treatment of this view, see Harvey C. Mansfield, Jr., *Taming the Prince: The Ambivalence of Modern Executive Power* (1989).

20. McLaughlin, "Lincoln, the Constitution, and Democracy," pp. 2–3, 5–7. Emphasizing the philosophical tendency of Lincoln's constitutionalism, McLaughlin pointed out that although he was an able lawyer, Lincoln did not undertake a critical examination of the legal right to exclude slavery from the territories, made no attack on the vulnerable parts of the fugitive slave law, and presented no technical argument against the validity of the main holding of the *Dred Scott* decision. Reflecting the same sense of intellectual priorities, McLaughlin, in analyzing Lincoln's position on some technical questions in constitutional law, did so "only that I may not appear to have wilfully ignored it" (ibid., p. 7). For recent commentary expounding on the idea of constitutional statesmanship, see Gary L. Jacobsohn, *The Supreme Court and the Decline of Constitutional Aspiration* (1986), and John Agresto, *The Supreme Court and Constitutional Democracy* (1984).

21. Andrew C. McLaughlin, "Teaching War and Peace in American History," *The History Teacher's Magazine* 7 (Oct. 1916): 259, 261. An illustration of this tension in McLaughlin's thinking is provided in the recollection of Philip S. Klein, the biographer of James Buchanan, of graduate instruction at Chicago in the 1920s. According to Klein, McLaughlin would "take a controversial subject, talk a bit, and say 'Who is to judge, who is to judge?' Well, *he* was to judge." Klein said McLaughlin "did not give the Democrats or the slaveowners a fair shake," and was "so pro-Republican and anti-Democratic in handling the years 1854 through 1933 that one could think he was a politician rather than a historian." Michael J. Birkner, "A Conversation with Philip S. Klein," *Pennsylvania History* 56 (Oct. 1989): 252.

22. Andrew C. McLaughlin to John A. Butler, Feb. 10, 1902, American Historical Association Papers, Box 258, B-1902, Manuscript Division, Library of Congress.

23. Andrew C. McLaughlin, "American History and American Democracy," *American Historical Review* 20 (Jan. 1915): 258.

24. Andrew C. McLaughlin to J. Franklin Jameson, April 25, 1917, Box 110, J. Franklin Jameson Papers, Manuscript Division, Library of Congress.

25. McLaughlin, "American History and American Democracy," p. 276.

26. Andrew C. McLaughlin to J. Franklin Jameson, Oct. 15, 1900, Box 110, J. Franklin Jameson Papers, Manuscript Division, Library of Congress.

27. Robert Livingston Schuyler, Book Review, *The Social Studies* 26 (Oct. 1935): 422.

28. Robert E. Cushman, Book Review, *American Political Science Review* 30 (June 1936): 565.

29. Henry Steele Commager, "Foreword," in Andrew C. McLaughlin, *The Confederation and the Constitution 1783–1789* (1962), pp. 7–8.

30. See Jack P. Greene, *Peripheries and Center: Constitutional Development in the Extended Polities of the British Empire and the United States 1607–1788* (1990), p. x; Peter S. Onuf, *The Origins of the Federal Republic: Jurisdictional Controversies in the United States 1775–1787* (1983), p. xiv; Ralph Lerner, *The Thinking Revolutionary: Principles and Practice in the New Republic* (1987); Michael P. Zuckert, "Federalisms and the Founding," *Review of Politics* 48 (Spring 1986): 166–210; William E. Nelson, "Reason and Compromise in the Establishment of the Constitution: 1787–1801," *William and Mary Quarterly* 44 (July 1987): 458–84.

31. Mark Tushnet, Book Review, *Law and History Review* 8 (Fall 1990): 311–12.

32. McLaughlin, "American History and American Democracy," pp. 274–75.

33. McLaughlin, *The Foundations of American Constitutionalism*, p. 156.

34. Michael Kammen, ed., *The Past Before Us: Contemporary Historical Writing in the United States* (1980); pp. 22–23.

35. James W. Ceaser, *Liberal Democracy and Political Science* (1990), pp. 114–18.

36. Ibid., p. 115.

37. McLaughlin, "Teaching War and Peace in American History," p. 259.

38. McLaughlin, "American History and American Democracy," p. 276.

39. Ibid.

40. Ibid., p. 263.

5

Changing Conceptions of Constitutionalism in the Era of World War II and the Cold War

Constitutionalism is one of the major themes in western political thought which has occupied a preeminent place in the American political tradition. Whatever else is said about the way Americans manage their governmental and political affairs, attention is invariably directed to the peculiarly important role that written constitutions have come to assume in defining the institutional framework and central purposes and values of the polity. Like most important political ideas, however, constitutionalism in its long history has acquired a variety of meanings and significations. The idea of the constitutional has become as basic to our political thought and discourse as the idea of the public interest—and as difficult to define. For what is regarded as constitutional by one person or group may seem unconstitutional or arbitrary to another. Nevertheless, though the concept may not readily lend itself to precise and rigorous application in the analysis of political behavior, few would deny its importance as a political idea or its validity in distinguishing between systems of government. Efforts to assess the nature, meaning, and significance of constitutionalism reflect major tendencies in the political and intellectual life of a society, in addition to providing insight into one of the central problems of political theory.

In the early years of the twentieth century American intellectual life was transformed by a shift of interest to the social and economic dimension of human affairs. Political and legal scholars, while not a principal source of this transformation, were nevertheless stimulated by it to adopt a new attitude of critical realism toward the Constitution and public law. Constitutional realism at a minimum involved description of the actual institutions of government and distribution of power be-

yond the formal prescriptions of the Constitution and laws. Often identified with reform efforts, constitutional realists criticized the judicial
process and the general tendency of traditional constitutionalism to
emphasize restraints on governmental power. They gave special attention, moreover, to the motivating forces behind constitutional
change—an intellectual pursuit which led them to become cynical and
disillusioned about constitutionalism itself.[1]

In the 1930s constitutional realism assumed an even greater degree
of relevance, especially as conservative judicial decisions blocked recovery and reform measures. Yet it was also in the 1930s that the challenge of European totalitarianism began to introduce new forces into
American intellectual life. The principal impact among students of law,
politics, and government was to stimulate a reconsideration of traditional constitutionalism. Those who insisted on the importance of the
rule of law spoke with a new immediacy which, by the end of World
War II, made neo-constitutionalism a major ideological force. In the era
of the Cold War neo-constitutionalism continued to have wide appeal
as Americans defined the struggle with the Soviet Union in essentially
political rather than economic terms. Soviet rule like Nazi rule was
arbitrary, coercive, totalitarian—the antithesis of a constitutional state.
In time, however, another shift in perceptions of constitutionalism occurred. Against the background of the civil rights movement and renewed demands for social and economic change in the 1960s, realist
criticism of neo-constitutionalism emerged and received further stimu-
lus from the widespread hostility toward democratic liberalism
aroused by American foreign policy. The angry denunciations of "the
system" that have punctuated the rhetoric of contemporary radicals
have been directed not so much to capitalism as to liberal democratic
constitutionalism—the political and legal foundations of the "vital center" and "mainstream" politics.

As reaction to the static legalism of traditional constitutional theory,
constitutional realism in the Progressive era provided the intellectual
basis for criticism of major principles of public law such as liberty of
contract. In the 1920s there was little interruption in the development
of this reform realist outlook. Targets of progressive constitutional criticism were numerous—ranging from reformers' old *bête noir*, the Supreme Court and judicial supremacy, to some of the newer regulatory
agencies such as the Federal Trade Commission. With the onset of the
Depression, the widened scope and heightened intensity of social and
economic problems that would have to be resolved in the arena of constitutional politics gave to the idea of constitutional realism an even
more urgent appeal.

The realist imperative rested on the assumption that American government and public law needed reform in order to meet the exigencies of the economic crisis and of modern industrial society. So far from separating facts and values in a rigorously scientific manner, constitutional realists treated facts as having normative force. Facts not only determined, or ought to determine, rules but also formed the basis for the value judgments implicit in policy decisions.[2] Thus to set forth the realities of the constitutional system was the first step in changing the system. According to the legal philosopher Karl Llewellyn, realism did not reject the normative and ideal element in constitutional law. What it did was to turn from the documentary constitution as a source of rules to the facts of actual governmental needs and practices. Words did not legitimate institutional practices, Llewellyn wrote; rather it was the other way around.[3] Not to be forgotten was the realists' belief that facts would dispel the ignorance on which conservative constitutionalism depended. When the people learned what was being done to them by conservative judicial oligarchs, Louis Boudin asserted, they would demand genuine self-government.[4]

Describing the actual Constitution was the realists' first task. This necessarily involved a good deal of demythologizing, especially when myths, as those surrounding the judiciary, served to protect conservative economic interests. Influenced by their aversion to judicial control of the organic law, reform realists defined the Constitution as essentially political rather than legal in character.[5] Charles Beard explained that very little of the Constitution was unambiguous fixed law. "The Constitution as practice," he reasoned, "is today what citizens, judges, administrators, lawmakers, and those concerned with the execution of the laws do in bringing about changes in the relations of persons and property in the United States, or in preserving existing relations. . . ."[6] Llewellyn described the Constitution as an institution: "a set of ways of living and doing. . . . not, *in first instance,* a matter of words or rules." A realist theory of constitutional law in Llewellyn's view would be based on politico-social units that he identified as governing specialists, interest groups, and the general public.[7]

To describe the Constitution in terms of institutional practices was to employ the old and important distinction between a written and an unwritten constitution.[8] Yet more was involved than mere description. The idea of thinking about the Constitution in political terms contained implications relevant to the very nature of American government. Edward S. Corwin considered some of the implications when he evaluated the constitutional impact of the New Deal. He predicted in 1934 that NRA would revolutionize the constitutional system. It not only signified coordination rather than separation of powers but also meant that "a change in the character of the Constitution itself would take place." Henceforth Americans would be less legalistic and more political in their constitutional outlook. "We shall value it for the aid it lends to considered social purpose," Corwin declared, "not as a lawyer's document."[9] The new Constitution must meet the test of serviceability, he wrote in 1938: "it was the People's Law and must meet their need."[10] The conception of the Constitution as the people's political law also informed the thinking of the well-known scholar-publicist on American government, William B. Munro. One of Munro's main reform suggestions in the 1930s was that a state constitution ought to contain precepts explaining what was expected but not legally required of public officials. To adopt this approach, he reasoned, would transfer responsibility for the constitution from the courts to the legislature and, thus, to the electorate where it properly belonged.[11]

In their attempt to establish "serviceability" as a criterion of public law constitutional realists faced serious obstacles in the traditions surrounding the judiciary. Here the principal work of constitutional de-mythologizing had to take place. Chief among the myths needing critical scrutiny was that which defined the Constitution as a fixed body of legal principles, and which had as a corollary the belief in impartial judicial guardianship of the fundamental law.[12] Yet the latter aspect, the impartiality of the judges aside, was of course not chimerical. On the contrary, the Supreme Court's involvement in major struggles concerning the New Deal gave judicial guardianship of the Constitution a substantial basis in reality and made it a matter of special concern to realist scholars.

For years constitutional realists had scored the simplistic notions of mechanical jurisprudence according to which judges declared or discovered law in an objective manner.[13] In the 1930s they argued even more vigorously against the notion that judges served as impartial instruments of the law or that the judiciary had a proprietary right to control constitutional change. The second of these points was implicit in the political conception of the Constitution that realists fashioned and would provide a basis for breaking the judicial hold on constitutional development. As for the judicial process, realists emphasized the wide range of nonlegal factors that shaped decision making, including the judges' environment, personality, conscience, policy preferences, and general social, political, and economic outlook.[14] The most extreme repudiation of the traditional judicial theory came from the group of lawyers and legal philosophers known as legal realists, who reduced the judicial process to the level of the personal and the idiosyncratic by a categorical denial of prescriptive rules.[15] Historians and political scientists generally took a wider view, calling attention to the social ideologies and economic institutions which shaped the contours of constitutional law, as well as individual differences in outlook and belief which determined divisions between judges.[16]

The Constitution conceived of politically and removed from the vise of legalistic judicial control provided the basis for the realists' demand for strong government, one of the central elements in their thinking. Negative, laissez-faire government was identified with the static ideal of conservative constitutionalism used by business interests to maintain freedom from public control. A start in the direction of energizing rather than restraining government had been made in the Progressive era, and studies of big government and centralization in the 1920s showed a continuation of the trend.[17] In the early years of the Depression, however, it was not so clear that the American Constitution could generate sufficient power to meet the emergency. Rexford G. Tugwell, critical of the system of deadlock known as checks and balances, lamented the impotence of the instruments of power available to the New Deal. To deal with the crisis he proposed a plan of positive government based on executive responsibility and delegation of legislative powers.[18] Max Lerner toward the end of the decade still exhorted: "We must release ourselves from the eighteenth century doctrine [of limited governmental powers] to the extent of accepting the necessity of a government with full powers." Instead of the separation of powers Lerner like most liberals argued for "the articulation of powers, which is aimed at getting things done."[19] Furthermore several works of constitutional history attempted to show that energetic national government, regulating and promoting economic development rather than letting it drift along in the manner of laissez-faire, was consistent with the outlook of the Founding Fathers.[20] Surveying American constitutional development, Carl B. Swisher saw efficient governmental operation as the outstanding problem of the future. "If government remains, or becomes, strong enough to rule over the economic units which constitute most of the producing and distributing agencies of our society," he wrote in 1943, "the government may well become the great center of power around which men of ability will congregate." Ultimately, Swisher believed, the key to efficient government was "a continuing one, demanding constant revitalization through an influx of new personnel and new leadership."[21]

The emphasis of Swisher and other constitutional realists on leadership and action revealed a concern for men rather than constitutional rules which affected the very meaning of constitutionalism. Swisher's constitutional history, observed Corwin, took the position that institutions did not much matter provided the right men managed them. This was a point of view which Corwin thought contradicted a basic premise of the framers of the Constitution.[22] Equally significant was the realists' emphasis on strong government. For it was not far to move from criticizing weak and ineffective government to questioning the value of limited government itself. Frequently the attack on laissez-faire government became an attack on constitutionalism itself, reinforced by a widespread cynicism toward the rule of law.

The Constitution as a dynamic process of government responsive to political forces and social pressures provided the intellectual foundation of the realist position. Yet to conceive of the Constitution in this way was to deny the normative, teleological meaning of constitutionalism as a system of legal restraints on government guaranteeing individual liberty. Disregarding the normative element—refusing to ask what the political purpose of a constitution was—realists held that every state had a constitution. Accordingly they found themselves unable to distinguish between a constitutional and a non-constitutional state. The United States, they reasoned, was not essentially different from other countries in the interaction between law and politics that characterized its constitutional life. Social movements, economic interests, and mass psychological pressures were the forces which determined the course of politics. Constitutions, if not valueless, were relatively unimportant and inconsequential. And constitutionalism was mere rationalization, a series of incantations comparable to word-magic.

This anti-constitutionalist attitude was often expressed in criticism, if not direct repudiation, of the principle of a government of law.[23] Typical was Munro's argument that the Constitution and laws were trivial in importance when compared to social and personal forces. Regarding a government of laws as a pure fiction of political fundamentalism, Munro held that the more complicated civilization became the more necessary it would be to widen the scope of administrative discretion and to have a government of men.[24] Turning to the problem of constitutional reform in 1935, Munro reasoned that a course of action clearly dictated by social interest would be followed irrespective of constitutional compulsion, while constitutional requirements not regarded in the public interest would, despite judicial enforcement, be evaded by governing officials. This fatalistic attitude led Munro to the extraordinary conclusion that a bill of rights ought to contain precepts indicating what public officials are expected to do, rather than legally enforceable guarantees and restraints. A more radical departure from traditional American constitutionalism would be hard to imagine.[25]

Though cognizant of the rise of totalitarianism in Europe, Beard in 1936 remained dubious about the idea of a government of law. Granting that Hitler's Germany showed the significance of the ideal, Beard nevertheless felt that "law itself is bewildering abstraction. There is something in it, but the reality is hard to grasp." If pushed too far the idea of the rule of law became "unreal," for it obscured the role played by men as legislators, administrators, judges. Beard's purpose was to refute the myth of the mechanical certitude of the law, but in the process he cast doubt on a central premise of constitutionalism.[26] Other constitutional realists, more skeptical toward the rule of law and influenced by a more thoroughgoing relativism, found distinctions between constitutional and non-constitutional states untenable. Max A. Shepard in 1939 illustrated this intellectual dilemma in an analysis of law and consent. Adopting a group theory of law derived from Arthur F. Bentley, Shepard defined law as those rules of conduct which are obeyed in accordance with community customs and feelings. Ethical considerations—the idea that law must be morally right in order to be law—he regarded as "a confusing factor" because they raised the question of whose standards should be the measure of what was right. And judgments about the motivation of obedience were less important than the fact of obedience, which Shepard took to signify consent. Accordingly he could disregard the apparently obvious difference between a constitutional democracy and a totalitarian regime, as when he concluded: "Thus Hiter, Mussolini, and Stalin keep large groups 'cowed,' inducing a grudging consent through 'ruthlessness.' It is not casuistry to say that here individuals have not been forced to obey, but have consented to obey. All governments, from the most peaceful representative government to the most Oriental of despotisms, rest on consent as I define the term."[27]

The failure or inability to make normative distinctions was related to a fundamental indifference to constitutional rules. It was impossible, wrote Edward McChesney Sait in 1938, to contend that a state, however autocratic it might be, could exist without a constitution or that a frame of government was not a constitution unless it guaranteed rights and privileges to citizens. Sait said that applying the term "constitutional" to the erection of safeguards of liberty, thus implying a contrast between arbitrary and lawful governments, was to use it in a restricted and specialized sense. Though the collapse of the Weimar Republic led him to think rigid constitutions were preferable to flexible ones, the whole question of constitutional structure seemed a minor matter. "While using them," Sait observed of constitutions, "we need not suppose that they plumb social realities or determine social conduct." Political affairs were shaped by men's actions, and a constitution would somehow be adjusted to the needs of the community.[28]

Constitutional realism, carried to its logical conclusion, dictated a cynical attitude toward political ideas in general and toward constitutionalism in particular. The concept of limited government under law seemed to lack any intrinsic validity. It was an axiom of modern social science, as Charles E. Merriam put it, that "the greater part of political theorizing on close analysis turns out to be more or less thinly veiled propaganda of particular social interests."[29] And although Beard by 1937 had abandoned the deterministic aspects of his economic interpretation, his principal conclusion at the 1937 meeting of the American Historical Association was that "the first and prime consideration of any realistic constitutional history is economic: whose property, what property, and what forms of regulation and protection?"[30] Under this kind of realistic analysis constitutionalism dissolved into a form of interest-seeking that protected the status quo.

The belief in law as an entity existing apart from men's opinions and will in a higher realm of pure reason, asserted A. K. Rogers, was a device for blocking the experimental spirit of democracy. Tugwell asserted in exasperation: "The Constitution is used as a holy of holies within which the ugly practices of free competition can be hid from vulgar eyes." And Harold J. Laski, answering a constitutionalist's plea to make *ultra vires* all exorbitant acts of government, asked: "How do we know what an 'exorbitant' act of government is?" Except for certain procedural aspects of personal liberty, Laski thought that the constitutionalist's formula for the rule of law "boils down to protecting certain property relations from reform by the will of a legislative assembly."[31] Even civil liberties were dismissed by Lerner, who stated that rather than setting boundaries of arbitrary power they were "a pack of tricks to defeat the purposes of majority rule." The only valid meaning of civil liberties for Lerner was the right of the majority to organize new economic alignments.[32]

Although constitutional realists professed to view the Constitution as a social symbol around which public life was organized, they could not quite overcome their sense of amazement or incredulity at what, from their reform perspective, seemed mere fetishism blocking progressive change.[33] In *The Encyclopedia of the Social Sciences*, for example, constitutionalism was not the theory and practice of limited government, with roots reaching back into ancient and medieval political thought. It was instead, wrote Walton H. Hamilton, "the name given to the trust which men repose in the power of words engrossed on parchment to keep a government in order." Not only did this definition seem to deny constitutionalism historical actuality or validity but it also was based on a simplistic, formalist view of constitution which realists criticized in other contexts. Hamilton identified his subject with the attempt to limit irresponsible authority, but dated it only from the first American state constitutions of 1776. Constitutionalism offered exact language as a test of official conduct "at the risk of imposing outworn standards upon current activities." Like other constitutional realists, Hamilton viewed constitutionalism as a form of word-magic, then seemed disillusioned at its failure to produce results. The Constitution "is not a self-regulating mechanism which automatically holds official conduct to conformity with its lines," he concluded.[34]

When Lerner adverted to Hamilton's essay as an account of the hold of constitution-worship on the American mind, he offered without intending it an implicit criticism of constitutional realism.[35] For what Hamilton described was not constitutionalism, at least not in the way it was conceived of by many intellectuals who in the mid-1930s took a more affirmative view of the reality and importance of the rule of law.

Insofar as constitutional realism referred to an awareness of social and economic influences on constitutional development and a recognition that political institutions were a vital part of the Constitution, it described the general outlook of most students of public law and policy. Realist tendencies of this sort were prominent even in the work of traditional scholars, such as Andrew C. McLaughlin and Homer C. Hockett, and before long took on the aspect of conventional wisdom in constitutional history textbooks.[36] Yet by no means all who applied the insights of constitutional realism accepted the anti-constitutionalist conclusions to which it led. On the contrary, against the background of anti-liberal movements sweeping Europe many political and legal scholars reasserted the principles of constitutionalism. Recognizing the need for strong government to deal with economic or international crisis, they looked on the Constitution as the basis for progressive change. But they also evinced special concern for the Constitution as formal law guaranteeing liberty and restraining governmental power. Accordingly judicial review in this outlook was a vital means of assuring limited and responsible government. Without denying the influence of men's actions these intellectuals renewed the ideal of a government of law. And they held that in the United States the rule of law was a substantial reality. Thus from within the realist movement came a neo-constitutionalist impulse. Resembling the nineteenth-century belief in the superiority and world-importance of American institutions, neo-constitutionalism became a major component of America's ideology in World War II and the Cold War.

Among the earliest and most influential of the intellectuals who explored the central themes of neo-constitutionalism were three Harvard political scientists, William Yandell Elliott, Charles H. McIlwain, and Carl J. Friedrich. Elliott clearly identified himself with the need for strong government. He agreed with many liberals that the executive should be given greater powers in the context of a more disciplined party system and recognized that the Constitution was a means of or-

ganizing as well as limiting power. He nonetheless showed special concern for the Constitution as formal law. And above all he insisted on
the value of constitutionalism. Elliott's first major work had defended
the constitutional state against the alternatives offered by syndicalism,
pluralism, and fascism.[37] In the 1930s he cautioned against cynicism
about constitutionalism. "I am not bent on debunking," he told the
American Historical Association in discussing the Constitution as a
social myth, "but on that more difficult thing—understanding the peculiar fact that is the American Constitution." In place of old symbols,
such as the Supreme Court as impartial arbiter, which the realists—
Elliott called them "sophists"—had shown to be no longer valid, he
proposed new ones.[38] For at stake ultimately was nothing less than the
survival of a method of politics that placed negative restraints on
power. "How much skepticism can be tolerated in a period of new
faiths that really clash?" Elliott asked as he speculated on whether the
United States could successfully resist the "universal drift" toward or
"contagion of a form of organization called the corporative state."[39]

An even more urgent sense of crisis informed Charles H. McIlwain's
contribution to neo-constitutionalism. An older scholar, firmly identified with traditional constitutionalism, McIlwain's major historical
work attempted to show that in medieval English history fundamental
law had operated to control acts of government in a manner similar to
the American doctrine of judicial review.[40] McIlwain also maintained
that sovereignty in its true meaning never signified unlimited, absolute
power, but always power subject to law.[41] "The one great issue that
overshadows all other," he wrote in 1936, "is the issue between constitutionalism and arbitrary government." Economic differences between
capitalism, socialism, and communism were less significant than the
fundamental question of "whether we shall be ruled by law at all, or
only by arbitrary will." At the 1937 meeting of the American Historical
Association, McIlwain reiterated his warning: "There is a tidal wave of
despotism sweeping over the world. On this anniversary of our Constitution we find constitutionalism itself threatened everywhere as it has
never been threatened since the founding of our government." The
immediate danger was despotism, explained McIlwain, but the cause
of the crisis was the feebleness of government. Like many of his liberal
critics, McIlwain would concentrate power in a government that was
unhampered by checks and balances, yet fully responsible to the people through the electoral system. As important as political responsibility, however, were legal limitations on government enforced by the
judiciary. Believing that the greatest contemporary danger lay in the
threat to individual liberty posed by government, McIlwain reasoned
that the protection of liberty was a problem of law. "And the one insti-

tution above all others essential to the preservation of law," he insisted, "has always been and still is an honest, able, learned, independent judiciary." McIlwain argued moreover that lasting and effective social reform depended upon orderly processes of law and courts free from governmental control. Recognizing the conflict between his own view of the judiciary and that of most liberals, he expressed the hope that the mutual suspicions of reformers and constitutionalists would be ended.[42]

In contrast to McIlwain the neo-constitutionalism of Friedrich placed less emphasis on concentration of authority and judicial supervision and much more on the division of power among the parts of government as the best means of achieving responsible rule. To Friedrich it was the division of power which was the basis of civilized government and the essence of constitutionalism. In Friedrich no more than in Elliott or McIlwain did constitutionalism mean a return to the negative laissez-faire state. Friedrich was aware of the historical importance of bureaucracy, but also of the political problem it created. Conservatives saw bureaucratization as anathema, liberals saw it as panacea; the latter, however, were unwilling to recognize the inherently political character of bureaucracy. Friedrich thought that bureaucratic organization was necessary for control of the industrial system, but recognizing its political nature he also saw the need to constitutionalize it. Furthermore, although historically constitutionalism had been in conflict with monarchical bureaucracies, its stress upon rationality and predictability made it compatible with modern bureaucratic organization. Sympathetic thus to positive government, Friedrich was also receptive to social and economic change. Indeed, it was not something to be feared, he wrote, "but is of the very warp and woof of modern constitutionalism."[43]

Concern for constitutional limitations spread through the 1930s. With reason Thomas I. Cook concluded in 1941 that political and social scientists were reviving the analysis of government in terms of arbitrariness versus the rule of law and were increasingly aware of the danger of attacking constitutional law in the desire for solutions to specific problems.[44] Arguing for a flexible Constitution adequate to the purposes of reform, Forrest R. Black as early as 1933 criticized the "dynamic" school of political scientists who dismissed a written constitution as a mere parchment barrier and looked to sociology as the main source and sanction of law. Arthur N. Holcombe's liberal appeal for government planning in 1935 focused on the need for constitutional limitations and responsibility. The creation of power was no longer the issue, but rather "what to do with all this power when generated, and how to keep it under public control." In response to this "baffling" problem Holcombe urged liberal reformers to seek the invention of political instruments combining "the power of a personal dictatorship with the sense of responsibility of a constitutional organ of government." His recommendations included formal representation of economic interests, a more disciplined party system, and a professional bureaucracy.[45]

Rather than political in tendency as in Holcombe's approach, neo-constitutionalism was more typically legalistic and juridical. Contributing to a symposium on the Constitution and social progress, assistant attorney general and former law professor John Dickinson attacked the idea of withdrawing from the courts the power to declare legislation unconstitutional. He warned that to do so, as some reformers proposed, "would in substance reduce the constitution to a mere anthology of hortatory platitudes." The Constitution must change in accordance with social forces, said Dickinson, but Americans lacked the habits of internalized political control which enabled a people to govern themselves without a charter of organic law.[46] Judicial enforcement of the Constitution was the principal theme in Benjamin F. Wright's 1942 account of American constitutional history. Wright held that although many constitutional changes occurred without legal sanction, "the central course of American constitutional development has been legal." Furthermore, constitutionalism—the limitation of government by law through judicial review—was an essential part of the democratic tradition. Not denying political influences on courts, Wright nevertheless defended the judiciary's reliance on rational debate and legalistic justification of its decisions. "This method," he pointed out, "enables us to hold before the whole people, majority and minorities alike, the ideal of discussion rather than violence as the only proper reliance in politics."[47]

The vigor with which the old and seemingly hopelessly theoretical problem of sovereignty was discussed in the 1930s was a further indication of the neo-constitutional revival. One of the great constructs of nineteenth-century political thought, the very idea of sovereignty had been rejected by theorists of pluralism who held that groups and voluntary associations rather than the state possessed power. Sovereignty was a perfect abstraction having no basis in reality.[48] Yet by the time of World War II the group conflict so admired in pluralist theory seemed badly in need of control. "Is there no supreme body which may take the place of parliaments, courts, and people as the final authority of last resort?" asked the emigré German legalist Otto Kirchheimer in 1944.[49] Theories of dictatorship provided one kind of solution. Neo-constitutionalism provided another. Elliott's early attack on pluralism and fascism defended "democratic constitutionalism and the sovereignty based upon it." "The very existence of government under law instead of a universal feudal regime of petty groups, knowing no other arbitration than the right of might," Elliott asserted, "shows to what a degree the state-purpose is real and operative in modern society." The state-purpose meant sovereignty, which McIlwain defended as the "central formula under which we try to rationalize the complicated facts of our modern political life."[50]

Succinctly stated this was a theory of the sovereignty of the constitution.[51] As was true of neo-constitutionalists in general, its proponents denied neither the idea of social forces behind law, nor the social reform program of the English pluralists or American liberals. They rejected, however, the idea that the formal legal unity of the state as expressed in the Constitution was illusory or insignificant, as the pluralists insisted. Sovereignty conceived of in this sense served as a point of reference useful in maintaining a standard of peace and order more definite than the claims of competing groups.[52] Even critics of the idea of sovereignty seemed to accept the sovereignty of the Constitution. Thus Heinz Eulau, though questioning the classic theory of depersonalized constitutionalism as patently unreal, proposed to combat the Nazis' dictatorial version of sovereignty with democratic popular sovereignty—expressed through "the organizational equipment of the constitutional State."[53]

The intellectual impact of neo-constitutionalism was strikingly apparent in the changed outlook of the constitutional realists themselves. In the crisis state which now existed, Lerner wrote in 1940, it was necessary to maintain state power without state monopoly of thought or action. Democratic survival demanded a commitment to constitutional principles and procedures as well as attention to economic matters. "We cannot continue to draw the sharp boundaries between the two realms that we have drawn in the past," Lerner concluded as he looked back on the crisis of the 1930s and congratulated Americans for retaining "the essential fabric of legality." Swisher also demonstrated the realist shift toward constitutionalism. A liberal political scientist who had been special assistant to Attorney General Homer Cummings at the time of the great court-packing controversy, Swisher in his realist history of 1943 emphasized efficiency in government and the availability of public power for social purposes as a test of constitutional development. In 1946, however, Swisher wrote that the significance of a constitution extended beyond that of giving power. Among its most important meanings were those that were restrictive and in some cases absolutely negative. Swisher admitted a tendency to describe political systems that one approved of as constitutional and those one disapproved of as arbitrary. Yet such judgments were not entirely subjective.

"There is value," he declared, "in the relative conception of orderliness and impersonality in the application of law." The positive state was clearly necessary, but it was all the more important that administrators "be held by constitutional restrictions."[54]

As perceptions of constitutionalism changed in the late 1930s realist and neo-constitutionalist ideas came into conflict. This intellectual confrontation was an important feature of the 1937 meeting of the American Historical Association, which was given over entirely to consideration of the United States Constitution on the sesquicentennial of its formation. Speaking in Independence Hall in Philadelphia, McIlwain issued his call to make *ultra vires* all exorbitant acts of government. In reply several scholars presented analyses in a realist framework of thought.[55] But the leading voice was that of Beard, who reiterated that economic interests remained the primary datum in constitutional history. In actuality, however, Beard's remarks gave evidence of a convergence of ideas with those of the neo-constitutionalist McIlwain.

As early as 1932 Beard displayed a more sympathetic attitude toward constitutionalism that was related to his reconsideration of political ideas in general.[56] Analyzing the problem of domestic reform in 1936 he remained skeptical about the rule of law, and at the Philadelphia meeting in 1937 he reaffirmed the primacy of economic interests in understanding constitutional change. Yet the very purpose of performing an economic interpretation, Beard explained before an overflow audience in Independence Hall, was to strengthen constitutionalism. Referring to the study of economic influences Beard averred: "This conception . . . has a profound meaning for the future of constitutional government as practice and for social living under the Constitution." Its special relevance lay in promoting government by discussion in contrast to government by force.[57] Beard made the same point in the 1935 edition of *An Economic Interpretation of the Constitution:* "By the assiduous study of their [the Founding Fathers'] works and by displaying their courage and their insight into the economic interests underlying all constitutional formalities, men and women of our generation may guarantee the perpetuity of government under law, as distinguished from the arbitrament of force."[58] Beard's revaluation of constitutionalism was completed in *The Republic* (1943). He not only set out a new interpretation, arguing that the Framers' greatest triumph was to avert military dictatorship, but also declared that "no other theme of national policy is so important for us as constitutionalism—the civilian way of living together in the Republic. . . ." How to preserve the idea of constitutional processes and impress it upon the minds of future generations was the "task of civilization, supreme over all others."[59]

Friedrich, who surely agreed with Beard, was confident enough in 1941 to conclude that the moment of deepest crisis for constitutionalism had already passed. He believed that many people who a few years earlier had been cynical or indifferent had rediscovered the importance of constitutionalism.[60] The necessity of making constitutions again, remarked Carl Becker in an attitude of pessimism and seeming reluctance in 1937, was transformed into a positive principle of the good society during World War II.[61] Becker himself acknowledged in 1941 that his view of constitutional democracy had become less detached and critical, more cordial and defensive. The European dictators, by reducing to an absurdity the idea that law and morality were nothing more than the right of the stronger, had accomplished what civil liberties organizations and constitutional defense leagues could not.[62] Friedrich, noting the reaction of intellectuals like Becker and Beard who now extolled the virtues of constitutional democracy, thought it all demonstrated what the realists had once denied: that the Constitution in its legal signification as the rule of law exerted a potent political force.[63]

The constellation of ideas that defined neo-constitutionalism formed a major part of American ideology during the Cold War. As in the realm of diplomacy, so in the intellectual sphere but to a much greater degree, the foundations of hostility toward the Soviet Union were established well before the end of World War II. As the United States faced the challenge of the Soviet Union both liberals and conservatives professed abiding commitment to the values of constitutionalism. The more noticeable tendency was the reform realist identification with constitutionalism. The widely used constitutional history textbook by Alfred H. Kelly and Winfred A. Harbison, which was liberal and pro–New Deal in outlook, minimized in typical realist fashion the causative force of constitutional ideas in favor of an economic interpretation. But the authors did not question the reality or importance of constitutionalism defined as the rule of law. The idea of limited government was the grand theme of American constitutional history.[64] In another work Kelly affirmed: "Our faith in constitutional government and individual liberty is not just a piece of outworn intellectual baggage from a dead age."[65]

The essence of Cold War constitutionalism remained the idea that "the power of the state ought to be checked and controlled according to the forms of law."[66] In the more prosperous economic situation of the 1940s and 1950s, however, neo-constitutionalists showed less concern with positive government than during the Depression. Liberty was more often defined in negative terms—as freedom from rather than freedom to—and with good reason in view of the ubiquitous loyalty programs inspired by anti-communism. Accordingly neo-constitutionalists focused on judicial protection of individual freedom in struggles over civil liberties. Thus, despite some backing-and-filling, the rule of law seemed to operate as a political force. The moral and religious aspect of neo-constitutionalism, which was present from its beginning, also became more prominent in the Cold War era. Reacting against relativism and positivism, neo-constitutionalists displayed normative tendencies of thought characteristic of the general revival of political philosophy after World War II. Indeed part of the latter development has consisted in attempts to restate the theory of constitutionalism in terms appropriate to modern industrial society.

The central place of constitutionalism in America's Cold War ideology was aptly illustrated in Walter Lippmann's 1955 analysis of the crisis in western civilization. Describing the disintegration of political authority in the modern world, Lippmann found the source of the crisis in the decline of the "public philosophy." This was a protean term for Lippmann; it meant variously natural law, the wisdom of a great society, the traditions of civility.[67] But the public philosophy was the antithesis of totalitarianism; it could be applied to problems such as the abuse of private property rights; and it could be most effectively communicated—its "imponderable truths" made immediate—by the methods of constitutional government. Indeed, the first principle of a civilized state, according to Lippmann, "is that power is legitimate only when it is under contract." The idea of "reciprocal rights and duties under law" as the essence of constitutionalism thus emerged as the practical meaning of the public philosophy.[68] Lippmann had presented essentially the same analysis in earlier works, but his Cold War treatise was more sharply focused on the value of constitutionalism.[69]

The broad appeal of constitutionalism was evident in two studies of American civilization written from different historiographical perspectives by the conservative Ralph Henry Gabriel and the liberal Lerner. According to Gabriel, as the Constitution of 1787 was a republican alternative to monarchy, so in the twentieth century it remained the American alternative to European dictatorship. Lerner thought that the Constitution counted most as a symbol of non-totalitarian social organization. Referring to the idea of constitutionalism he wrote: "Even among those skeptical of spread-eagle patriotism, there is a sober sense that the American political genius has here added something of its own to the tradition of government." From the ranks of the social scientists Alfred deGrazia cautioned against dismissing respect for constitutionalism as a mere psychological state. Constitutionalism was one of the great ideas around which human activity was organized, de-Grazia explained, adding: "Science can describe and analyze it but is not permitted to dismiss or depreciate it. Its dismissal or depreciation is purely a political affair—to be left to people attached to different values . . . or even to cynicism."[70]

The political importance of constitutionalism was evident in the 1950s in struggles over civil rights and liberties. The judiciary was at the center of these conflicts, attempting to make the rule of law a reality and create a viable tradition of libertarianism.[71] It was in this context that the well-known debate over the democratic character of judicial review occurred. Judicial activists urged vigorous exercise of judicial review to shape constitutional law in accordance with democratic values, while supporters of judicial restraint, disliking judge-made law, would defer to popularly elected legislatures and confine courts to a narrowly circumscribed role.[72] Although the two groups differed sharply over the meaning of democracy and the scope of judicial review, both accepted the institution of review. Both, moreover, regarded their positions as expressions of the constitutional idea of the rule of law. And despite some recriminations on this point, both were right. According to activist Charles E. Wyzanski, the essence of constitutionalism was the right of individual liberty and property against governmental interference, and the existence of independent courts to vindicate the right.[73] None of the judicially modest could object to this view, just as no activist could disavow the ideal enunciated by restraint advocate Herbert Wechsler. In an article on neutral principles of constitutional law, Wechsler wrote that courts should decide cases on the basis of "reasons that in their generality and their neutrality transcend any immediate result that is involved."[74] The debate turned on the method of realizing constitutionalism through courts of law. The Italian scholar Giovanni Sartori concluded astringently that constitutional guarantees were protected not by a pervasive conception of law, but by devices of juridical defense.[75] To most neo-constitutionalists, however, the rule of law meant more than the positive fact of court decisions. It was the character of judicial decisions—the result of a deliberative process involving a pluralism of views—which gave reality to the rule of law and distinguished it from arbitrary authoritarianism.[76]

One of the most distinctive features of Cold War constitutionalism was its moral impulse—a tendency consciously developed as an antidote to relativistic positivism. Reflecting on the influence of his early work, *The Pragmatic Revolt in Politics,* Elliott wrote in 1940 that its chief importance lay in its insistence on evaluating politics in the light of moral norms.[77] Indeed by the beginning of World War II an important intellectual struggle was being waged between advocates of a value-free and a normative study of law and political science.[78] As Cold War attitudes intensified in the 1950s and the enormities of Nazism were fully considered, the apparent connection between totalitarianism and positivism in political science provoked strong reaction from neo-constitutionalists. The positivistic social scientist, declaimed Cook, had no convincing answer to give to the totalitarian nihilist because he "had abandoned by implication (whatever his nominal professions) the full method of freedom of constitutional government and the rule of law." Rejecting relativism yet unable to accept moral absolutism, Cook fell back on a form of "natural law with a changing content" which he called "universalist relationism."[79] Lippmann, who also turned to natural law, deplored the tendency to reduce ideas and principles concerning right political and social action to the sphere of private, subjective relevance. The liberal democracies of the West, he observed in a harshly critical tone, "became the first great society to treat as a private concern the formative beliefs that shape the character of its citizens."[80]

Analytical or positivist jurisprudence, starting with John Austin in the nineteenth century and culminating in Hans Kelsen's pure theory of law in the twentieth century, found incomprehensible the idea that law must accord with reason or some conception of right higher than the state in order to be authoritative. Rejecting natural law or natural rights thinking, positivist jurists defined law as command.[81] Neo-constitutionalists maintained, however, that by dismissing the idea of the rule of law as a metaphysical superstition and by teaching that every state had a constitution and was a *rechtstaat,* legal positivists prepared the way for fascism and communism.[82] It was necessary therefore to insist on a normative conception of a constitution. Sartori urged political and legal scholars to think of a constitution in teleological terms as a guarantee of liberty, rather than as the institutional and organizational framework of the state in the manner of realism or positivism. The *"garantiste"* approach, as Sartori termed it, gave moral content to constitutionalism and could be ignored only at peril. "When the time of trial comes," he summarized, "one discovers that what the 'pure' jurists have really been doing—under the shield of their juridical indifference to metajuridical matters—was to pave the way for allowing unscrupulous politicians to make a discretionary use of power under the camouflage of a good word"—namely, the constitution. Ironically constitutional realism, which had placed such a heavy emphasis on the non-legal character of constitutional rules, now seemed to be an attempt to depoliticize a problem that was inescapably political, that is, constitutionalism itself.[83] Friedrich, writing in 1968, underscored the conclusion that realist or positivist conceptions of constitution failed because they did not ask: "What is the political function of a constitution?"[84]

In rejecting positivism neo-constitutionalists reflected one of the major tendencies of the renewal of political philosophy that took place following World War II. Philosophers such as Eric Voegelin, Leo Strauss, Michael Oakeshott, and Bertrand deJouvenel sought to identify the principles of right order in human society.[85] At a less general level neo-constitutionalists attempted to set forth the principles of good government. This endeavor followed from the belief that in answering the ultimate problem of politics—how to be governed well—it was possible on empirical grounds to describe a general model of which particular forms of rule are specific applications.[86] A further consideration stimulated efforts to restate constitutional theory. During World War II and in the early years of the Cold War the superiority of the constitutional to the totalitarian state was a sufficient theme of neo-constitutional writing. As it became evident, however, that the crisis of political order of which totalitarianism was a symptom could not be met simply by resorting to old formulas, neo-constitutionalists sought to adapt theories of the rule of law to the dominant concerns and aspirations of the contemporary age.

In general, law remains the essence of the constitutional state. The central meaning of law, moreover, is that of formal institutionalized rules rather than informal countervailing power or influence, although the latter is recognized as having a place in the constitutional order.[87] The rule of law means that the rules under which government operates and men live must be general and prospective.[88] It also means that people who are under the law can find out what it is and know the consequences of actions they may take. A degree of predictability is thus introduced into public life that reflects the ancient quest for political stability.[89] The elemental beliefs on which constitutionalism rests are the dignity of the individual person and his fundamental rights and the distrust of men in power and the consequent need to check and control them.[90]

In reformulating constitutional theory neo-constitutionalists have responded to political and social forces such as the demand for equality of civil rights, economic progress, and social justice. They have also felt obligated to meet the imperative of a scientific study of politics deriving from a persistent realist or behavioralist tendency in modern social science scholarship.

The concept of responsibility forms the central theme of Herbert Spiro's theory of comparative politics. Rejecting the value-neutral approach, Spiro holds that modern man thinks of himself as controlling his future, as being *responsible* for himself. This fundamental fact creates for Spiro a preeminent value which can be used to judge all political systems. According to his analytical scheme, individuals should have opportunities to form policies from several alternative choices, resources for implementing policies, and foreknowledge of the consequences of their actions. Neither a bureaucratized, a totalitarian, nor a constitutional state satisfies all of these requirements; but, concludes Spiro, "the basic goal of constitutional democracy is . . . the creation of better situations of responsibility," and it meets and holds in balance these varied demands more effectively than any other form of government. Spiro in 1959 conceived of his theory as avoiding what he called the Anglophile and Cold War fallacies of assuming that western constitutional democracy was the final expression of man's political genius. The norm of individual responsibility, he argued, was more easily referable to concrete reality than the values ordinarily used in Cold War political analysis such as freedom, equality, or security. Even the communists could agree with the standard of responsibility.[91]

Spiro's intention of transcending Cold War ideology notwithstanding, his theory of comparative politics was a restatement of the theory of constitutionalism. The same may be said of Friedrich's magisterial work, *Man and His Government*. Undertaking a systematic theory of politics, Friedrich addressed himself to the disintegration of authority and legitimacy in the political order, signified by widespread dissatisfaction with government and the failure to settle disputes such as those involving race. As against their growing disenchantment, however, Friedrich observed, people have demanded ever more of government in solving modern social problems. By the 1960s according to Friedrich, totalitarianism was recognized as a false solution to the crisis in the political order. Traditional democratic constitutionalism was not fully satisfactory, either, in providing justice, equality, and freedom. But in charting the "leap into the unknown," said Friedrich, it was necessary to start with the methods of governing that had once been adequate. Accordingly the basic features of Friedrich's model political order derived from the constitutional state which he had defended for thirty years. Those features were effective government action; enforceable restraints on government to enable individuals to become political persons; participation of citizens in making rules; the existence of general rules; an independent judiciary; and voluntary associations coordinating these elements and providing a decisional framework.[92]

Still another defense of constitutionalism was presented by the British scholar, M. J. C. Vile, as part of an historical study of the separation of powers. The historical record, Vile argued, shows a persistent concern for the idea of the separation of powers which demonstrates its relevance. Even empirical political scientists, he pointed out, continue to rely upon it in fashioning theories of political development. Significant also was Vile's refutation of the realist-behavioralist attack on constitutionalism, in which he shows that behavioralists have simply taken for granted the stability provided by the constitutional rules which they have considered unimportant.[93] Vile's principal concern, however, was to posit a theory of constitutionalism based upon the modern concepts of function, structure, and process in political science. Functions such as the making, application, and interpretation of rules were most effectively carried out and were best controlled and coordinated by basic organizational structures, either collegial (legislature) or hierarchical (executive). Process describes the comprehensive manner in which functions were performed (for example the legislative process), including the participation of informal or non-official elements like parties, pressure groups, and the media. But at the center of each process, Vile emphasized, must be a *procedure:* an institutionalized, rule-prescribed action. These procedures were important because they reflect the dominant values of the society. Historically in western civilization the basic procedures have been the legislative, executive, and judicial, expressing the values of democracy, efficiency, and justice. But in the twentieth century, Vile observed, the additional value of social justice has emerged and through the agency of the mass political party, and in other ways, has nearly overwhelmed the older values. Writing toward the end of the 1960s, Vile urged placing social justice in a perspective where it could be reconciled with the older values. This he considered the task of modern constitutional theory.[94]

Neo-constitutionalism has thus been a major expression of American political thought in the era of the Cold War. Nevertheless it has not ended debate on the way in which law and politics interact in constitutional development. There persists a realist tendency in behavioralist scholarship that is heavily concerned with social forces and processes rather than formal rules and institutions. As the civil rights movement of the late 1950s broadened into the more far-reaching reform demands of the 1960s, the insights of constitutional realism distinguished the work of a number of neo-realists.

Behavioralist students of public law have applied a realist point of view in emphasizing the value preferences and policy attitudes which they believe determine judicial decisions. Although most of these new realists would support the position of judicial activism, they are not concerned with the normative question of the proper role of the judiciary. Instead they concentrate on the dynamics of decision making in the manner of the realists of the 1930s. Their understanding of the Constitution is essentially similar, moreover, to that of the older realist movement. From a behavioral standpoint, writes Glendon Schubert, the Constitution is what a majority of justices agree it ought to be said to mean, or what the president or Congress may proclaim by word or deed. In an even broader sense Schubert holds that the Constitution is embedded in "the consensually dominant patterns of values that constitute American political ideologies."[95] Other of the new realists focus on courts—rather than individual judges—as participants in the political process. This approach denies any essential difference between the character of legal and political questions. Judicial actions, according to one of the advocates of this approach, are "neither more nor less reflections of the legal rules which have the support of the most powerful interests of society than are the activities of legislators, administrators, and other groups."[96] For years of course it was recognized that courts were politically involved. The new realists have rigorously applied this insight in studies of the Supreme Court's actions and results, as distinct from its legal rhetoric. In urging a jurisprudence based on "impact analysis" of Supreme Court decisions they consciously direct their attention to the social consequences of judicial action. And they set themselves squarely against the neo-constitutionalist appeal for neutral principles of constitutional law. The new realism, explains Martin Shapiro, "is basically an attempt to treat the Supreme Court as one government agency among many—as part of the American political process, rather than as a unique body of impervious legal technicians above and beyond the political struggle."[97]

Another and far more serious challenge to Cold War constitutionalism, however, has appeared in the attack on the liberal democratic state that has been made manifest in student strikes, ghetto riots, and the general phenomenon on the left known as "the movement," including both revolutionary theorists and Weatherman activists. In evaluating the crisis of public authority that seems to exist today care must be taken to separate drama and rhetoric from genuine thought. Nevertheless there has emerged in recent years, paralleling the demand for participatory democracy, an intellectual quest for a renewal of political life that raises important questions about constitutionalism.

Insofar as it is critical of existing tendencies, this intellectual appeal makes the point that American constitutionalism has become atrophied in what was originally its unique strength: political action by citizens through republican institutions. In the post–New Deal era the Supreme Court has admirably protected freedom of speech, press, and religion. Yet these civil liberties, identified as the very soul of democracy by neo-constitutionalist liberals, no longer seem to provide meaningful political freedom in the eyes of a growing number of critics. Constitutionalism, say the critics, contains no theory of political action.

This is because it was the creation of intellectuals aspiring toward a mechanistic science of politics in which the personal, human element would be eliminated or reduced to a minimum, and in which decisions would be shifted from men to institutional structures or avoided altogether by rule prescriptions. The result of these constitutional theories in modern times has been the debasement of politics and the discouragement of political education and leadership. In tones of decided hostility Sheldon Wolin thus writes: "A constitutional government is a system for directing stimuli which will control human actions and outlooks and, by so doing, make them predictable."[98] Critics like Wolin charge that constitutionalism, seeking as it does to produce uniformities of behavior, takes no account of the need for political action.

In this context the term "political action" takes on a special meaning, referring to acts that are defined as consequential, purposive, novel, and indeterminate. All other actions, including the predictable responses and knowable results that constitutionalism seeks to promote, are defined as behavior.[99] The emphasis that is placed on action in this analysis marks it as neo-realist in character, an expression of the personalism that has so often been a distinctive feature of attacks on constitutionalism.[100] Like their counterparts of the 1930s, the neo-realist critics charge that constitutionalism reduces momentous human choices to the single standard of legality.[101] The failure of constitutionalism to consider the need for political action is in turn related to lack of true awareness of the need for public space in which citizens can act. "Public space" is another rather freighted term, but it may be thought of as opportunities for debate, deliberation, and speech.[102] This criticism recalls C. Wright Mills's strictures on the trivialization of public life and the eclipse of the idea that a community of publics should be a source of governmental action and legitimacy.[103] It is related furthermore to the current interest in decentralization, which seems to rest on the belief that political life can be regenerated by resort to town-meeting methods of action at the local level.[104] Constitutional theory, however, is most seriously defective according to the neo-realist critique in its narrowly economic conception of man. In the traditional constitutionalist view, writes Kirk Thompson, freedom is private not public, and negative in character being defined as the absence of governmental restraints on economic pursuits. The conclusion of Thompson and other neo-realist critics is that constitutional theory posits no true political freedom.[105]

At the heart of the neo-realists' quest for political renewal is the restoration of citizenship.[106] In traditional constitutionalism citizenship is merely protection for economic interest; it is not, as Thompson puts it, "a vital and active membership in a political community."[107] Not providing for political action, constitutionalism minimizes dependence on citizens. Indeed, writes another critic of the liberal constitutional state, it "rejects the notion of citizenship as the ennobling and educative experience of participation in the definition of justice."[108] This is a serious weakness, however, for if the state is to ask for the degree of commitment and cooperation necessary to meeting contemporary problems, it must give citizens a sense of controlling the government.[109] Yet everywhere, according to this critique, citizens are overborne: a situation of tyranny exists in which the public citizen is excluded from the political. In part this is the result of bureaucratization. In Hannah Arendt's description, "Bureaucracy is the form of government in which everybody is deprived of political freedom, of the power to act; for the rule by Nobody is not no-rule, and where all are equally powerless we have a tyranny without a tyrant." Corporate power, acting through forms of voluntary associations originally conceived as instruments of citizen action, is seen as further undermining the vitality of citizenship. In the situation that is thus created civil disobedience becomes a means of gaining access to the political sphere. Wilson Carey McWilliams in a recent analysis treats civil disobedience not as an appeal to a higher moral law nor to individual conscience, but rather as a way of restoring to citizenship the possibility of political action. Another critic of neo-constitutionalism writes of theories of civil disobedience as "strategies for democratic citizenship in a time when the deficiencies of American political life are becoming known to increasing numbers and varieties of people. . . ."[110]

Though critical of constitutionalism, the neo-realists do not evince the cynical attitude of earlier constitutional realists. Rather they seek to revitalize and reformulate constitutional theory. Constitutionalism, argues Thompson, has not provided a proper balance between order and liberty, and he evidently considers the task of critics such as himself to be to help define a proper balance. Their theory and practice would be more political and libertarian, but it would remain within the framework of the existing constitutional order.[111]

Meanwhile other critics of the liberal democratic state adopt an outlook that is more clearly continuous with traditional constitutionalism. Several studies of the public power of corporations, trade organizations, labor unions, and other "voluntary associations" of pluralist theory call for the application of constitutional limitations and standards of public responsibility.[112] One of the keenest critics of contemporary liberalism is Theodore J. Lowi, who attacks the "vital center" for elevating to the status of principles of government the political process of group bargaining and special interest promotion. To remedy the constitutional defects of a flaccid liberal state Lowi urges "some contemporary version of the rule of law."[113] Thus, although there are differences between rule of law critics such as Lowi and the neo-realist theorists of political action, there does not appear to be the deep division over the value of constitutionalism (reformulated or revised) that characterized the conflict between constitutional realists and neo-constitutionalists in the 1930s.

Constitutional politics has often seemed more rhetorical than substantive, the chief concern of its practitioners appearing to be expediency rather than principle, power rather than right. It may be, however, that historians witness an ironic reversal: revolutionary politics may be more rhetorical than substantive, professions of armed insurrection or resistance concealing a willingness to work within the constitutional framework.[114] Arendt has advanced the thesis that the civil disobedience of student radicals, despite their leaders' protestations to the contrary, is a form of voluntary association and an expression of dissent by an organized minority that is compatible with the spirit and practice of American constitutionalism.[115] And it is at least suggestive, as well perhaps as being enigmatic, that the Black Panther party has issued a call for a constitutional convention.[116] While the principles of a Black Panther constitution remain unclear, there is in the very suggestion of such a project presumably a realization of the necessity, value, and importance of constitutional rules. Undoubtedly the same idea informs the new model constitution that a group far removed politically from the Black Panthers, the Center for the Study of Democratic Institutions, has brought forth.[117] Thus from sources as divergent as the radical Panthers and liberal reformers such as Tugwell, the principal author of the Center's proposed constitution and an old constitutional realist at that, come initiatives for constitutional reform. The ironies are numerous and worth cogitating, but the significance seems clear. Both groups recognize that a constitution is not only an important expression of values and principles but also the source of authority for legal and political rules and institutions which affect the course of social change.

Constitutionalism must remain a complex and shifting set of values, ideas, and institutional practices. As long as it has to do with law, the nature of which has never been and will never be agreed upon, this will be so. And since it is preeminently a method of conducting politics, constitutionalism must also have a strongly political character and tendency. But regardless of how political the Constitution may seem, the very idea of the constitutional will carry an inescapable legal meaning. The use of the term "constitutional" in a descriptive way in analyzing public problems—be they questions of corporate responsibility, civil rights, regulatory authority, or military power—will have a normative connotation, implying a commitment to managing public affairs in accordance with fundamental values and through certain formally legitimate procedures. Awareness of this inner tension is one of the major consequences of the reassessment of constitutionalism that has taken place in the past three decades of world crisis and turbulent change.

Notes

1. Herman Belz, "The Realist Critique of Constitutionalism in the Era of Reform," *American Journal of Legal History*, XV (Oct. 1971), 288–306.

2. John A. Hobbs, "The Rise of Scientific Value Relativism in American Political Science" (doctoral dissertation, Princeton, 1961), 67–70.

3. Karl Llewellyn, "The Constitution as an Institution," *Columbia Law Review*, XXXIV (Jan. 1934), 33.

4. Louis B. Boudin, *Government by Judiciary* (2 vols., New York, 1932), I, x.

5. Charles Grove Haines, *The Role of the Supreme Court in American Government and Politics, 1789–1835* (Berkeley, 1944), 1–44.

6. Charles A Beard, "The Living Constitution," *Annuals of the American Academy of Political and Social Science*, CLXXXV (May 1936), 31.

7. Llewellyn, "The Constitution as an Institution," 17–26; Karl Llewellyn, "The Real Constitution—and the Supreme Court," *Survey Graphic*, XXV (April 1936), 233–35.

8. For example, see Howard L. McBain, *The Living Constitution: A Consideration of the Realities and Legends of Our Fundamental Law* (New York, 1927); William Bennett Munro, *The Makers of the Unwritten Constitution: The Fred Morgan Kirby Lectures, delivered at Lafayette College, 1929* (New York, 1930); Charles E. Merriam, *The Written Constitution and the Unwritten Attitude* (New York, 1931); Walton H. Hamilton, "1937 to 1787, Dr.," *The Constitution Reconsidered*, Conyers Read, ed. (New York, 1938), xiii–xvi.

9. Edward S. Corwin, "Some Probable Repercussions of 'Nira' on Our Constitutional System," *Annals of the American Academy of Political and Social Science*, CLXXII (March 1934), 139–44.

10. Edward S. Corwin, *Court over Constitution: A Study of Judicial Review as an Instrument of Popular Government* (Princeton, 1938), 228–29.

11. William Bennett Munro, "An Ideal State Constitution," *Annals of the American Academy of Political and Social Science*, CLXXXI (Sept. 1935), 6.

12. T. Swann Harding, "The Myth of Constitutional Absolutism," *Journal of Social Philosophy*, II (Oct. 1936), 69–84; James Hart, "A Unified Economy and States' Rights," *Annals of the American Academy of Political and Social Science*, CLXXXV (May 1936), 102–14.

13. T. R. Powell, "The Logic and Rhetoric of Constitutional Law," *Journal of Philosophy, Psychology, and Scientific Method*, XV (Nov. 21, 1918), 645–58.

14. Carl B. Swisher, *Stephen J. Field, Craftsman of the Law* (Washington, 1930), 4, 166–67; Charles Grove Haines, *The American Doctrine of Judicial Supremacy* (Berkeley, 1932), 500–40; Boudin, *Government by Judiciary*, I, iv–x; Howard Lee

McBain, "Some Aspects of Judicial Review," *The Bacon Lectures On The Constitution of the United States Given at Boston University* 1928–1938 (Boston, 1938), 375–90; Harding, "The Myth of Constitutional Absolutism," 69–84; C. Herman Pritchett, "Divisions of Opinion Among Justices of the U.S. Supreme Court, 1939–1941," *American Political Science Review*, XXXV (Oct. 1941), 890–98.

15. Wilfrid E. Rumble, Jr., *American Legal Realism: Skepticism, Reform, and the Judicial Process* (Ithaca, 1968); Edward F. Purcell, Jr., "American Jurisprudence Between the Wars: Legal Realism and the Crisis of Democratic Theory," *American Historical Review*, LXXV (Dec. 1969), 424–46.

16. Max Lerner, "The Supreme Court and American Capitalism," *Yale Law Journal*, XLII (Feb. 1933), 696–701; Henry Steele Commager, "Constitutional History and the Higher Law," *The Constitution Reconsidered*, Conyers Read, ed. (New York, 1938), 225–45.

17. Charles McKinley, "The Constitution and the Tasks Ahead," *American Political Science Review*, XLIX (Dec. 1955), 962–63; Felix Frankfurter, *The Public and Its Government* (New Haven, 1930), 24; Walter Thompson, *Federal Centralization: A Study and Criticism of the Expanding Scope of Congressional Legislation* (New York, 1923); Charles A. Beard and William Beard, *The American Leviathan: The Republic in the Machine Age* (New York, 1930).

18. Rexford G. Tugwell, "Design for Government," *Political Science Quarterly*, XLVIII (Sept. 1933), 321–32; Rexford G. Tugwell, "The New Deal: The Available Instruments of Governmental Power," *Western Political Quarterly*, II (Dec. 1949), 545–80.

19. Max Lerner, *It Is Later Than You Think: The Need for a Militant Democracy* (New York, 1938), 233.

20. Walton H. Hamilton and Douglass Adair, *The Power to Govern: The Constitution—Then and Now* (New York, 1937); Irving Brant, *Storm over the Constitution* (Indianapolis, 1936); Beryl H. Levy, *Our Constitution: Tool or Testament?* (New York, 1941). The most extreme statement of the thesis of a powerful national government, W. W. Crosskey, *Politics and the Constitution: In the History of the United States* (2 vols., Chicago, 1953), was undertaken in the 1930s in the belief that the exercises of congressional power urged by the Roosevelt administration were historically legitimate and consistent with the views of the framers of the Constitution. Charles O. Gregory, "William Winslow Crosskey—As I Remember Him," *University of Chicago Law Review*, XXXV (Winter 1968), 245.

21. Carl B. Swisher, *American Constitutional Development* (Boston, 1943), 1019, 1025–27. Rexford G. Tugwell made the same point: "The executive branch of the government is not a piece of mechanism, it is a body of men. If the new program is to succeed, those men must be wise, able, ingenious and honest." Tugwell, "Design for Government," 331.

22. *American Historical Review*, L. (Oct. 1944), 127–31. Edward S. Corwin expressed a similar view a few years earlier. Corwin, *Court over Constitution*, 228–29.

23. McBain, *The Living Constitution*, 3–5.

24. Munro, *The Invisible Government* (New York, 1928), 4–5l, 20, 113; William Bennett Munro, *Personality in Politics* (New York, 1924).

25. Munro, "An Ideal State Constitution," 6.

26. Beard, "The Living Constitution," 29–30.

27. Max A. Shepard, "Law and Obedience," *American Political Science Review*, XXXIII (Oct. 1939), 783–87. Shepard revealed the abstract, formalistic quality of his approach in protesting that he did not mean to imply that ordinary speech might not refer to important social realities in drawing a line between free and involuntary consent.

28. Edward McChesney Sait, *Political Institutions: A Preface* (New York, 1938), 314, 338–40.

29. Charles E. Merriam, *New Aspects of Politics* (New York, 1925), 53–54.

30. Charles A. Beard, "Historiography and the Constitution," *The Constitution Reconsidered*, Conyers Read, ed. (New York, 1938), 165. Beard's address was viewed as a reaffirmation of his earlier position, the New York *Times* reporting that he appealed to historians "to regard economic interests as determining features of history. . . ." New York *Times*, Dec. 30, 1937. See also Bernard C. Borning, *The Political and Social Thought of Charles A. Beard* (Seattle, 1962), 165–81.

31. A. K. Rogers, "Constitutionalism," *The International Journal of Ethics*, XL (April 1930), 289; Tugwell, "Design for Government," 322–23; *American Historical Review*, XLIV (April 1939), 650–51. Harold J. Laski was referring to views of Charles H. McIlwain.

32. Lerner, *It Is Later Than You Think*, 118–19. See also Robert N. Baldwin, "Personal Liberty," *Annals of the American Academy of Political and Social Science*, CLXXXV (May 1936), 162–69.

33. Thurman Arnold, *The Symbols of Government* (New York, 1935); Thurman Arnold, *The Folklore of Capitalism* (New York, 1937).

34. Walton H. Hamilton, "Constitutionalism," *The Encyclopedia of the Social Sciences* (7 vols., New York, 1935), IV, 255–59. See also Carl Becker, "Afterthoughts on Constitutions," *The Constitution Reconsidered*, Conyers Read, ed. (New York, 1938), 384–400; Merriam, *The Written Constitution*, 11; Max Lerner, "Constitution and Court as Symbols," *Yale Law Journal*, XLVI (June 1937), 1290–1319.

35. Max Lerner, "The Supreme Court and American Capitalism," *Yale Law Journal*, XLII (Feb. 1933), 674.

36. Andrew C. McLaughlin, *A Constitutional History of the United States* (New York, 1935); Homer C. Hockett, *The Constitutional History of the United States, 1776–1826: The Blessings of Liberty* (2 vols., New York, 1939); Erik M. Eriksson and David N. Rowe, *American Constitutional History* (New York, 1933); Carl B. Swisher, *American Constitutional Development* (Boston, 1943); Alfred H. Kelly and Winfred A. Harbison, *The American Constitution: Its Origins and Development* (New York, 1948).

37. W. Y. Elliott, *The Pragmatic Revolt in Politics: Syndicalism, Fascism and the Constitutional State* (New York, 1928).

38. For example, when the government is a partner with industry in regulating national economic life.

39. W. Y. Elliott, "The Crisis of the American Constitution," *Bulletin of the*

College of William and Mary, XXXII (June, 1938), 12–14; W. Y. Elliott, *The Need for Constitutional Reform: A Program for National Security* (New York, 1935), 186–93; W. Y. Elliott, "Getting a New Constitution," *Annals of the American Academy of Political and Social Science*, CLXXXV (May, 1936), 115–22, W. Y. Elliott, "The Constitution as the American Social Myth," *The Constitution Reconsidered*, Conyers Read, ed. (New York, 1938), 209–12, 219–24.

40. Charles H. McIlwain, *The High Court of Parliament and Its Supremacy: An Historical Essay on the Boundaries between Legislation and Adjudication in England* (New Haven, 1910); J. W. Gough, *Fundamental Law in English Constitutional History* (Oxford, 1955), 1–11.

41. Charles H. McIlwain, *The Growth of Political Thought in the West: From the Greeks to the End of the Middle Ages* (New York, 1932).

42. Charles H. McIlwain, "Government by Law," *Foreign Affairs*, XIV (Jan. 1936), 185, 189; Charles H. McIlwain, *Constitutionalism and the Changing World* (New York, 1939), 257; Charles H. McIlwain, *Constitutionalism, Ancient and Modern* (Ithaca, 1947), 139–46.

43. Carl J. Friedrich, *Constitutional Government and Democracy: Theory and Practice in Europe and America* (rev. ed., Waltham, Mass., 1950), 5–6, 17–19, 26, 35, 57; Carl J. Friedrich, "Some Thoughts on the Politics of Governmental Control," *Journal of Social Philosophy*. I (Jan. 1936), 122–33.

44. *American Historical Review*, XLVI (April 1941), 598.

45. Forrest R. Black, "Constitutions and Democracy," *Annals of the American Academy of Political and Social Science*, CLXIX (Sept. 1933), 2–3; Arthur N. Holcombe, *Government in a Planned Democracy* (New York, 1935), 25–37.

46. John Dickinson, "The Constitution and Progress," *Annals of the American Academy of Political and Social Science*, CLXXXI (Sept. 1935), 11–18.

47. Benjamin F. Wright, *The Growth of American Constitutional Law* (Chicago, 1967), 4–5, 260.

48. See Henry S. Kariel, *The Decline of American Pluralism* (Stanford, 1961).

49. Otto Kirchheimer, "In Quest of Sovereignty," *Journal of Politics*, VI (May 1944), 170.

50. Elliott, *The Pragmatic Revolt in Politics*, viii, 425–28, 433; Charles H. McIlwain, "A Fragment on Sovereignty," *Political Science Quarterly*, XLVIII (March 1933), 94.

51. Lewis Rockow, "The Doctrine of the Sovereignty of the Constitution," *American Political Science Review*, XXV (Aug. 1931), 573–88.

52. Francis G. Wilson, "A Relativistic View of Sovereignty," *Poltiical Science Quarterly*, XLIX (Sept. 1934), 392–95.

53. Heinz Eulau, "The Depersonalization of the Concept of Sovereignty," *Journal of Politics*, IV (Feb. 1942), 5–6, 15–18.

54. Max Lerner, "Constitutional Crisis and the Crisis State," *Ideas for the Ice Age: Studies in a Revolutionary Era* (New York, 1941), 306–08, 319; Carl Swisher, *The Growth of Constitutional Power in the United States* (Chicago, 1963), 3–4, 10–11, 249–50.

55. See essays by Lerner, Carl Becker, and Commager, in Read, ed., *The Constitution Reconsidered*.

56. See Charles A. Beard's "Introduction" to J. B. Bury, *The Idea of Progress* (New York, 1932), ix; Charles A. Beard and John D. Lewis, "Representative Government in Evolution," *American Political Science Review,* XXVI (April, 1932), 223–40.

57. Beard, "Historiography and the Constitution," 164–65.

58. Charles A. Beard, *An Economic Interpretation of the Constitution* (New York, 1935), xvii.

59. Charles A. Beard, *The Republic: Conversations on Fundamentals* (New York, 1943), 16–21, 26. F. A. Hermens, a European neo-constitutionalist, called this "one of the best books ever written on constitutionalism in general, and American constitutionalism in particular." *Review of Politics,* VI (Jan. 1944), 107. See also Beard's "Introduction" to Merlo Pusey, *Big Government: Can We Control It?* (New York, 1945).

60. Friedrich, *Constitutional Government and Democracy,* ix.

61. Becker, "Afterthoughts on Constitutions," 396–97.

62. Carl Becker, *New Liberties for Old* (New Haven, 1941), xvi, 146.

63. Friedrich, *Constitutional Government and Democracy,* 156–57, 617.

64. Alfred H. Kelly and Winfred A. Harbison, *The American Constitution* (New York, 1963), 1–6, 64, 251, 984–86.

65. Alfred H. Kelly, ed., *Foundations of Freedom in the American Constitution* (New York, 1958), 51.

66. *Ibid.,* 14–15.

67. Walter Lippmann, *Essays in the Public Philosophy* (Boston, 1955), 99, 101.

68. *Ibid.,* 161–71.

69. Walter Lippmann, *The Good Society* (Boston, 1936).

70. R. H. Gabriel, *The Course of American Democratic Thought* (New York, 1956), 445; Max Lerner, *America as a Civilization* (2 vols., New York, 1957), I, 29–30; Alfred deGrazia, *The Elements of Political Science* (New York, 1952), 305.

71. For a statement of this view, see John P. Roche, "American Liberty: An Examination of the 'Tradition' of Freedom," *Aspects of Liberty: Essays in Honor of Robert E. Cushman,* M. Konvitz and C. Rossiter, eds. (Ithaca, 1958), 129–62.

72. C. L. Black, Jr., *The People and the Court* (New York, 1960); Alexander M. Bickel, *The Least Dangerous Branch: The Supreme Court at the Bar of Politics* (Indianapolis, 1962).

73. Charles E. Wyzanski, Jr., "Constitutionalism: Limitation and Affirmation," *Government Under Law,* Arthur Sutherland, ed. (Cambridge, Mass., 1955), 480–81. Charles E. Wyzanski, Jr., criticized Learned Hand, an advocate of judicial restraint, for his skepticism about constitutionalism. This was reflected, said Wyzanski, in Hand's belief that courts could not save a society that lacked the spirit of moderation, and need not save a society in which that spirit flourished. To the judicial activist this was an admission that the Constitution as a legal instrument played such an insignificant role that it could be dispensed with. *Ibid.,* 478–79.

74. Herbert Wechsler, "Toward Neutral Principles of Constitutional Law," *Harvard Law Review,* LXXIII (Nov. 1959), 19.

75. Giovanni Sartori, *Democratic Theory* (Detroit, 1962), 311.

76. Robert Goedecke, "What Are the Principles of American Constitutional Law?" *Ethics,* LXXVIII (Oct. 1967), 17–31. See also Robert Goedecke, *Change and the Law* (Tallahassee, 1969).

77. W. Y. Elliott, "The Pragmatic Revolt in Politics: Twenty Years in Retrospect," *Review of Politics,* II (Jan. 1940), 1–11.

78. Hobbs, "The Rise of Scientific Value Relativism," 233; Purcell, "American Jurisprudence Between the Wars," 441–46.

79. Thomas I. Cook, "The Prospects of Political Science," *Journal of Politics,* XVII (May 1955), 271–74.

80. Lippmann, *The Public Philosophy,* 99–100.

81. J. U. Lewis, "Jean Bodin's 'Logic of Sovereignty,'" *Political Studies,* XVI (June 1968), 206.

82. F. A. Hayek, *The Constitution of Liberty* (Chicago, 1960), 236–46.

83. Giovanni Sartori, "Constitutionalism: A Preliminary Discussion," *American Political Science Review,* LVI (Dec. 1962), 854–56, 864.

84. C. J. Friedrich, "Constitutions and Constitutionalism," *International Encyclopedia of the Social Sciences* (17 vols., New York, 1968), III, 318–26.

85. Dante Germino, *Beyond Ideology: The Revival of Political Theory* (New York, 1967).

86. C. J. Friedrich, *Man and His Government: An Empirical Theory of Politics* (New York, 1963), 19.

87. *Ibid.,* 271–72, Sartori, *Democratic Theory,* 311–13.

88. Francis D. Wormuth, *The Origins of Modern Constitutionalism* (New York, 1949), 215.

89. R. G. Collingwood, *The New Leviathan, or Man, Society, Civilization and Barbarism* (Oxford, 1942), 328; Lippmann, *The Public Philosophy,* 167.

90. Friedrich, *Man and His Government,* 271; Carl J. Friedrich, *Transcendent Justice: The Religious Dimension of Constitutionalism* (Durham, N.C., 1964).

91. Herbert Spiro, *Government by Constitution: The Political Systems of Democracy* (New York, 1959), 33–40; Herbert Spiro, "Comparative Politics: A Comprehensive Approach," *American Political Science Review,* LVI (Sept. 1962), 588–89.

92. Friedrich, *Man and His Government,* 658–69.

93. M. J. C. Vile, *Constitutionalism and the Separation of Powers* (Oxford, 1967), 294–314.

94. *Ibid.,* 315–50.

95. Glendon A. Schubert, *Quantitative Analysis of Judicial Behavior* (Glencoe, Ill., 1959), 2–11; Glendon A. Schubert, "The Future of Public Law," *George Washington Law Review,* XXXIV (May 1966), 593–614; Glendon A. Schubert, "The Rhetoric of Constitutional Change," *Journal of Public Law,* XVI (1967), 38; Glendon A. Schubert, *The Constitutional Polity* (Boston, 1970). See David Ingersoll, "Karl Llewellyn, American Legal Realism and Contemporary Legal Behavioralism," *Ethics,* LXXVI (July 1966), 253–66, on the connection between recent political scientists and the realist movement.

96. Jack W. Peltason, "A Political Science of Public Law," *Southwestern Social Science Quarterly,* XXXIV (Sept. 1953), 53.

97. Arthur Selwyn Miller, "On the Need for 'Impact Analysis' of Supreme

Court Decisions," *Georgetown Law Journal*, LIII (Winter 1965), 365–401; Martin Shapiro, *Law and Politics in the Supreme Court: New Approaches to Political Jurisprudence* (New York, 1964), 15–23.

98. Sheldon Wolin, *Politics and Vision: Continuity and Innovation in Western Political Thought* (Boston, 1960), 392.

99. Kirk Thompson, "Constitutional Theory and Political Action," *Journal of Politics*, XXXI (Aug. 1969), 655–81. Thompson's conception of political action is based on the philosophy of Hannah Arendt. Hannah Arendt, *The Human Condition* (Chicago, 1958), 175–247.

100. For example, see the views of Samuel Beer in Sutherland, ed., *Government Under Law*, 548–50. He argues for actions and judgments that do not follow from rules, but arise from the pursuit of justice, a value higher than constitutionalism.

101. Wilson Cary McWilliams, "Civil Disobedience and Contemporary Constitutionalism: The American Case," *Comparative Politics*, I (Jan. 1969), 211.

102. Thompson, "Constitutional Theory and Political Action," 669; Robert J. Pranger, *Action, Symbolism and Order: The Existential Dimensions of Politics in Modern Citizenship* (Nashville, Tenn., 1968), 29.

103. C. Wright Mills, *The Power Elite* (New York, 1956), 253, 298–324.

104. An example is *Public Life*, a journal edited by H. R. Shapiro, which attacks government bureaucracies and the national political parties and urges the formation of urban townships as units of local self-government. See *Public Life*, II (Oct.-Nov. 1970).

105. Thompson, "Constitutional Theory and Political Action," 674–79; David M. Ricci, "Democracy Attenuated: Schumpeter, the Process Theory, and American Democratic Thought," *Journal of Politics*, XXXII (May 1970), 239–67; Michael Parenti, "Power and Pluralism: A View from the Bottom," *ibid.* (Aug. 1970), 501–30.

106. Pranger, *Action, Symbolism, and Order*; Robert J. Pranger, *The Eclipse of Citizenship: Power and Participation in Contemporary Politics* (New York, 1968).

107. Thompson, "Constitutional Theory and Political Action," 677.

108. Darryl Baskin, "American Pluralism: Theory, Practice, and Ideology," *Journal of Politics*, XXXII (Feb. 1970).

109. McWilliams, "Civil Disobedience and Contemporary Constitutionalism," 220.

110. Hannah Arendt, "Reflections on Violence," *New York Review*, XII (Feb. 27, 1969), 30; Hannah Arendt, "Reflections: Civil Disobedience," *New Yorker* (Sept. 12, 1970), 78–105; McWilliams, "Civil Disobedience and Contemporary Constitutionalism," 221–23; Paul F. Power, "On Civil Disobedience in Recent American Democratic Thought," *American Political Science Review*, LXIV (March 1970), 35.

111. Thompson, "Constitutional Theory and Political Action," 655, 681; McWilliams, "Civil Disobedience and Contemporary Constitutionalism," 221; Power, "On Civil Disobedience in Recent American Democratic Thought," 35–47.

112. See Kariel, *The Decline of American Pluralism*; Corinne Gilb, *Hidden Hierar-*

chies: The Professions and Government (New York, 1966); Grant McConnell, *Private Power and American Democracy* (New York, 1966); Wolfgang G. Friedmann, "Corporate Power, Government by Private Groups, and the Law," *Columbia Law Review*, LVII (Feb. 1957), 155–86; Arthur Selwyn Miller, "Technology, Social Change, and the Constitution," *George Washington Law Review*, XXXIII (Oct. 1964), 17–46.

113. Theodore J. Lowi, "The Public Philosophy: Interest-Group Liberalism," *American Political Science Review*, LXI (March 1967), 5–24; Theodore J. Lowi, *The End of Liberalism: Ideology, Policy, and the Crisis of Public Authority* (New York, 1969), 298–313. As example, Theodore J. Lowi calls for a revival of the principle invoked by the Supreme Court in the *Schechter* decision invalidating NRA, that delegations of legislative power to administrative agencies be accompanied by clear standards of implementation.

114. Murray Kempton, "The Panthers on Trial," *New York Review*, XIV (May 7, 1970), 38–42.

115. Arendt, "Reflections: Civil Disobedience," 86–105.

116. New York *Times,* Sept. 6, 1970.

117. "Constitution for a United Republics of America," *The Center Magazine,* III (Sept.-Oct. 1970).

6

The New Left Attack on Constitutionalism

Every state has a constitution—a body of principles, institutions, laws, and customs that forms the framework of government—but not every state is a constitutional state. The latter is distinguished by a commitment to constitutionalism, which in essence is the idea that political life ought to be carried on according to procedures and rules that paradoxically are in some degree placed beyond politics: procedures in other words that are fundamental. Nothing so positive as a written constitution, but rather the belief that the law as the embodiment of a society's most important values is powerful, characterizes government under the rule of law.

Apprehension about the future of constitutional government in the United States has increased in recent years. Political assassination, urban riots, the resort to civil disobedience by groups as disparate as striking postal workers and university students, the idea that politics is important enough to be the object of secret intelligence operations—all of this is evidence of a crisis in which the very legitimacy of public authority is called into question. In the long run, however, perhaps even more unsettling than these turbulent events is the intellectual and ideological challenge to constitutionalism that they have produced.

This challenge appears most significantly, I believe, not in the revelations of former White House aides, alarming as these are, but rather in the crisis literature of political science which has attempted to explain the upheaval of the past several years and offer a new theory of politics. The most obvious feature of this literature is its critique of pluralism. Interest-group liberalism, the antipluralists emphatically conclude, is the dead end, not the vital center, of American democracy. Dissatisfaction with liberal pluralism is not new, however, and in the recent literature it does not provide the special animus of the attack on the liberal state. Rather impatience with constitutionalism, which runs pretty deep amid the consciousness raising and political involvement of our time, forms the essential theme of the attack on pluralism.

The fundamental charge against pluralism is that it is not real democracy, but rather a system of special privilege by which the rich and powerful protect their interests at the expense of the people. American politics, the antipluralists insist, simply does not work the way it is supposed to in theory. It is fatuous, they say, to think that a vast number of competing and roughly equal groups interact freely in the political decision-making structure. On the contrary, a few corporate giants control the political system. An even more damning indictment of pluralism is that it excludes many groups from the political process entirely. Blacks, the poor, students, women, and sundry minorities are all seen as relegated to a condition of noncitizenship outside the political arena.[1]

If it is suggested that American politics is actually responsive to demands from nonelite groups, the antipluralist answer is that the system may work after a fashion, but the workings are all trivial and irrelevant. The root of the trouble is said to be the biased context in which interest-group politics operates. The political process may be open, the media relatively accessible, freedom of speech and of the press secure. All this is beside the point, however, for what is really important, say the critics, is "the other face of power," that is, the class bias of pluralist politics which prevents issues of real concern to the community from being brought into the political arena. The groups which control the system ignore problems such as urban blight, public transportation, worker alienation, and environmental destruction. What officials do not do, the argument runs—the nondecisions they make—are more important than the decisions they make about insignificant matters.[2]

From here it is but a short distance to the doctrine of repressive tolerance. Because the political system is managed in the interests of dominant economic groups, Herbert Marcuse argues, there is an objective contradiction between the political structure and the theory of pluralist toleration. In practice equality of tolerance becomes abstract and spurious, an instrument of coordination and control rather than a means of effecting change. Benjamin R. Barber holds that when toleration is examined in the context of liberalism, with its assumption of a utilitarian and individualistic ethic, it is revealed as negligence of the public interest. The attitude which this kind of criticism encourages will be recognized by anyone who has been on a college campus the past five years. Student radicals take part in an election, work hard for a candidate, and then if the candidate loses decry the system for failing once again. In a gloss on this attitude, Barber states that the contemporary crisis is rooted in skepticism about the ability of the system to serve the interests of fixed minorities, who cannot or will not be assimilated into it. The procedures of democratic pluralism become in this view mere legitimizing rituals and the right of dissent an instrument of oppression. Barber concludes ominously: "The politics which concerns itself with the good life, . . . which aims at virtue rather than at mechanistic freedom, may not find much room for, or be particularly interested in, tolerance."[3]

As Barber's statement suggests, the critique of pluralism goes beyond an accounting of the specific failures of the liberal state in America. What is being challenged is the very idea of constitutionalism itself. This is most apparent in the antipluralists' preoccupation with political action.

Constitutionalism, they contend, even in its original eighteenth-century formulation, was flawed by its failure to contain a concept of political action. Beguiled by the idea of applying science to politics, the founders of constitutionalism sought to control human behavior by devising rules and procedures for the conduct of government that would eliminate the need for political leadership and citizen participation. Placing their faith in institutions rather than men, they provided no space for political action and designed a mechanistic system which depersonalized, trivialized, and fragmentized political life. Antipluralists charge further that constitutionalism comprehends and protects mere private economic interests. It thus denies the vision of politics as an educational and salvational activity, and the possibility of defining and achieving a true public purpose. In liberal society a "nondirective constitutionalism" aimed at containing competing interests is substituted for authentic political community.[4]

Those who think of politics as the art of achieving the possible and see in the constitutional system broad scope for political action may wonder about the criteria used to reach these negative conclusions. And indeed skepticism is warranted, for the antipluralists' critique of constitutionalism depends heavily upon a conception of political action drawn more from philosophy than from ordinary language and experience.

Following Hannah Arendt, critics of pluralism hold that political action refers to acts which are novel, consequential, purposive, irreversible, and indeterminate. All else, including the routine and often predictable responses which characterize a stable constitutional regime, are defined—and dismissed—as behavior. Perhaps not every antipluralist critic would subscribe to precisely this formulation of the issue, but the demands for relevant action and meaningful change heard so often these days come pretty close to capturing the more technical definition. A corollary notion taken also from Arendt is the idea of public space. As used by the antipluralists, public space refers to opportunities in which men can appear to others and disclose themselves in speech and action. This seems familiar enough, and we readily think of the range of legally protected liberties under the first and fourteenth amendments. But if speech and action and petitioning of the government avail nothing in the way of boundless, novel, unanticipated, and indeterminate results—nothing that meets the criteria of political action—then there is evidently no true public space or genuine political freedom.[5]

If constitutionalism is seen as defective in its original conception, it is criticized all the more in its present-day reality for suppressing authentic politics. This emerges most clearly in the attack on the "process theory" of democracy. Classical democratic thought, the critics argue, posited broad popular participation in politics in pursuit of the common good. In the Cold War era, however, pluralists revised the classical theory by concluding that democracy consisted in procedures and practices which assured a stable political system characterized by low popular participation. Liberal democracy became in essence a process distinguished by voter apathy and elite manipulation.[6]

Although the antipluralists do not quite say that procedure is unimportant, they believe it has too often been honored at the expense of higher values. John Schaar thus decries "the liberal fear of politics and the inability to see that the politics of a free people both depend upon and promise more than a machinery of offices, procedures, statutes, and programs." After students shut down many universities in 1970, Schaar and Sheldon S. Wolin explained that a major factor in the domestic crisis was Americans' unduly narrow conception of politics as bargaining, compromise, and electoral contests. The "rules of the game are many and confining," the Berkeley professors commented, and "hence small novelties look like major violations." In similar fashion Wilson Carey McWilliams has suggested that any solution to the contemporary political crisis must involve an abandonment of our fascination for a government of mechanical contrivances designed to avoid conflict, if not to eliminate politics altogether.[7]

Impatient, if not scornful of procedure, antipluralists regard politics as a matter of commitment and values and substantive results. Pluralism in contrast is seen as excessively concerned with stability and efficiency and, therefore, as essentially antipolitical. Christian Bay epitomizes the antipluralist animus in condemning what he calls the liberal myth that American society is democratic and that only by working within the constitutional system can a more just society be created. The most urgent contemporary need, says Bay, is to destroy this myth.[8]

Certainly the critics of liberal pluralism have done their demythologizing best. It remains to ask, however, what they would have in its place and how their reform ideas stand in relation to constitutionalism.

In the recent crisis literature three tendencies can be discerned on the question, what is to be done? One looks to civil disobedience as a source of political renewal, a second contemplates the democratization of economic organizations, and a third urges a new theory of politics based upon a revival of citizenship.

Although practitioners of civil disobedience may see it as a way of bringing down the system, scholarly interpreters contend on the contrary that it can make the political system work better. Civil disobedience, they reason, can become a new form of representation with the potential to revitalize democratic citizenship. Those who engage in civil disobedience are seen as a legitimate opposition whose political actions may enlighten the government and, by informing it of its misuse of power, actually enhance the rule of law. Tyranny being the exclusion of the public from the political, reasons Wilson Carey McWilliams, we are perilously near that condition now. Yet a way out is provided by civil disobedience, which by enabling citizens to gain access to the public can be a means of constitutional reform. Hannah Arendt views civil disobedients as organized minorities expressing their disagreement with the majority. Placing recent protesters in the tradition of voluntary associations, Arendt's novel argument envisions formal recognition of a lobbyist, group representation role for civil-disobedient minorities.[9]

The hostility that people feel toward a nameless bureaucracy may lead in the future to further spasms of civil disobedience. It is hard to take seriously, however, the suggestion that "disciplined civil disobedience is possibly a creative way to ask citizens of the state if they are satisfied with other aspects of the delegational model that has served well but which may not have produced the most equitable and efficient allocation of power and resources to deal with emergent disaffection and unmet needs in the national polity."[10] If civil-disobedient groups do somehow become "constitutionalized" they will be part of the pluralist political structure, a curious and disappointing conclusion, it would seem, from the radical point of view. Should civil disobedience increase, however, and produce a body of concerned participating magistrates as McWilliams urges,[11] the result will more likely be an expedient people's justice than constitutional government as we have known it historically.

A second reformist theme of the antipluralists concerns the enforcing of accountability and responsibility in the economic power structure. It has become a commonplace to observe that corporations wield political power and make policies no different in substance and effect from those of public officials. What is needed is to broaden the definition of the political to include these nominally private but actually public institutions.

One way of constitutionalizing corporations is through judicial and administrative regulation. Because this would mean more of the same sort of centralized national regulation that has seemed so ineffectual in the past, however, antipluralists take a dim view of it. They argue instead for "participatory democracy." This is surely one of the more imprecise terms of contemporary political discourse, but in the present context it means control of corporations by those who work in and are affected by them. The system of self-management that exists in Yugoslavia is taken as model. Workers would form the board of directors or governing council of a business or industry, or in larger enterprises elect delegates to a council. The point is not to redistribute property, but rather to encourage democratic participation at the place of work in order to reduce people's sense of powerlessness and contribute to their self-development. Industrial democracy would make workers citizens of the enterprise rather than corporate subjects. And by enabling them to see the relationship between public and private spheres it would in turn make them better citizens of the state.[12]

A politically engaged citizenry, the ultimate objective of both civil disobedience strategy and participatory economic democracy, lies at the very center of the third tendency in antipluralist reformism, the quest of a new theory of politics. The immediate purpose of this quest is a regeneration of citizenship and the creation of opportunities for genuine political action. But for this to take place a new way of thinking about politics is required. And this means rejecting as the proper method of political science the point of view known as behavioralism, defined generally as empirical, positivistic, value-free description of the existing political system.

The trouble with behavioralism, the antipluralists argue, is that it takes what is for what ought to be: professing to be morally neutral and rigorously objective, it turns out to be normative after all. What is more, this unacknowledged normative influence is exerted in support of pluralist constitutionalism. The techniques of behavioral political science, the antipluralists observe, can be most effectively applied to organized, predictable, routine processes. As constitutionalism produces exactly this kind of political and social phenomenon, it encourages behavioralist studies, which in turn reinforce the constitutional order. According to its critics, behavioralism perpetuates faith in the utilitarian, technical rationality characteristic of liberal constitutionalism.[13]

Antipluralists propose a new political theory that will not be restrained, as behavioralism is said to be, by facts selected as functional prerequisites of the existing order. On the contrary, political theory must recognize the facts of the real world that do not accord with the received liberal wisdom, and thus open itself to new possibilities. Rejecting the ideal of an objective social science, antipluralists contend that factual knowledge about what is or has been should not dominate political education, as it usually has. Sheldon Wolin states that the knowledge characteristic of the new theory of politics is suggestive and illuminative, rather than explicit and determinative. Instead of accepting the assumptions of the established system, the new political theory will acknowledge as all-important the context in which events occur and will show respect for the people who engage in political action.[14]

Taking the argument several steps farther, Henry S. Kariel calls for a social science that instead of reconciling us to our fate will expand political reality. In Kariel's view the new political theory must provide metaphors, models, languages, forms, and conceptual frameworks that will make it possible to identify the contours and meaning of political life lying below the surface of society. Sharing the sense of failure that many political scientists felt at their inability to predict the upheavals of the sixties and early seventies, the antipluralists are warning us to grasp and make sense of this new reality. The social scientist, says Kariel, must interpret the actions of previously suppressed persons in such a way as to bring them into—and thus expand—the political present. Sheldon S. Wolin similarly declares that with the world seemingly coming apart, a theoretical imagination is needed which will admit new facts and restate new possibilities.[15]

Wolin's appeal has not gone unanswered. Indeed the antipluralist theoretical imagination has been exceedingly active in trying to discern the political meaning of recent events. With a kind of apocalyptic zeal it projects the vision of a dynamic politics of commitment in which participating citizens find a new ground of being and realize their true humanity and potential as individuals. The apathy and indifference of pluralism are not only condemned on moral grounds, they are stood on their heads and transformed into a throbbing political activism. Full participation—"nothing less than a society all of whose members are active participants in an interminable process—and who will not mind such activity," says Kariel—is the goal. The key to attaining it lies in enlarging the public space within which true political action can take place. Outsiders, the underclass, apolitical men and women who desire to speak and act in public and gain recognition, are to be brought into the political arena. To overcome people's feelings of alienation and powerlessness, the distance between them and government must be reduced, the height of government scaled down, the veil of secrecy about government lifted. A public life of common involvements will be the result.[16]

Empirical as we are, we think of public space in concrete terms and wonder which new modes and forms and jurisdictional arrangements will implement this vision. In their reaction against positivistic social science, however, the antipluralists incline toward a symbolic view of the problem of public space. Robert J. Pranger writes that the boundaries of the political arena may be territorial and organizational, but also spiritual and intellectual. Pranger finds inspiration in Hannah Arendt's description of the ancient polis as "the organization of the people as it arises out of acting and speaking together," its true space lying "between people living together for this purpose, no matter where they happen to be." The political space, time, distance, and choice in which citizenship consists are thus more a matter of psychological perception than objective reality. In an age when alienation is assumed to be a mass phenomenon this is perhaps to be expected. It is striking nevertheless to learn that the picture of the French resistance during World War II—as a "republic of silence" without formal institutions or leaders, in which political actions were taken with a sense of common involvement and responsibility for the freedom of others—is taken as a model of participatory politics completely irrespective of its empirical or historical accuracy.[17]

Citizenship in the new political theory, instead of being an empty catalogue of subjects' rights, becomes an opportunity for creative political action. Citizens acting in true community define themselves as human beings, gain knowledge of themselves and others, and discover that which unites them as brothers. Participation in decision making becomes an ennobling and educational venture which overcomes the separation between man and citizen, unites personal and social forces, and eliminates the dichotomy between public and private.[18] In the upper reaches of the new political consciousness, Sheldon Wolin and John Schaar tell us, "knowledge, personal identity, and public commitment are part of the same quest." Benjamin R. Barber offers a new word—"philopoly"—to describe the love of politics for its own sake that will characterize true democratic participation. Equally optimistic, Henry S. Kariel urges that the pleasures and rewards of political discourse and deliberation be extended to everyone rather than kept by the elite for themselves. Politics, Kariel suggests, ought to be regarded "as a form of play, as characteristically a performing art" which becomes a manifestation of human freedom and "the determination to . . . create publicly meaningful structures of being. . . ." The outer limits of the new political universe seem to be reached in Herbert Reid's definition of politics as "the tendency of men in general to resist, whatever the means, the severing of meaningful self-world relationships. . . ."[19]

In view of the quasi-religious character of the appeal, one might ask by what signs a second coming of authentic citizenship and true democracy would be known. Although the antipluralists profess an attitude of openness toward the future rather than an ability to predict it, they have at times assessed contemporary affairs in the light of the new political theory and indicated what the new politics might look like in the real world.

Despite their impatience with pluralist politics, some antipluralists regard voting as a possibly significant form of political action. The catch is that there must be a real choice, which according to one writer means following the candidates into office and affecting their policy decisions, and voting should be perceived as a manifestation of man's desire to appear in public and display his freedom.[20] These are large qualifications which, together with an awareness that an activated silent majority might well be "unprogressive" in outlook, lead the critics of pluralism to take only a reluctant interest in the usual forms of liberal politics. Organizing projects—in urban slums, on college campuses, and in factories—are a more likely expression of the new politics. Such efforts reflect the current interest in decentralization, with its assumption that the consensus-forming methods of small-group interaction can be applied to political and social problems. A few years ago attempts to incorporate "maximum feasible participation" in the federal government's war on poverty seemed to embody this approach. Yet none of these undertakings has seriously challenged the structure of pluralist politics.[21]

The events which have given antipluralists the clearest vision of a new politics, leading Wolin and Schaar to think that "perhaps even the birth of the American as a political man" was imminent, were the student strikes, ghetto riots, and general upheaval of the late 1960s. These developments, so disturbing to most people, were regarded with hope and expectation by the critics of liberal pluralism. Thus Henry S. Kariel suggested that what seemed to be violent and irrational actions were really controlled efforts to break with present actualities and create a new reality. Though threatening to middle-class sensibilities, they were rational actions which ought not to have been dismissed as "dysfunctional" to the system. Describing the youth of the 1960s, Wolin and Schaar recorded "a rich variety of truly political actions [which] showed a genuine concern for public things, thereby reversing the long trend toward privatization." In particular young people "argued, sang, marched, organized, sat in, milled around, walked out, and disrupted.[22]

Even brighter promise appeared in the swiftly explosive reaction to the U.S. incursion into Cambodia in May 1970. Thousands of students who would have nothing to do with politics as usual engaged in the spontaneous and unpredictable political action that unfolded on the nation's campuses. According to Wolin and Schaar, this was a new politics, impatient with routine and contemptuous of compromise. Kinetic, pulsating, and shaped toward experiencing a climactic moment, it gathers energy and when confronted with abstract rules spills over into overt, unpremeditated, and collective violence. This violence, however, say these interpreters of the New Left, is to be understood as a protest against the pedestrian politics and stale rhetoric of liberalism. Assaulting the police is "a way of asserting that there is a human reality to the world, that the world is not all plastic and steel." Wilson Carey McWilliams reasons similarly that the politics of involvement demanded by the present crisis necessarily brings with it a kind of violence. It is the kind of violence, McWilliams writes, "that best enables a man to find himself, his friends, and a standard of legitimacy."[23]

McWilliams is not talking about violence in the usual sense of physical assault, and I do not wish to imply that he and like-minded critics are advocating a brass-knuckles approach to political action. But one does wonder what they are driving at, and what the implications and effect of their analysis might be. These are not easy questions to answer, in part because the new political theory seems to disdain, not just politics as usual, but critical rational thinking as usual.

Wolin says that political life is elusive, and meaningful statements about it must be allusive and intimative. The new theory he advocates would deal in "tacit political knowledge" rather than "methodistic truths." Pranger goes further in declaring that there may be differences between the demands of theory construction and simple description of empirical facts. He suggests that a "suspension of the empirical" is involved in the formulation of the new political theory. When in the face of widespread social disorder Kariel advises the social scientist to "publicly ponder and implicitly exalt the sheer appearance of political life—the inexplicable fact that it is present at all"—suspension of the empirical seems to have become abandonment of common sense. Indeed an apocalyptic note, not dominant perhaps but distinctive nonetheless, enters the antipluralist crisis literature. It can be seen, for example, in Aristide Zolberg's speculation about "moments of madness" when the wall between the instrumental and the expressive collapses. "Is it farfetched," he asks, "to believe that those imbued with extraordinary sensibility provoke moments of exaltation, when the meek can more easily enter the kingdom?"[24]

It may be, as anthropologist Stanley Diamond argues, that the rule of law is a symptom of the disorder of customary institutions and the decline of a civilization.[25] Believing that the second coming of true democracy, community, and participation would obviate the whole rule structure of the modern liberal state, the antipluralists seem to share this view. Until our political salvation is assured, however, we are justified in asking what the implications of the new politics and the new political theory are for constitutionalism.

Although the question usually is of interest to liberals and conservatives, some radical antipluralists, despite intense criticism of the liberal state, profess concern for constitutionalism. Theorists of civil disobedience and economic democracy seek ways of legitimizing new forms of dissent and constitutionalizing the great aggregates of economic power. A few theorists of the new politics say their purpose is to revise constitutionalism to provide greater scope for political action, diminishing the height of government but not removing the restraints upon it. In fighting for their causes, moreover, radicals will rely on constitutional rules for protection. Some caution further against rejecting bourgeois liberal constitutional ideals simply because they have often been a cloak for oppression, and express concern for constitutional processes within the radical movement, lest violence and brutality obliterate peaceful procedures. This is evidence that the attack on the pluralist system does not necessarily mean repudiation of the idea of constitutionalism.[26]

Nevertheless, the new political theory of the antipluralists contradicts the fundamental ideas of constitutionalism. Those critics who profess to revise the theory of constitutionalism are mistaken, I believe, in their understanding of its essential meaning. To them—and inferentially to the antipluralists in general—constitutionalism means, or ought to mean, the people as constituent power, the source of authority and ground of law. It means further the people creating political power by forming a social compact and exercising that power in governing themselves. The ancient notion of popular sovereignty, dating from the founding of the republic, epitomizes this conception of constitutionalism.

Its root idea is politicism, the belief, that is, that political will and the force of personality, knowledge of the good and the will to realize it in acts of wisdom, are more important for good government—and more decisive in determining the course of events—than any institutional framework or procedural arrangements. Governments are like clocks, runs the old aphorism, and go from the motion men give them, not from anything in themselves. This politicist argument has always had considerable appeal. When it is applied to the people has a whole, and they are invested with the power of political action—especially as the antipluralists would define political action—it acquires even greater force, if indeed it does not become irresistible.

But while flexibility, discretion, personal character, and freedom of political action—the elements of politicism—have had a place in the constitutional tradition, they have not formed the essence of it. In essence constitutionalism has meant adherence to certain formal procedures embodying and promoting the fundamental values of liberty, equality, and justice; to ways of conducting politics and managing public affairs which preserve a space immune to or beyond politics. In other words, while the people have been the constituent power, their power to govern—popular sovereignty—has been limited by their own constitutional creation. At its inception in the eighteenth century American constitutionalism was marked by an extraordinarily democratic basis, and the people as constituent power was the most startling of the revolutionary ideas.[27] Yet the idea that a constitution was superior to and controlling of the political power of government, even when the people themselves exercised that power either through established institutions or outside them, was also part of revolutionary constitutionalism.

In the history of Western political thought this idea of fundamental law was as remarkable an innovation as the notion of the people as constituent power. In the long run it became the truly distinctive feature of American constitutionalism. The Constitution was conceived of as a means of conducting politics, but it did not consist in a mere declaration of purposes or a set of exhortations, as the French constitution of 1791 did. It was on the contrary explicitly declared to be law, the supreme law of the land along with treaties of the United States and acts of Congress made in pursuance of it. Ordinary law, as between private persons, was to be used to regulate the acts of government and the energies and passions of politics. And this political law maintaining the structure of the body public and protecting individual liberty against encroachment by the government, a paradoxical and contradictory thing according to the best learning of the day, was to be enforced by ordinary courts of justice. It was altogether a curious amalgam which, in conjunction with the division of power between national and state governments known as federalism, effectively destroyed sovereignty as it was then known. And it meant too that popular sovereignty must be stillborn, must be placed under constitutional restraints as well.

It is the age-old politicist drive to be free of procedural restraints which informs the antipluralist appeal for a new politics. Expressing this appeal in modern terms of commitment, transcendence, and self-fulfillment, the critics resurrect the classic democratic ideal of an engaged citizenry exercising political and legal sovereignty and standing above institutions. But no better than anyone else are the antipluralists able to explain how fundamental fairness can obtain in a system of government in which all is politicized.

The essence of the political is discretion, discrimination, expediency, adjustment of conflicting claims on a pragmatic basis. The essence of the legal is general and prospective rules that result in regular and predictable procedure. A constitution must of course generate power as well as channel it. It must comprehend both the political and legal dimension. And in a strict sense we cannot say that one is more important than the other; both are essential. Yet while we can be certain that political energies and passions and conflicts will continue to manifest themselves, with the insistence and power seemingly of natural forces, the experience of the twentieth century tells us that the existence of a stable and just system for restraining these forces cannot be taken for granted. The opposite of constitutionalism—arbitrary and coercive government which denies political liberty and free public criticism—must be guarded against. And this means keeping in mind, to use the language of social science, a contrast-model.

From the 1930s to the 1950s totalitarian regimes in Europe provided a vivid contrast-model which led intellectuals in the United States to reconsider their own constitutional tradition. Instead of dismissing the rule of law as a conservative fiction and a device for maintaining the status quo, as many had done, they came to see it as a valid distinction between systems of government. A revival of interest in constitutionalism occurred which made it a principal theme in modern liberalism.[28]

The antipluralists have reacted against liberal constitutionalism as though it were entirely ideological—a reflection of the false consciousness of its adherents—and lacking any basis in historical reality. They deny the validity of the totalitarian contrast-model on the ground that it fosters complacency and, by failing to emphasize problems, forecloses the possibility of change.[29] Yet it is difficult to ignore recent history—right down to the latest interdiction of free speech and academic inquiry by student radicals—and hard not to be apprehensive about a political theory that exalts popular participation and political action to the extent that the new politics does. It may seem entirely clear to the heralds of the new citizenship that the mass participation of modern technological society is completely different from the true democratic participation they envision, but a skeptical view of this distinction seems warranted. How realistic is it to think that men and women will engage in politics for the sheer love of it, apart from practical purposes? Benjamin R. Barber states that "a new era of *philopoly* might help to make life for man in the post-historical epoch livable."[30] It would be more accurate to say that only after history ends—in the world to come—will people play at politics for the love of the thing itself, as some antipluralists believe.

If the present crisis is rooted in an erosion of community which has released proliferating forces of conflict, calling into question the authority of government and politicizing all manner of social processes and relationships, the solution lies not in further encouragement of politicist tendencies but in their being brought into a more stable equilibrium with the essential ideas and procedures of constitutionalism. This will not be accomplished by stern admonitions from high officials to respect law and order, especially now in the light of the Watergate revelations. Whether the crisis can be surmounted according to prescriptions offered meanwhile by political scientists in the liberal constitutional tradition may also be doubted. These solutions range from Lowi's juridical democracy, to Friedrich's call for inspirational democratic leadership, to Tugwell's new model constitution. Appealing as these suggestions are, they seem to assume against the evidence that someone somewhere has the knowledge and power to set things right.[31]

The crux of the matter is the tendency and habit of ordinary citizens to regard political institutions and procedures as legitimate. In the United States legitimate authority derives in large part from the direct link with the eighteenth-century Framers' act of foundation and the consensual basis on which it rested. This basis has been seriously challenged, but how far the disintegration of community has gone is not clear. Probably it has not gone as far as the dramatic events of a few years ago seemed to indicate. The structure of assumptions, beliefs, and practices in which constitutionalism consists may be more solidly based than it appears in the crisis literature. Nevertheless, the antipluralists' insistence on ever greater political participation and action reflects and represents a challenge to constitutionalism that is not merely academic.[32] If the liberal constitutional order collapses, the critics of pluralism might consider, it is not at all likely that a left-wing movement dedicated to participatory democracy will take its place.

Notes

Research for this article was supported by a grant from the American Bar Foundation for research in constitutional and legal history.

1. Peter Bachrach, ed., *Political Elites in a Democracy* (New York, 1971), pp. 4–11; Michael Parenti, "Power and Pluralism: A View from the Bottom," *Journal of Politics*, XXII (August, 1970), pp. 501–30, and "The Possibilities for Political Change," *Politics and Society*, I (November, 1970), pp. 79–90; C. George Benello and Dimitrios Roussopoulos, eds., *The Case for Participatory Democracy: Some Prospects for a Radical Society* (New York, 1971), pp. 4–5; Christian Bay, "Hayek's Liberalism: The Constitution of Perpetual Privilege," *The Political Science Reviewer*, I (Fall, 1971), pp. 93–124; Duane Lockard, *The Perverted Priorities of American Politics* (New York, 1971), 18, pp. 314–15.

2. David M. Ricci, *Community Power and Democratic Theory: The Logic of Political Analysis* (New York, 1971), pp. 62–63; William E. Connolly, ed., *The Bias of Pluralism* (New York, 1969), pp. 13–17; Peter Bachrach and Morton Baratz, "Decisions and Non-Decisions: An Analytic Framework," *American Political Science Review*, LVII (December, 1963), pp. 632–42.

3. Herbert Marcuse, "Repressive Tolerance," in Bachrach, ed., *Political Elites in a Democracy*, 138–69; Benjamin R. Barber, *Superman and Common Men: Freedom, Anarchy, and the Revolution* (New York, 1971), pp. 94–96, 101–02.

4. Kirk Thompson, "Constitutional Theory and Political Action," *Journal of Politics*, XXXI (August, 1969), pp. 655–81; Sheldon S. Wolin, *Politics and Vision: Continuity and Innovation in Western Political Thought* (Boston, 1960), pp. 388–92, 433–34; Darryl Baskin, *American Pluralist Democracy: A Critique* (New York, 1971), pp. 59–73, 96–98, 175–76.

5. Thompson, "Constitutional Theory and Political Action," pp. 657–61; Hannah Arendt, *The Human Condition* (Chicago, 1958), pp. 175–247; Robert J. Pranger, *Action, Symbolism, and Order: The Existential Dimensions of Politics in Modern Citizenship* (Nashville, 1968), 10, pp. 100–02.

6. Graeme Duncan and Steven Lukes, "The New Democracy," *Political Studies*, XI (June, 1963), pp. 156–77; Lane Davis, "The Cost of Realism: Contemporary Statements of Democracy," *Western Political Quarterly*, XVII (March, 1964), pp. 37–46; Jack L. Walker, "A Critique of the Elitist Theory of Democracy," *American Political Science Review*, LX (June, 1966), pp. 285–94; David M. Ricci, "Democracy Attenuated: Schumpeter, the Process Theory, and American Democratic Thought," *Journal of Politics*, XXXII (May, 1970), pp. 239–67.

7. John H. Schaar, book review, *American Political Science Review*, LXIV (December, 1970), p. 1259; Sheldon S. Wolin and John H. Schaar, "Is a New Politics Possible?" *New York Review of Books*, XV (September 3, 1970), p. 3; Wilson Carey McWilliams, "On Violence and Legitimacy," *Yale Law Journal*, LXXIX (March, 1970), p. 645.

8. Christian Bay, "Politics and Pseudopolitics: A Critical Evaluation of Some Behavioral Literature," *American Political Science Review*, LIX (March, 1965), pp. 39–51, and "Foundations of the Liberal Make-Believe: Some Implica-

tions of Contract Theory Versus Freedom Theory," *Inquiry,* XIV (Autumn, 1971), pp. 213–37.

9. Paul F. Power, "On Civil Disobedience in Recent American Democratic Thought," *American Political Science Review,* LXIV (March, 1970), pp. 35–47, and "Civil Disobedience as Functional Opposition," *Journal of Politics,* XXXIV (February, 1972), pp. 37–55; Wilson Carey McWilliams, "Civil Disobedience and Contemporary Constitutionalism: The American Case," *Comparative Politics,* I (January, 1969), pp. 211–27; Hannah Arendt, "Reflections: Civil Disobedience," *New Yorker* (September 12, 1970), pp. 78–105.

10. Power, "On Civil Disobedience in Recent American Democratic Thought," p. 47.

11. McWilliams, "Civil Disobedience and Contemporary Constitutionalism," p. 222.

12. Peter Bachrach, *The Theory of Democratic Elitism: A Critique* (Boston, 1967), pp. 72–104; Carole Pateman, *Participation and Democratic Theory* (Cambridge, 1970), *passim;* Kenneth A. Megill, *The New Democratic Theory* (New York, 1970), pp. 89–120. Robert A. Dahl, not otherwise an antipluralist, has endorsed this approach in "Power to the Workers?" *New York Review of Books,* XV (November 19, 1970), pp. 20–24. See also "The New Corporatism," the entire issue of the January 1974 *Review of Politics,* to be published with some additions as a book in the spring of 1974 by the University of Notre Dame Press.

13. Shelton S. Wolin, "Political Theory as a Vocation," *APSR,* LXIII (December, 1969), pp. 1062–82; Herbert Reid, "Contemporary American Political Science," *Midwest Journal of Political Science,* XVI (August, 1972), p. 365; Ricci, *Community Power and Democratic Theory,* pp. 62–63, 211; Bay, "Politics and Pseudopolitics"; Charles A. McCoy and John Playford, eds., *Apolitical Parties: A Critique of Behavioralism* (New York, 1967).

14. Wolin, "Political Theory as a Vocation," pp. 1070–71.

15. Henry S. Kariel, *Open Systems: Arenas for Political Action* (Itasca, Ill., 1969), p. 7; Kariel, "Expanding the Political Present," *APSR,* LXIII (September, 1969), pp. 774–75, "Terminal Cases," *The Political Science Reviewer,* I (Fall, 1971), pp. 84–85; Wolin, "Political Theory as a Vocation," p. 1081.

16. Kariel, *Open Systems,* p. 73, and "Terminal Cases," pp. 85–91; Pranger, *Action, Symbolism, and Order,* pp. 6, 29, and *The Eclipse of Citizenship: Power and Participation in Contemporary Politics* (New York, 1968), pp. 68–72.

17. Barber, *Superman and Common Men,* p. 109; Pranger, *Action, Symbolism, and Order,* p. 6, and *Eclipse of Citizenship,* p. 97.

18. *Ibid.,* p. 89; Pranger, *Action, Symbolism, and Order,* p. 107; Darryl Baskin, "American Pluralism: Theory, Practice, and Ideology," *Journal of Politics,* XXXII (Fall, 1970), pp. 71–95, and *American Pluralist Democracy,* pp. 173–74; David Kettler, "The Politics of Social Change: The Relevance of Democratic Approaches," in Connolly, ed., *The Bias of Pluralism,* pp. 213–49; Connolly, "Liberalism under Pressure," *Polity,* II (Spring, 1970), pp. 365–66; Wolin and Schaar, "Is a New Politics Possible?" p. 4.

19. *Ibid.,* p. 10; Barber, *Superman and Common Men,* pp. 96, 122; Kariel, "Expanding the Political Present," p. 773; Reid, "Contemporary American Political Science," p. 365.

20. Pranger, *Eclipse of Citizenship*, p. 71; Kariel, "Expanding the Political Present," p. 774.

21. Pranger, *Eclipse of Citizenship*, p. 92; Kariel, "Expanding the Political Present," p. 774; Dorothy Buckton James, "The Limits of Liberal Reform," *Politics and Society*, II (Spring, 1972), pp. 309–22.

22. Kariel, "Expanding the Political Present," p. 771; Wolin and Schaar, "Where We Are Now," *New York Review of Books*, XIV (May 7, 1970), p. 3.

23. Wolin and Schaar, "Is a New Politics Possible?" p. 4; McWilliiams, "On Violence and Legitimacy," pp. 645–46.

24. Wolin, "Political Theory as a Vocation," p. 1070; Pranger, *Action, Symbolism, and Order*, p. 105; Kariel, "Expanding the Political Present," p. 774; Aristide R. Zolberg, "Moments of Madness," *Politics and Society*, II (Winter, 1972), pp. 183–207.

25. Stanley Diamond, "The Rule of Law versus the Order of Custom," *Social Research*, XXXVIII (Spring, 1971), pp. 42–72.

26. Thompson, "Constitutional Theory and Political Action"; Pranger, *Eclipse of Citizenship*, pp. 68–72; Barrington Moore, Jr., *Reflections on the Causes of Human Misery and Upon Certain Proposals to Eliminate Them* (Boston, 1972), pp. 112–14; Kettler, "The Politics of Social Change"; Wolin and Schaar, "Is a New Politics Possible?" p. 4.

27. R. R. Palmer, *The Age of the Democratic Revolution: A Political History of Europe and America 1760–1800* (2 vols., Princeton, 1959–64), I, pp. 213–35.

28. Herman Belz, "Changing Conceptions of Constitutionalism in the Era of World War Two and the Cold War," *Journal of American History*, LIX (December, 1972), pp. 640–69.

29. Lockard, *Perverted Priorities of American Politics*, p. 18; Connolly, ed., *The Bias of Pluralism*, p. 23; Duncan and Lukes, "The New Democracy," pp. 174–77. The intellectual discrediting of the idea of totalitarianism is described in Robert Burrowes, "Totalitarianism: The Revised Standard Version," *World Politics*, XXI (January, 1969), pp. 272–94, and Herbert J. Spiro and Benjamin R. Barber, "Counter-Ideological Uses of 'Totalitarianism,'" *Politics and Society*, I (November, 1970), pp. 3–22.

30. Barber, *Superman and Common Men*, p. 122.

31. Theodore J. Lowi, *The End of Liberalism: Ideology, Policy, and the Crisis of Public Authority* (New York, 1969), pp. 287–314; Carl J. Friedrich, "Bureaucracy Faces Anarchy," *Canadian Public Administration*, XIII (Fall, 1970), pp. 219-31; Rexford G. Tugwell, "Constitution for a United Republics of America," *The Center Magazine*, III (September/October, 1970), pp. 24–45; Robert Y. Fluno, "The Floundering Leviathan: Pluralism in an Age of Ungovernability," *Western Political Quarterly*, XXIV (September, 1971), pp. 563.

32. How literally unacademic the challenge is can be seen in a sympathetic critic's observation that to achieve true community advocates of the new political theory will not undertake empirical research, but rather will become actively involved in social movements, teach "skills of criticism to large numbers of people," and engage in "philosophical investigations into the structure of openness, integrity, and self-knowledge." Michael A. Weinstein, "The Inclusive Polity: New Directions in Political Theory," *Polity*, V (Spring, 1973), p. 372.

7

Bureaucracy and Constitutionalism

Although plans are well underway for celebrating the bicentennial of the U.S. Constitution in 1987, it is doubtful that many of the public will be aware—or if aware would care to celebrate—a centennial milestone in the history of American government that teachers of political science will recognize as having great importance for American constitutionalism. I refer to what may be described, with some historical license, as the birth of the administrative state. This event was announced by the publication in 1887 of Woodrow Wilson's famous essay, "The Study of Administration," and by the creation in the same year of the Interstate Commerce Commission, the prototype of the independent regulatory agencies that were to affect so profoundly the nature of American government in the twentieth century. The anticipation of this dual commemoration provides occasion for considering the relationship between constitutionalism and bureaucracy, two basic issues in contemporary political life which are too seldom studied in relation to each other.

We have long been accustomed to think of the twentieth century as an age of bureaucracy, positive government, the omni-competent state. We are equally familiar in recent years with attacks on bureaucratic government that verge on repudiation of the very idea of scientific public administration. These attacks come from different directions, but the implicit perspective of the most common charge—that bureaucracy is out of control—is a constitutional one.

If dissatisfaction with the administrative state reflects attention to constitutional limitations, it is nevertheless true that interest in constitutionalism revived in the mid-twentieth century for reasons other than bureaucratic excesses. After a period of debunking and demythologizing in the era of reform (1900–1940), constitutional values, principles, and rules came to be appreciated in the era of World War II and the Cold War as a political method and ideology essential to the preservation of free institutions against totalitarian assault. This lesson was forgotten by radicals and reformers in the 1960s, who while primarily concerned with attacking the liberal bureaucratic state, offered a fundamental challenge to constitutionalism.[1] By a kind of democratic dialectic, however, the Watergate affair, a ready symbol of the dangers of bureaucratic power, transposed the radical threat into an establishment-based brush with executive tyranny. Richard Nixon abruptly ended the development of the liberal activist presidency, at least for the time being, and converted many tough-minded pragmatists into constitutionalists.

In the past decade demands for constitutionalizing the bureaucracy have persisted, even as courts have complicated matters by adopting the techniques of administrative policy making in further derogation of the requirement of democratic accountability.[2] Meanwhile the advent of a conservative administration urging deregulation as an approach to the problem of bureaucracy has raised liberal fears, with respect to civil rights, social welfare, and other issues, of wholesale policy changes that are seen as a violation of fixed legal and constitutional rules and principles. The continued appeal to constitutionalism and the persistence of the problem of bureaucracy suggest the timeliness of reflection on the bearing these issues have on each other in contemporary political life.

A curious disparity appears when one surveys the materials dealing with this question. Bureaucracy, or public administration, is a relatively clearly defined field with specialized journals, a well-developed curriculum, and academic departments and schools devoted to its study. Most scholars outside the field, as well as citizens, have definite views about bureaucracy. Constitutionalism by contrast suffers from want of attention. It is seldom the subject of direct and explicit study, although, to be sure, teachers and practitioners in government and politics readily employ constitutional notions in evaluating institutions and events. In the organization of scholarship and teaching, constitutionalism tends to break down into its principal components. These are the constitutional document, including constitutional law; governmental and political institutions derived from or related to the founding charter; and political and constitutional theory, including popular attitudes toward liberty, authority, social justice, and so on. If constitutionalism is not necessarily greater than the sum of its parts, it ought at least to be recognized as a distinctive ideology and approach to political life that warrants holistic analysis. Constitutionalism not only establishes the institutional and intellectual framework, but it also supplies much of the rhetorical currency with which political transactions are carried on. This very ubiquity and utility suggest that it possesses a variety of meanings.

Liberal Constitutionalism

Recent work on constitutionalism builds on the classic accounts of, among others, Charles H. McIlwain, Andrew C. McLaughlin, Edward S. Corwin, William Yandell Elliott, Carl J. Friedrich, J. W. Gough, Francis D. Wormuth, and M. J. C. Vile. The principal theme in this literature is the emergence of modern constitutionalism from the seventeenth to the nineteenth century as the theory and practice of limited government, for the protection of individual liberty and property against despotic rule. The twentieth-century story concerns the adaptation of liberal constitutional principles and institutions to the demand for social justice and economic regulation, in the face of challenge from revolutionary and totalitarian political systems and ideologies. Two basic techniques or approaches implement traditional constitutionalism. The first is the rule-of-law tradition, which seeks to limit power through the judicial application of fundamental law external and superior to governmental institutions, and to make it responsible through popularly controlled instruments of political accountability. The second constitutionalist technique is structural, and consists in so arranging the forms and institutions of government as to provide limited yet effective power.

In the twentieth century, constitutions have become universal as a formal requirement in state making or political reconstruction. Yet at the same time they appear less relevant to the actual conduct of government. In a well-known essay of 1962 Giovanni Sartori analyzed this phenomenon from a liberal constitutionalist perspective that offers a framework in which to consider contemporary treatments of the subject. Rejecting the positivist view of constitution as descriptive of political institutions in general, Sartori insists on a normative and prescriptive meaning. Properly understood through historical development, he writes, a constitution prescribes and limits governmental power in order to guarantee the rights of individual liberty and property. If we grant the positivist contention that every state has a constitution, it is nevertheless not true that every state is a constitutional state. Against the fact-value distinction of modern social science and the totalitarian obliteration of values to which it logically leads, Sartori asserts a normative constitutionalism aimed at securing negative liberty against government. This teleological purpose rather than any specific institutional configuration distinguishes the constitutionist outlook in Sartori's view.[3]

Sartori can be criticized for ignoring ancient constitutionalism, in which constitutions were enactments of the sovereign intended to establish, regulate, and set limits to the political order and the institutions of government. In this still relevant view constitutions exist to create power for the conduct of the public business as well as to prevent the abuse of power. Although it runs the risk of equating constitutional government with the pursuit of desirable political ends or problem-solving purposes, this broader conception accommodates the modern demand for socially constructive government more readily than does negative-liberty constitutionalism. Accordingly its influence is considerable in contemporary discussions.[4]

Citizen-Activist Constitutionalism

Although a suitable doctrine for defending the western democracies in the Cold War, liberal constitutionalism appeared increasingly irrelevant in the 1960s. The antipluralist "crisis literature" of political science that dominated the latter part of the decade might have been mistaken for a wholesale repudiation of the purposes and methods of checks and balances and the rule of law. It is nevertheless possible to see in the radical critique an alternative constitutional outlook which regards the exercise of governmental power to promote positive liberty as the controlling purpose of political life. In this view liberty is not the right of individuals to pursue economic and other private interests free from government supervision. It is rather the ability of virtuous citizens, either individually or collectively, to fulfill their human potential through political participation and action. Citizen-activist constitutionalism transcends the dichotomy between the public and private spheres by confining the latter within narrow bounds, if not actually abolishing it. It thus enables individuals to overcome the alienation from the public good that is caused by pluralistic democracy under the rule of law. A further dimension of human freedom in citizen-activist constitutionalism results from the imposition of participatory democratic controls on corporate economic power, and on the political power of public and private bureaucracies.[5]

Perhaps illogically, the radical critique of pluralistic institutions attracted less attention during the Watergate affair, which insofar as it illustrated the abuse of executive power recalled the importance of traditional rule-of-law and checks-and-balances constitutionalism. Whether the resolution of the affair signified vitality or infirmity in the

American polity was and perhaps remains an open question. In any event, as radicalism waned a sympathetic reform impulse superseded it, extending government regulation throughout the 1970s into new environmental and social-welfare areas and applying the rule of democratic citizen participation to political and governmental institutions in a wholesale way. Though with nothing like the hostility evinced by its radical antecedent, this reformism seemed to confirm the long-range irrelevance of negative-liberty constitutionalism.

Support for this view appeared in a major publication of the political science profession in the mid-1970s, *Handbook of Political Science* (1975). In the essay on constitutionalism, Harvey Wheeler declared that liberal constitutionalism was inadequate to contemporary needs. The old constitutionalism no longer serves governmental purposes, Wheeler reasons, because the assumptions on which it rested—individualism and rationality in the conduct of political life—have been obliterated by the complexities of corporate and group social existence, and by scientific and psychological advances. Wheeler holds that the American Constitution in particular, in its fragmentation of power and functional division of government, is incongruous with modern realities and incapable of achieving necessary social ends. He therefore asserts that a new constitutionalism is needed. But Wheeler is unable to delineate its characteristics with any clarity. Offering an attenuated version of the citizen-activist ideal, he defines constitutionalism as a way of directing government and law toward the achievement of the common good, through the application of democratic civic wisdom to political problems. Constitutionalism is unworkable, Wheeler concludes pessimistically, but it continues to be necessary because it is the only effective way to enlist popular energies in the pursuit of the common good. Seeking refuge in symbols, he suggests that constitutionalism can become a self-fulfilling myth possessing existential and functional validity.[6]

Into the 1980s: Constitutional Pluralism

If this is all that can be said for constitutionalism, new or old, the prospect is grim indeed. Fortunately it is not, as the essays in *Constitutionalism* (1979), a volume in the Nomos series attest.[7] To some extent Gordon J. Schochet's account of the recent intellectual history of constitutionalism confirms Wheeler's pessimism. Constitutionalism has fallen into intellectual disrepute and is no longer part of our vocabulary of politics, Schochet states. In part this is because constitutions, existing everywhere but in many places only as a facade, have been trivialized; because of the alleged inadequacy of limited government to modern social problems; and because the revolt against liberalism and the behavioralist rejection of formalism became a repudiation of constitutionalism. Yet Schochet and the contributors to the Nomos volume resist this trend.

Defining constitutionalism in limited-government, rule-of-law terms, Schochet criticizes the realist attack on formalism and proceduralism. He is further skeptical of citizen-activist constitutionalism of the 1960s, observing that the capacity for accomplishing the public good and promoting civic education by political action is also the capacity to do public evil. Schochet's preference is for a pluralistic and procedural constitutionalism, characterized by formal rules and a clear public-private distinction intended to confine the sphere of politics and the scope of governmental intervention.[8] George Kateb argues that constitutional procedures, usually dismissed by pragmatic realists as less important than ends and goals expressing moral purpose, themselves possess moral significance that redefines political ends. Indeed, Kateb reasons that procedures like due process and democratic elections may transcend their instrumental nature and become the real ends of society. He thus attempts to demonstrate the intrinsic value of constitutional procedures.[9] In a concluding essay J. Roland Pennock observes signs of constitutional vigor in the exercise of judicial power, preferable he suggests to government by bureaucracy; in the continued operation of institutional checks and balances among the branches of government; and in a still strong popular hostility to government authority.[10]

If there has been little general theory of constitutionalism, there has been much theorizing about a key institution in the contemporary polity—constitutional adjudication by the judiciary. The continued expansion of judicial power has been a major development of the post–New Deal era, and like earlier aggrandizements has required democratic sanction. Theories of judicial review are intended to supply this need and reconcile government by judiciary with the principles of liberal constitutionalism.

Illustrative of this literature and relevant to the present inquiry is William F. Harris's essay, "Bonding Word and Polity: The Logic of American Constitutionalism" (1982).[11] Harris presents his analysis in the fashionable idiom of semiotics, but it is really an updated version of the old legal-realist contention that the Constitution is not just the formal document, but also the effective governing institutions of the political order.[12] The words of the Constitution create the polity, Harris reasons, and the institutions of the polity in turn become a "text" requiring interpretation. Using the polarities of word and institution and immanence (text-bound) and transcendence (non-text-bound), he describes four styles of constitutional interpretation.[13] He states that as long as courts stay within these several modes of adjudication they do not abuse their power. Harris does not consider, however, the possibility that other constitutional actors may use these techniques, nor the potential usefulness of the method of "transcendent structuralism," in particular. This method regards the political order and the external structure of institutions as an "organized text," available as a source of inferences to be applied in settling constitutional disputes.

Harris describes this "two-text Intepretable Constitution" as a bounded construction. Yet it is difficult to see where the limits come from or who will establish them, especially when, as he stipulates, original constitutional intention is rejected as authoritative. Using semantic theory, he states that as a work when it is written leaves the control of the author, so the words of the Constitution lose their connection with the intent of the Framers. "Because the polity changes in accordance with the logic incorporated in it," Harris writes, "the regulative link with the framers' thoughts could not plausibly endure." To adhere to original intent, he adds, would be to revert to the rule of will over the rule of law. When Harris defines the rule of law as adherence to the constitutional text, however, and then treats the structure of institutions as the text, one begins to doubt the boundedness or confining effect of his Constitution.[14] The practical conclusion to which this logic points is that existing institutions and the actions of government officials are by definition constitutional. If this be constitutionalism, its flexibility is remarkable indeed.

The implicit question behind Harris's model building is *how* the Constitution works rather than *whether* it works. That the issue should be posed in this way is no doubt encouraging. But if the "two-text" Constitution does not do what it is supposed to—namely, set boundaries on power, provide a basis for rights, and make the political and governmental system "legible" to citizens—there is little cause for optimism. There is, however, another way of thinking about constitutional text, principles, institutions, and values which enables us to understand more clearly the effect of constitutionalism on political life.

Constitutionalism and Political Action

In addressing this question we confront the argument that because constitutions are concerned with forms and procedures rather than the substantive ends thought to motivate political action, they do not deal with the basic reality of political life. The short answer to this line of reasoning is that constitutional text, rules, principles, and values—and constitutionalism as the coherent ordering of these elements into an ideology—*are* political and social reality.

Constitutionalism shapes political life in a variety of ways. Constitutional principles can become matters of commitment and belief possessing intrinsic value that motivate political action. Does this not explain the zeal with which civil libertarians defend unpopular agitators or neighborhood associations oppose forced busing? When citizens and governing officials internalize constitutional values, acting out of fidelity to law rather than expediency, constitutionalism gives direction to political life.

Constitutionalism has a configurative effect also in providing the forms, rhetoric, and symbols by which politics is carried on. Political groups and individuals ordinarily try to choose courses of action that are consistent with or required by the Constitution. They do so not because they are in each instance committed to the constitutional principle or value at issue; in different circumstances they may employ an alternative or conflicting principle. Rather, political and governmental actors adhere to constitutional standards because they know that the public takes the Constitution seriously, believing that it embodies fundamental values and formal procedures that are the touchstone of political legitimacy.[15] In American politics the Constitution is a justifying concept, and groups that invoke constitutional arguments do so, from their own perspective perhaps and in an immediate sense, instrumentally. Considered from an external and long-range view in relation to the polity as a whole, however, reliance on constitutional principles and rules is normative and noninstrumental. In this way constitutionalism shapes political events.

Is this happening in the United States today? Certainly there has been no surcease of constitutional controversy; indeed, quite the opposite is the case as new issues and aspects of social life are brought within the ambit of government through the reach of the due process clause or the equal protection requirement. Are the basic purposes of constitutionalism—to limit government in the interest of individual liberty while assuring effective government for the accomplishment of collective social ends—being fulfilled? We may agree that as long as peaceful methods of political change are employed and violence eschewed, constitutionalism is effective at a minimal level. But there is much to demand of a constitutional state beyond keeping the peace.

Some observers, for example, believe unwillingness or inability to control private economic power by democratic means renders government too weak for the preservation of constitutional liberty and the public good.[16] Lack of public confidence in political institutions is similarly regarded as evidence of a constitutional problem of governmental weakness and incompetence.[17] More often, however, government's far-reaching power, exercised for national security purposes and egalitarian social interventions, appears to threaten constitutional liberty.[18] Courts, Congress, and the executive can all be criticized on this score, under the negative-liberty principle that public opinion continues to hold in high esteem. The principal danger to liberty, however, is thought to come from administrative institutions. The existence of impersonal, remote, and irresponsible bureaucracy appears as a challenge to constitutionalism.

The Problem of Bureaucracy: Historical Origin

From the constitutionalist point of view the problem of bureaucracy arises not from the mere fact of hierarchically organized institutions performing specialized functions, but from the exercise of unauthorized political and governmental power by administrative bodies. The problem of bureaucracy, in other words, is the ancient problem of discretion versus law.

In early modern constitutionalism this problem took the form of the struggle to bring the executive under legal limitation. Administrative capacity was a necessary attribute of government; it was the king's abuse of discretionary power inherent in the administrative role that was objectionable. When the separation of powers was introduced briefly in seventeenth-century England and permanently in revolutionary America as an alternative to mixed government, its purpose was to deprive the executive of law- and policy-making authority and confine it to the nondiscretionary duties that properly defined the executive office. Although an administrative system emerged in the United States and became an object of political controversy in the early nineteenth century, the problem of law versus discretion was fought out between Congress and the executive or the judiciary and the political branches. It was not until administrative institutions began to exercise law- and policy-making authority independently of the political branches, contradicting the separation-of-powers requirement that governmental measures interfering with liberty and property must be authorized by politically responsible institutions, that the problem of bureaucracy assumed its recognizably modern form.

To consider the historical relationship between bureaucracy and constitutionalism is to ask not only when but why administrative power became problematic. Bureaucratic organization is usually regarded as a functional requirement of modernizing societies, and as the United States experienced this transformation in the late nineteenth and early twentieth century, the problem of bureaucracy is often viewed as a necessary corollary of the creation of an industrial capitalist economy. Closer examination suggests, however, that the growth of discretionary administrative power was the result of political decisions rather than an inevitable constitutional development.

Americans have always desired limited, responsible, democratic government, and also rational, efficient, and economical government. In the post-Civil War period and continuing for fifty years, reformers, politicians, academics, professionals, businessmen, publicists, and enlightened opinion in general supported efforts to create a structure of administrative authority that could secure these often incompatible goals. A central purpose of progressive reform was to confer governmental authority on new administrative institutions to regulate a rapidly changing society and economy. Rejecting popularly elected, corrupt, inefficient legislatures, reformers favored the delegation of legislative power to independent administrative agencies. They believed this would lead to nonpolitical yet democratically legitimate policy making by trained and knowledgeable administrative experts, acting in accordance with broad statutory mandate to promote the public good.[19]

This was a normative vision intended to guide political reform, not an empirical description of the governmental system.[20] In fact power conferred by Congress on executive and administrative bodies in moments of exuberant reform, from the creation of the Interstate Commerce Commission in 1887 to the proliferation of regulatory agencies during the New Deal, was discretionary and decidedly political. Moreover the exercise of power in the regulatory state of the twentieth century did not proceed in the rational, coherent, and unified manner predicted by public administration theory, but rather conformed to the pluralistic and decentralized pattern encouraged if not always required by the constitutional order. The administrative state adapted to the existing political culture.

This adaptation did not occur naturally or automatically, however. The institutions whose power was threatened by the new administrative state—the judiciary, the legislature, political parties—mounted effective resistance. Using their power of judicial review, courts rejected the notion of independent regulatory agencies interfering with individual liberty and property to promote the public interest under the presumptive legitimacy of the European idea of administrative law.[21] Congress, expressing the reaction of localistic political parties to centralized coordination, maintained an effective hold on administration through its committee system and power over appropriations. Aligned with private interest groups, party-legislative managers absorbed the regulatory apparatus into the constitutional order. Administrative agencies were by no means powerless; they acquired broad policy-making authority under the delegation of legislative power. Nevertheless, because Congress was unwilling to make political choices in the face of conflicting constituent demands, major regulatory enactments often failed to provide clear standards for administrators to follow. Pluralistic group conflict was extended from the legislature where it belonged into the arena of bureaucratic policy making where according to administrative theory it did not. The result, clearly evident by the 1950s, was the problem of bureaucracy: discretion versus law, or as Theodore J. Lowi put it in his classic study, policy without law.[22]

Constitutionalizing Bureaucratic Government: The Contemporary Debate

The problem of bureaucracy may be viewed as the historical manifestation of tendencies immanent in the polity. Administrative science places a high value on rationality, unity, energy, efficiency, and substantive policy results in the conduct of government. Many public administration scholars describe a different set of values as constitutional: decentralized power, institutional restraints, guarantees of individual liberty, an emphasis on forms and procedures rather than substantive ends. This way of posing the issue requires a more narrow and traditional liberal conception of constitutionalism than many would accept. But a persuasive case can be made that the framers of the Constitution, reacting to the excesses of British rule, obfuscated if they did not deny basic requirements and realities of administrative authority.[23] There is much truth in the view which regards American political history as a continual conflict between modernizing attempts to create effective policy-making and administrative institutions, and a deeply ingrained premodern hostility toward government authority.[24]

Depending on how one defines constitutionalism, under the variety of meanings and emphases shown to be available in this discussion, one may accommodate administrative power and discretion as legitimate policy making or regard it as suspect.[25] Most of the time, however, bureaucracy is viewed in the perspective of limited-government constitutionalism: the student of contemporary politics must account for the widespread belief that public and private bureaucracies are too big, too powerful, and all but impervious to effective control. And it appears things may be getting worse, not better. Not only do traditional economic, professional, and ethno-cultural interest associations maintain their place in the subgovernments of administration, but, as a result of the reformism of the past decade, morally committed policy experts in fields such as nuclear energy and environmental protection also now constitute an important sector of the bureaucracy, either as appointed officials or representatives of private issue organizations.[26] Appealing to substantive rationality and enlightened morality, policy bureaucrats, like judges, justify their governmental role by standards outside the framework of conventional democratic accountability.

Several means of constitutionalizing the bureaucracy have been proposed in recent years. The most traditional, akin to fighting fire with fire, is judicial review of agency actions under standards of substantive rationality or procedural regularity which are intended to ensure correct policies and full participation by interested groups in administrative decision making. Another method is for Congress to impose clear standards of accountability on administrators when it delegates legislative power. The Supreme Court's recent invalidation of the legislative veto may encourage this technique. Still another way to check the bureaucracy is to pass a constitutional amendment for a balanced budget that would restrict big government's source of supply. Meanwhile the bureaucratic solution for the problem of bureaucracy, favored by politicians and especially presidents, is executive reorganization, a time-honored ritual of more symbolic than practical importance.[27] At the opposite conceptual pole deregulation, or reliance on market mechanisms, is the neo-laissez-faire approach to the problem.

Public administration scholars are divided in their assessment of bureaucracy. Some accept the basic critique of the administrative state as constitutionally suspect, and argue that it can be legitimated by what may be called training in applied constitutionalism. Acknowledging the discretionary power of administrative agencies, they suggest that restraints can be derived from knowledge of the Constitution as an independent source of political morality. By treating the Constitution as both a source of legal rules and a covenant sanctifying regime values and political processes, administrators can reconcile bureaucracy with constitutionalism.[28] A related approach would have public administrators receive training in ethical analysis to guide responsible policy making.[29] Without a conscious bias toward democratic values, however, it is difficult to see how ethical training can dispel doubts about the constitutional legitimacy of bureaucratic power.[30]

While conceding the political force of the attack on bureaucracy, other scholars deny the constitutional infirmity of the administrative state. The charge that the bureaucracy is out of control, they point out, upon closer examiantion often expresses mere disagreement with an administrative decision, or dissatisfaction that an agency has not followed a congressional directive or allowed the fullest public participation in decision making.[31] If by control one means accountability of administrators to elected officials, citizen and interest-group involvement in policy making, and effective implementation of programs, then the bureaucratic state can be shown to operate under a system of flexible controls and in conformance with check-and-balance limitations.[32] Moreover, although bureaucratic adherence to existing statutes and legal-rational procedures may appear arbitrary to outsiders, it is consistent with the rule-of-law requirement of constitutionalism.[33] A strong argument can be made, finally, that the bureaucratic civil service in its social, economic, and cultural diversity is more representative of the American people than the assembled members of Congress. There is undoubted merit in Norton E. Long's classic statement of the view that modern bureaucracy serves to reinforce the constitutionalizing elements of democratic representation and restraints on legislative and executive power.[34]

The Constitutional and Bureaucratic Future

Bureaucratic discretion in American government is real, and discretionary power is the bugbear of constitutional order and regularity. But constitutionalism, although it must ever guard against government by mere will and political expediency, requires discretionary power. Schochet puts it well when he observes that constitutionalism propounds a logical paradox: it seeks to place limits on supreme political authority without denying its existence.[35] In the United States the bureaucratic state has been adapted to the political culture. It has been democratized, politicized, and fragmented, sometimes at the expense of the general, prospective, and clearly defined rule making that characterizes the rule of law. Yet the rule of law is not the sum and substance of constitutionalism. Since its origins in the late nineteenth century the administrative state has conjured up the vision—approved by supporters and condemned by critics—of unified and concentrated power. To the chagrin of reformers from Woodrow Wilson's time to our own, however, political reality has frustrated this design. Diffusion of authority and reciprocal restraints under the separation of powers have remained the constitutional norm. In all but the formal amendatory sense the administrative state has been constitutionalized as a fourth branch of government, and in its episodic development has adapted to the pluralistic Madisonian principle.

This doesn't mean it is always clear where proper constitutional limits lie or what effective restraints on power are in particular situations. The science of politics seeks to prevent tyranny, and constitutionalism is a method of conducting politics. Its operation therefore involves political values and judgments. Constitutions establish the general rules to be followed in making specific laws and policies. In order to be effective they must be upheld for intrinsic rather than instrumental reasons, at least by some people at some times.[36] Constitutionalism as a way of organizing political life paradoxically places these basic rules and principles beyond politics. Yet the very circumstances in which constitutions become useful cause constitutional decisions and actions to reflect the conflicting political aspirations, ends, and values that produced controversy in the first place. This makes agreement on constitutional standards and restraints unlikely, although it does not mean they are irrelevant in shaping political action.

M. J. C. Vile has written that because subjective political judgments are involved, discussion of constitutionalism must begin by pointing to examples of societies which are regarded as non-tyrannical.[37] Few would deny that the United States has been a constitutional state since its eighteenth-century foundation, or, unless liberals succeed in having the present conservative administration declared unconstitutional, that it continues to be one in the 1980s. The United States is also very clearly a bureaucratic state. Attacks on the bureaucracy as out of control may question its constitutional legitimacy, but a century of administrative history offers a persuasive rebuttal. Nevertheless, the Constitution is not a living organism, nor constitutionalism a natural development. It is a form of political action, and to make it work effectively placing limits on power usually demands more attention than creating or augmenting power. From this perspective criticism of discretionary power in the administrative state can have the salubrious effect of reinforcing constitutionalism as the American way of politics.

Powerful as the bureaucratic state has become, it has generally followed public policies determined by the political branches in accordance with public opinion organized and expressed through party competition. It is not certain, however, that this situation will continue. In the twentieth century political parties and legislative policy making have grown weaker, while administrative, executive, and judicial institutions have become more powerful. In the heyday of the liberal activist presidency, Congress was often the odd man out, its policy preferences frustrated by the other branches. Since the election of a conservative president in 1980, this may also be happening to the executive branch. If executive policy making in response to public opinion is thwarted by the "permanent government" of courts and bureaucratic agencies, applying standards of substantive rationality and correct morality that are intended to end political debate, a significant constitutional change will have occurred. Do the political branches represent the society and make the basic policies and rules, or do bureaucrats and judges? Constitutional democracy is not direct democracy, but legitimacy derives from consent, and American constitutionalism has always required not only the form but the substance of electoral accountability. Perhaps by 1987 we will have a clearer view of the changes in constitutionalism we are presently making.

Notes

1. Herman Belz, "New Left Reverberations in the Academy: The Antipluralist Critique of Constitutionalism," *Review of Politics*, Vol. 36 (April 1974), 265–83.

2. Jeremy Rabkin, "The Judiciary in the Administrative State," *The Public Interest*, No. 71 (Spring 1983), 62–84.

3. Giovanni Sartori, "Constitutionalism: A Preliminary Discussion," *American Political Science Review*, Vol. 56 (Dec. 1962), 853–64.

4. Graham Maddox, "A Note on the Meaning of 'Constitution,'" *APSR*, Vol. 76 (Dec. 1982), 805–09.

5. See, for example, Kirk Thompson, "Constitutional Theory and Political Action," *Journal of Politics*, Vol. 31 (Aug. 1969), 655–81; Sheldon S. Wolin, "Political Theory as a Vocation," APSR, Vol. 63 (Dec. 1969); Henry S. Kariel, *Open Systems: Arenas for Political Action* (Itasca, Ill., 1969). Modified recent expressions of this outlook appear in Robert Dahl, "On Removing Certain Impediments to Democracy in the United States," *Political Science Quarterly*, Vol. 92 (Spring 1977), 1–20; Lawrence B. Joseph, "Democratic Revisionism Revisited," *American Journal of Political Science*, Vol. 25 (Feb. 1981), 160–187. John Manley, "Neopluralism: A class analysis of Pluralism I and Pluralism II," *APSR*, Vol. 77 (June 1983), 368–83.

6. Harvey Wheeler, "Constitutionalism," in Fred I. Greenstein and Nelson W. Polsby, eds., *Handbook of Political Science*, Vol. 5: *Governmental Institutions and Processes* (Reading, Mass., 1975), 76–87.

7. J. Roland Pennock and John W. Chapman, eds., *Constitutionalism: Nomos* Vol. 20 (New York, 1979).

8. Gordon J. Schochet, "Introduction: Constitutionalism, Liberalism, and the Study of Politics," *Constitutionalism*, 1–11.

9. George Kateb, "Remarks on the Procedures of Constitutional Democracy," *Constitutionalism*, 215–37.

10. J. Roland Pennock, "Epilogue: Constitutionism," *Constitutionalism*, 378–83.

11. William F. Harris, II, "Bonding Word and Polity: The Logic of American Constitutionalism," *APSR*, Vol. 76 (March 1982), 34–45.

12. Karl N. Llewellyn, "The Constitution as an Institution," *Columbia Law Review*, Vol. 34 (Jan. 1934), 1–40.

13. The styles are immanent positivism, transcendent positivism, immanent structuralism, and transcendent structuralism. These are similar to the catego-

ries developed in John Hart Ely, *Democracy and Distrust* (Cambridge, 1980), and Philip Bobbitt, *Constitutional Fate* (New York, 1982).

14. Harris, "Bonding Word and Polity," *loc. cit.*, 43–45.

15. Cf. Martin Spencer, "Rhetorics and Politics," *Social Research*, Vol. 37 (Winter 1970), 597–623; Sartori, "Constitutionalism," *loc. cit.*, 864; Stuart A. Scheingold, *The Politics of Rights: Lawyers, Public Policy, and Political Change* (New Haven, 1974).

16. Dahl, "On Removing Certain Impediments to Democracy in the United States," *loc. cit.*

17. James L. Sundquist, "The Crisis of Competence in Our National Government," *Pol. Sci. Q.*, Vol. 95 (Summer 1980), 183–208.

18. Pennock, "Epilogue," *loc. cit.*

19. This is of course the ideal presented in Woodrow Wilson, "The Study of Administration," *PSQ.* Vol. 2 (June 1887), 197–220.

20. Douglas Yates, *Bureaucratic Democracy: The Search for Democracy and Efficiency in American Government* (Cambridge, 1982), 46–47.

21. Martin Shapiro, "On Predicting the Future of Administrative Law," *Regulation*, Vol. 6 (May–June 1982), 18–25.

22. Theodore J. Lowi, *The End of Liberalism: The Second Republic of the United States*, second ed. (New York, 1979); Stephen J. Skowronek, *Building a New Administrative State: The Expansion of National Administrative Capacities, 1877–1920* (New York, 1982); Morton Keller, *Affairs of State: Public Life in Late Nineteenth Century America* (Cambridge, 1977); Richard B. Stewart, "The Reformation of American Administrative Law," *Harvard Law Review*, Vol. 88 (June 1975), 1669–1813; James Q. Wilson, "The Rise of the Bureaucratic State," *The Public Interest*, No. 41 (Fall 1975), 77–103; Michael T. Hayes, "The Semi-Sovereign Pressure Groups: A Critique of Current Theory and an Alternative Typology," *Journal of Politics*, Vol. 40 (Feb. 1978), 134–61; James O. Freedman, *Crisis and Legitimacy: The Administrative Process and American Government* (New York, 1978).

23. Michael Nelson, "A Short, Ironic History of American National Bureaucracy," *JP,* Vol. 44 (Aug. 1982), 747–78.

24. Samuel P. Huntington, *American Politics: The Promise of Disharmony* (Cambridge, 1981).

25. A good expression of the legitimacy view is William F. West, "Institutionalizing Rationality in Regulatory Administration," *Public Administration Review*, Vol. 43 (July–Aug. 1983), 326–34.

26. Hugh Heclo, "Issue Networks and the Executive Establishment," in Anthony King, ed., *The New American Political System* (Washington, 1978).

27. Cf. James G. March and Johan P. Olson, "Organizing Political Life: What Administrative Reorganization Tells Us About Government," *APSR*, Vol. 77 (June 1983), 281–96.

28. John A. Rohr, "Public Administration and the Constitutional Bicentennial: An Essay on Research," *International Journal of Public Administration*, Vol. 4 (1982), 349–80; David H. Rosenbloom, "Constitutionalism and Public Bureaucratics," *The Bureaucrat*, Vol. 11 (Fall 1982), 54–56.

29. Frank Fischer, "Ethical Discourse in Public Administration," *Administration and Society*, Vol. 15 (May 1983), 5–42.

30. Mark T. Lilla, "Ethos, 'Ethics,' and Public Service," *The Public Interest,* No. 63 (Spring 1981), 3–17.

31. Herbert Kaufman, "Fear of Bureaucracy: A Raging Pandemic," *Public Admin. Rev.,* Vol. 41 (Jan.–Feb. 1981), 1–9.

32. Yates, *Bureaucratic Democracy,* 152–55.

33. Kaufman, "Fear of Bureaucracy," *loc. cit.,* 7; Timothy J. O'Neill, "Does the Separation of Powers Violate the Rule of Law?" unpublished manuscript, p. 4.

34. Norton E. Long, "Bureaucracy and Constitutionalism," *APSR,* Vol. 46 (Sept. 1952), 808–18. Long's thesis has an historical analogue in the argument that the bureaucratic state originated in attempts to preserve individual and group minority rights against majoritarian encroachment. See William E. Nelson, *The Roots of American Bureaucracy 1830–1900* (Cambridge, 1982).

35. Schochet, "Constitutionalism, Liberalism, and the Study of Politics," *loc. cit.,* 11.

36. Cf. Shirley Letwin, "Law without Law," *Policy Review,* No. 26 (Fall 1983), 7–16.

37. M. J. C. Vile, *Constitutionalism and the Separation of Powers* (New York, 1967), 308.

8

Constitutional and Legal History in the 1980s: Reflections on American Constitutionalism

As communist governments in the late twentieth century become subject to disintegration under the aspiration for human freedom, we are reminded once again of the practical importance of constitutionalism.[1] Fortunately the American people have enjoyed the benefits of constitutionalism from the beginning of their historical existence.[2] Even in our Revolution, because of the persistence of community self-government under the rule of law, we avoided regression into pre-political revolutionary violence.[3] Accordingly, whereas other nations have struggled to achieve constitutional government, maintaining the Constitution has been a principal purpose of American politics.

Americans require knowledge and understanding of the Constitution to carry on their political life. To a significant extent this knowledge and understanding are historical. It would be reassuring to think that our long if not yet ancient experience in constitutionalism, commemorated in the recent bicentennial, provides guidance for dealing with problems in contemporary political life and a safeguard against the erosion of essential constitutional principles.[4] In fact, however, our constitutional history has become so contested that it may not provide the usable past that our constitutionalism requires.

The relevance of history to our constitutional system is widely attested. It appears to have become more pertinent in light of recent controversy over original-intent jurisprudence. Explaining the "rediscovery" of constitutional history, Harry N. Scheiber states that political and ideological confrontation in the 1970s and 1980s stimulated constitutional and legal studies. The debate over original intent gave an additional sharp edge to public sensitivity on matters relating to constitutional law and history.[5] Political scientist Stanley C. Brubaker points out that a proper understanding of the role of the courts requires historical inquiry into the emergence of judicial review.[6] Legal scholar Robert N. Clinton observes that the original-intent debate has created a political schism over the value of constitutional history in constitutional interpretation.[7] And historian Michael Kammen, asserting that the American people have failed to understand the Constitution, more broadly attributes this result in part to the failure of constitutional historians to perform their proper educational function.[8]

In view of renewed recognition of the significance of history in American constitutionalism, it is pertinent to examine recent tendencies in constitutional and legal history. The present inquiry will focus first on how scholars conceive of the nature and purpose of constitutional and legal history. Discussions of this question necessarily transcend the issue of historical method to consider the substantive question of the nature of the Constitution and American constitutionalism in general. In order further to pursue this issue we shall consider recent writings on the three most important events in American constitutional history: the founding of the republic and the framing and ratification of the Constitution; the amendment of the Constitution during the Civil War and Reconstruction; and the transformation of judicial review as an aspect of New Deal and post–New Deal governance. Our survey indicates deep scholarly division on whether continuity or discontinuity characterizes American constitutional development; on the effect of the Constitution and constitutionalism on American politics and society; and on the extent to which constitutional government may truly be said to exist in the United States.

I

Constitutional and legal historians in the 1980s believe that history has practical and normative significance for American society. In holding this view they share the outlook of historians, philosophers, and statesmen of earlier ages who regarded history as having a morally didactic purpose. Within the tradition of modern scholarship a similar conception of history guided the writings of historians who took as their purpose to explain how human liberty had advanced, and to teach that reason and liberty were essential to human progress.[9] In the field of constitutional history this approach guided the efforts of scholars in the late nineteenth and early twentieth century who sought to show the intrinsic value and positive benefits of the Constitution.[10]

Since the 1960s, according to a study published by the American

Historical Association, historians have generally rejected the values of nationalism, liberalism, and intellectual detachment that traditionally underlay historical scholarship. National self-criticism and subjective ideological engagement have become far more widely accepted as professional norms.[11] Constitutional and legal historians in the 1980s reflect these tendencies. Many of them follow a tradition of reform scholarship that since the early twentieth century has criticized constitutionalism as an expedient strategy for defending the status quo. Repudiating the theory of declaratory, text-based, formalist legal decision making, reform-minded scholars have sought to assimilate law and history to the social sciences.[12]

In a widely noted article that anticipated the concerns of liberal scholarship in the 1980s, Paul L. Murphy in 1963 called for a revival of constitutional history. Ostensibly exhorting historians to reclaim the field from ahistorical political scientists and lawyers, Murphy projected an agenda for constitutional history in the service of liberal reform. Dismissing major works of previous constitutional scholarship as " 'revealed' history" that used "philosophic-metaphysical analysis" to underwrite the virtue of established institutions, he argued that history should be used to promote change. The judicial function, Murphy claimed, was naturally directed toward historical analysis, and the willingness of the Supreme Court to assume a policy-making role further implicated history in the task of reform. Moreover the advent of positive government since the New Deal signified a break from the past that required historical reassessment of the Constitution. Murphy envisioned for constitutional history "a new role as an auxiliary tool for the jurist, not for 'the consecration of an already established order of things,' but for a new order seeking a new level of equal rights and social justice through law." "If the Court is intent upon building new and dramatic legal structures to meet the requirements of a dynamic society," he concluded, "the historian can at least furnish it with complementary modern architectural materials. . . ."[13]

While Murphy expressed the resurgent spirit of liberal scholarship, the major influence on liberal historians' understanding of the nature of the legal and constitutional order were the writings of James Willard Hurst. Beginning his career under the influence of legal realism in the 1930s, Hurst took for granted the reformist purpose of modern social science. Accordingly he dedicated himself to reorienting legal historical study toward a social and instrumental conception of law, in contrast to the idealist conception that characterized traditional constitutional and legal history.

At a descriptive level Hurst was intent on going beyond formal doctrines to discover the realities of the legal process. The basic reality he discerned was law as a social institution. Law was an instrument of individual, interest-group, or community purpose to be defined in terms of social functions, rather than a self-contained body of concepts, principles, and procedures consisting of timeless essences and values. The legal system also contained a constitutional ideal, which Hurst defined as the belief that all power should be accountable and should serve life outside public and private power structures according to standards of utility and justice. The constitutional ideal in the broadest sense meant using law to enlarge the meaningful content of life against formless experience. Although Hurst was able to maintain a constructive balance between the instrumental and constitutional aspects of the legal order, the problem in his work as a whole is that it explores the former dimension so thoroughly and with such a sense of intellectual excitement as to reduce the constitutional component to insignificance.[14] Although conceding that "Constitutionalism must be reckoned with in a realistically comprehensive legal history," Hurst taught mainly that "A realistic history of law in the United States will be a social history of law. . . ."[15]

Hurst's followers in the Wisconsin school of legal history adopted a severely instrumental view of law, virtually excluding constitutional considerations. Lawrence M. Friedman, perhaps the leading disciple, wrote in his *History of American Law:* "This is a *social* history of American law. . . . [It] treats American law, then, not as a kingdom unto itself, not as a set of rules and concepts . . . , but as a mirror of society. It takes nothing as historical accident, nothing as autonomous, everything as relative and molded by economy and society."[16] Basing his work on "the theory . . . that law moves with its times and is eternally new," Friedman said "real economic interests" and "concrete political groups" determined the meaning of law. He acknowledged that "Constitutionalism answered to a deep-seated need among members of the articulate public, for formal, outward signs of political legitimacy." Yet he dismissed constitutional arguments as "masks" concealing interests and demands, and doubted that a constitution was essentially different from ordinary law. The function of a constitution in enumerating essential rules, rights, and limitations on government "has no natural boundaries," Friedman asserted, because "opinions differ from generation to generation on what rights and duties are most fundamental." Rejecting any idealist or normative element in law, Friedman's instrumentalism ultimately dissolved the boundaries between law and society.[17] "As long as the country endures," he wrote, "so will its system of law, coextensive with society. . . . A full history of American law would be nothing more or less than a full history of American life."[18]

Conceived as a work of social science, Friedman's study rejected the traditional concept of the nature and purpose of legal history.[19] Law was previously thought to embody idealist elements, expressed in formalist properties of the legal process considered to be in some sense autonomous, and legal history was intended to assist judges in developing the law by showing how modern legal rules came to exist.[20] This type of "internal" legal history was largely superseded by the "external" "law and society" approach of the Wisconsin school. In the 1970s, however, the Hurst school was challenged by radical historians who saw in its pragmatic and relativistic functionalism a form of liberal complacency that accepted the existing order. Proposing a more sophisticated version of instrumentalism, radical critics called for a legal history to assist the cause of social transformation.

In a leading work of radical legal history, Morton J. Horwitz accepted the Hurstians' instrumental conception of law, but criticized their view that legal interventions to promote economic change benefited the society as a whole. Horwitz contended that nineteenth-century economic development was managed by courts in a deliberately instrumental way—i.e., by the use of a self-consciously instrumental as opposed to a formalist-declaratory concept of law—to redistribute wealth to the advantage of entrepreneurial groups.[21] More recently Horwitz has pursued a vision of legal history that can be described as anti-constitutionalist in tendency. Criticizing traditional legal history as simply a justification of the world as it is, he argues that legal historians should penetrate the distinction between law and politics by seeing legal and jurisprudential change as a product of social forces.[22] Asserting that law and politics are essentially the same, he destroys the distinction between the two fields by rejecting the idea of law as neutral and autonomous principles or ideals. He goes so far as to question the rule of law as an unqualified good because it prevents the benevolent exercise of power and promotes substantive inequality by creating a consciousness that separates law from politics.[23] The purpose of legal history, then, is to demystify the law, breaking down its power as an instrument of conservative social control.[24] In a positive sense Horwitz sees legal history raising questions of legal and political theory that can assist in using law to constitute genuine community and establish a vision of the good society. Urging historians to become conscious of the use of legal history arguments as proxies for more general political controversies, Horwitz advises: "It is time for us to bridge the chasm between legal theory and legal history."[25] In fact his advice is tantamount to a recommendation that history be absorbed into theory and abandoned as a separate discipline.

Still another version of legal history instrumentalism, so sophisticated that its practitioners do not recognize it as such, is offered by

radical scholar Robert W. Gordon. Rejecting the functional and pragmatic social view of the Wisconsin school, Gordon states that law is
ideology. Law consists in cultural codes, social text, "deep structures"
of consciousness, discursive practices, political language—things that
may be considered embedded in relatively autonomous structures.
Gordon disavows instrumentalism, which he defines as the belief that
legal doctrines and rules are made and used by groups and classes in
their own interest. He contends, in contrast, that legal decisions are
made by persons who are "prisoners of their conventional categories
of discourse." The codes, categories, and languages of discourse "organize and make sense of reality" for decision makers.[26]

If in liberal instrumentalism political actors use legal principles and
rules to promote group and class interests, in radical instrumentalism
cultural codes and structures of consciousness, directed by we know
not what, control legal and constitutional decision making. In liberal
instrumentalism constitutional principles possess no intrinsic validity,
but merely expedient practical utility in the hands of political actors.
In radical instrumentalism political and legal decision makers are the
instruments of structures and consciousness and language that function beyond the reason and will of human agents. "The discourses of
law," Gordon writes, "connect with other social discourses to form
complex overlapping systems of ideology that help to constitute and
shape the desires and powers of interest groups themselves."[27]

The purpose of legal history in this view is to discover "the sunken
codes of shared inarticulate assumptions" that underlie apparently
neutral legal systems. Legal history discloses that no "rule of law" exists, only contradictory systems struggling for dominance in a deeply
divided society. The political task is radical reformation of "the teeming jungle of plural, contradictory orders struggling for recognition,"
Gordon declares. Legal history has the role of describing "how constraints upon freedom get socially manufactured and how people acting collectively through politics sometimes succeed and sometimes fail
in breaking through the constraints."[28]

Comparable to Gordon's theory of legal history is the radical conception of constitutional history that informs the bicentennial volume published by the Organization of American Historians. The OAH history
is conventionally radical in its view of the impact of the Constitution
on American life. The unifying themes describing this impact are that
corporate interests control constitutional development; that the hegemonic function of constitutional law is "to educate, to gloss power with
high moral and intellectual standards"; and that "constitutionalism
aided the 'winners' in American history."[29] The distinctive feature of
the OAH radical history is its normative, aspirational dimension. Stud-

ies of social groups and rights consciousness define the Constitution as the ground of social and cultural conflict on which plain people—workers, farmers, blacks, immigrants, women—struggle for emancipation. The OAH volume in effect applies Horwitz's dictum that the task of legal history is to bridge the chasm between history and legal and political theory.

Hendrik Hartog captures the spirit and describes the method of radical constitutional history in the OAH volume. He dismisses traditional constitutional history, concerned to preserve the constitutional order, as "an apologetic discourse" that justifies the power of ruling elites. Dismissed along with it is the concept of the Constitution as an authoritative text with a permanent and fixed meaning. Radical history also rejects the more realistic liberal history that considers the impact of social, cultural, ideological, political, and economic forces on constitutional change. Hartog says the realist approach treats the "constitutional faiths and values of blacks and others of the constitutionally disinherited" merely as inputs that help produce constitutional law doctrines. Like traditional constitutional history, liberal history assumes that "only certain authoritative texts and certain authoritative textual interpretations can have the status of constitutional input." Hartog protests that emphasis on authoritative texts "tends to imply the near inevitability of the American pattern of discovering constitutional meaning and of establishing constitutional legitimacy."[30]

Radicals seek a new method of discovering constitutional meaning and establishing constitutional legitimacy. Through political and social struggle by the "disinherited," retrospectively realized in constitutional history, constitutional rights consciousness becomes the Constitution. This might be called the method of historically imagined constitutional aspiration, offered as a model for contemporary political action. According to the OAH volume, disinherited groups attacked the existing structure of rights and yearned for permanent statements of rights. Hartog says these groups made "aspirations to a life free from recognized hierarchies—to a life without badges and incidents of slavery—into a super-constitution that has taken permanent precedence over any merely transitory determination of constitutional meaning." History written from the point of view of constitutional aspiration, Hartog suggests, may force historians "to abandon notions of a distinctively legal or constitutional history, abandoning a perspective founded on the American Constitution's separation from the indeterminacies of American social and political history."[31]

Calling for "the social construction of constitutional history,"[32] radical history concludes that the Constitution is coeval with society. This means that the Constitution has no independent, objective existence.

Constitutional history in the radical perspective, Hartog notes, describes the conflicts of everyday life involving rights claims, treating labor contracts, divorce decrees, zoning variances, and municipal ordinances as equally important with Supreme Court decisions. Constitutional history, and by necessary implication the Constitution, is in the radical view important not for itself, but only as a way of learning about "the history of a people contending about power, identity, and justice."[33]

Constitutional interpretation in the United States in some sense inevitably derives from the Founding, a rule to which the OAH history forms no exception. Joyce Appleby supplies the obligatory originalist component in discussing the unfulfilled intent of the anti-Federalist critics of the Constitution. They were republicans, she tells us, whose aim was to establish populist legislative sovereignty. This purpose, which she believes can revitalize contemporary American politics, would have prevented the rhetorical "sacralization" of private property rights and enabled the people to decide the course of economic development. Appleby furthermore explains the intellectual rationale by which radical historians reconceptualize—and in reality seek to escape—the Constitution.[34] This is the theory of literary deconstruction or philosophical hermeneutics.[35] The "contemporary crisis of Western metaphysics," she asserts, has led to repudiation of the belief in reason, objective knowledge, and the concept of human nature that is essential to the "mystification of fundamental law." The result has been a "decentering of European culture, which threatens the elite and gives hope to the disinherited of "liberation from a language of rights accompanied by a practice of denial."[36]

Although ultimately directed at traditional constitutionalism, radical legal and constitutional history more immediately attacks liberal reform scholarship. To their credit, liberal historians have responded to the challenge. Harry N. Scheiber, for example, critically observes that radical history rejects the controlling premise of public law and constitutional history, namely, "that traditional constitutional principles have a content and historical importance that go beyond mere rhetoric." Scheiber objects to the dismissal of rule formalism and proceduralism in constitutional law as "empty pretension."[37] In his view realist instrumentalism is reconcilable with constitutionalism. Arguing that law is at once the product of social change and an autonomous force, he holds that the rule of law has been effective in correcting abuses, protecting the weak, and making power responsible.[38]

Lawrence M. Friedman concedes much of the force of the radical critique of Hurstian functionalism. He acknowledges that the Wisconsin school carried the law-in-society approach to such an extreme that it "may have . . . killed off the idea of law altogether, or at least the idea that law makes much of a difference." Legal history reduced to social history "eliminates law altogether as an independent entity with any kind of meaningful boundaries." Friedman's response to radical criticism is to accuse radical legal scholars of "neo-doctrinalism." Moreover, he insists that in order for the radical theory of law as a legitimating myth or symbol to have any effect, it must be understood as possessing an instrumentalist function or base. Friedman concludes that law has a double nature: instrumentally it represents a monopoly of force, while symbolically it expresses the moral hegemony of dominant political and economic elements.[39]

The dilemma of liberal legal history, rooted in the realist instrumentalism of the reform tradition yet concerned also with the defense of constitutionalism, can be seen in the writing of William E. Nelson. In the 1970s Nelson agreed with the radical view that law is an expression of social forces and that legal rules ultimately reflect the policy preferences of dominant elites.[40] Yet he believed law must also be seen as an autonomous body of principles and ideals. Quoting a conservative scholar, Nelson wrote: ". . . in order to avoid 'the intellectual and moral anarchy underlying the realist's conception of the law,' it is necessary 'to establish an ethical and moral basis for authority through the incorporation' into American jurisprudence of at least some autonomous values."[41] Rejecting natural law and original intent as sources of enduring legal values, Nelson relied on history. Although legal rules are instrumental in origin, he reasoned, some rules survive beyond the period of their usefulness to dominant groups and assume an autonomous status. He believed the task of the legal historian was to identify the traditions that were an essential part of the legal culture and that restrained judges and decision makers from initiating revolutionary changes in the legal order.[42]

Nelson has recently deemphasized the instrumental nature of law and recognized more clearly the value of traditional constitutionalism. He now attacks radical legal history for teaching that law is incapable of autonomous development and is ultimately no different from politics.[43] He asserts that radical legal history, defining law in terms of a hegemonic function of mystification, is simply another form of instrumentalism which rests on the idea that legal decisions result "from the impact of political and social forces on the law, and not from any neutral content in the law."[44] Nelson claims that some constitutional and political decision making is based on concern for the public interest and is guided by considerations of reason and justice, in contrast to ordinary politics grounded in interest-group conflict.[45] And he observes that traditional constitutional and legal history contributes to an

understanding of the neutral principles of constitutional law. It identifies "how determinate principles of constitutionalism can provide determinate answers to issues of constitutional law." Ultimately the
purpose of constitutional history, Nelson affirms, is "to preserve the
existing American political order designed to enhance individual autonomy or freedom to participate in imposing some new collective vision of the good on the polity."[46]

The liberal-radical split within the tradition of reform scholarship
raises the issue of a conservative approach to constitutional and legal
history. There is much to be said on this score, but little that is new.
Whatever novelty the conservative view may have arises from the circumstance of its being so long obscured by liberal realist instrumentalism. In fact the conservative approach to constitutional history is really
that of traditional American constitutionalism. To call it conservative
reflects mainly its rejection of the liberalism that has dominated American intellectual life since the 1930s. In any event the traditional or conservative approach to constitutional history seeks knowledge and
understanding of the Constitution with a view toward affirming and
maintaining American constitutionalism. While it includes political-
institutional analysis as well as studies of constitutional doctrine, the
organizing principle of this approach is the documentary Constitution
and the principles, forms, and procedures contained therein. Rejecting
the various instrumental views of the Constitution, the traditional approach regards constitutional and legal principles as things of enduring and intrinsic validity, proper historical understanding of which
requires consideration of the political and social context.[47] It takes the
view that despite continual change in the practical meaning of the Constitution, as Alfred de Grazia has written, "the term itself has always
conjured a firm image of a real thing to most people, changeless and
weighty."[48] The traditional approach to constitutional history treats the
Constitution as fundamental, paramount, and binding law—what
legal philosophers have called "hard law."[49]

Numerous works reflecting a traditional constitutionalist perspective might be noted.[50] Several scholars have recently affirmed the relationship between constitutionalism and constitutional history and law.
Discussing the problem of how to conceptualize and define constitutional history, Charles A. Lofgren suggests more analysis of the meaning of constitutions and constitutionalism.[51] Robert Faulkner states that
the purpose of constitutional scholarship remains "the grand old task
kept alive by a few scholars: taking the Constitution seriously." He
believes that in the present crisis of American constitutionalism, historical studies of the old constitutionalism are indispensable as a guide in
recovering what the liberal reform tradition rejected.[52] Edward J. Erler

declares: "A scholarship that takes constitutional government seriously must therefore be one which intends to elaborate and apply those permanent and fundamental principles in the spirit of the 'original and supreme will' of the people which established the Constitution."[53] Michael Zuckert urges historical studies of the Founding and the Reconstruction amendments in order to recover the original political character of the Constitution and depoliticize constitutional adjudication.[54]

The constitutionalist approach to constitutional history can be seen in Philip B. Kurland and Ralph Lerner's *The Founders' Constitution*. A five-volume collection of documents from the seventeenth and eighteenth centuries, the work gives a general view of the range of arguments concerning questions of political theory and governmental practice that were expressed in specific provisions of the Constitution. Unlike scholars whose approach to the Constitution rests on realist-instrumentalist assumptions, Kurland and Lerner take into account considerations of truth and timelessness or universality. They write: "This is an anthology of reasons and of the political arguments that thoughtful men and women drew from, and used to support, those reasons. We believe that those reasons have enduring interest and significance for anyone who purports to think about constitutional government in general and the Constitution of the United States in particular." Kurland and Lerner furthermore seek to recover an original understanding of those who argued for and against the Constitution. Their aim is to assist in detecting the "simplistic truisms" that pass for political thought today, in the belief that "the Constitution still matters—as a framework, as a statement of broad purposes, as a point of recurring reference, as a legitimation of further developments, as a restraint on the overbearing and the righteous. . . ."[55]

II

The liberal, radical, and conservative approaches to legal and constitutional history find expression in discussions of three critical turning points in American constitutional development. Accordingly we shall examine some of the principal interpretive problems raised in recent scholarship on the Founding, the Civil War and Reconstruction, and modern judicial review as an aspect of New Deal governance. Our concern will be with how scholars have defined or conceived of the Constitution and how they have evaluated the nature and tendency of constitutional government in the United States.

Scholarship on the Founding deals with two main issues: the nature of the Constitution, in the sense of identifying the forces, interests, ideas, purposes, motives, and intentions that led to the writing and adoption of the document; and the philosophical or ideological character and content of the Constitution. The former question has usually been posed by asking whether the Constitution is more accurately understood as an expedient response to problems of class, group, and sectional conflicts of interest, or as an action based on reason, reflection, and sound principles of political science, the purpose of which was to secure justice and the common good. In modern scholarship this question has usually been debated in the terms of Beardian economic analysis, with significant implications for American constitutional history in general. If the Constitution can be shown to rest on economic motives and interests, constitutionalism and the rule of law in general may be presumed to operate on the same basis. The way then becomes clear to regard the Constitution as a reflection of the hegemonic function of the law justifying the existing order.

The Beardian view of the Constitution as a reactionary document imposed on a democratic people by self-interested politicians has long since been refuted. Nevertheless the so-called Beardian insight into the role of economic and social class interests in the making of the Constitution has continued to influence neo-progressive scholarship.[56] More important than arguments about the conservative or democratic character of the Constitution, however, has been the transposing of the debate into the language of ideological analysis. This historiographical shift was accomplished two decades ago in the writings of Bernard Bailyn, Gordon S. Wood, and J. G. A. Pocock, who argued that the ideology of classical republicanism formed the intellectual framework and shaped the content of the Revolution and Constitution. The republican interpretation was subsequently challenged by scholars arguing that liberalism was the ideological basis of American institutions.[57] Nevertheless historians on both sides of the controversy agree about the nature of constitutional thinking, action, and decision making in the revolutionary era. The linguistic-ideological analysis of political thought provides the approach to constitutionalism employed by these scholars.

Although Pocock is the leading theoretician of linguistic historical analysis, Gordon S. Wood is its most influential practitioner.[58] Wood and the ideological school have been seen as refuting the economic-instrumental interpretation of political thought and upholding the autonomy of ideas.[59] In fact linguistic-ideological analysis is but another form of instrumentalism. Wood states that ideas are essential to behavior, but it is not thinking, reflecting, deliberating individuals who in his account formulate ideas to guide action. Ideas or ideology accompany action; they do not motivate or cause it. "Ideology creates behavior," Wood asserts, adding that the meanings we give to what we do are public ones and are defined and delimited by the conventions and languages of the culture of our time. Culture or ideology creates behavior "by forcing us to describe our behavior in its terms." According to Wood, what is liberal or tyrannical, monarchical or republican, democratic or aristocratic, "is determined by this cultural structure of meanings."[60]

This is a deconstructionist approach to history which separates intelligence from the senses and the reading of texts from the experience of life.[61] Because it treats the Constitution as having no determinate meaning, it has serious implications for constitutionalism. Historians faced with different meanings attributed to the Constitution, Wood advises, should not try to determine which is the more true or correct one. The task of the historian rather is to explain why opposing sides in constitutional debate argued as they did. There was not in 1787, nor is there today, Wood avers, a true meaning of the real Constitution. Indeed, he argues that "there was and is no 'real' Constitution against which we can measure the conflicting statements" in a constitutional controversy.[62] Wood dismisses the notion of an objective and intelligible Constitution as a legal fiction necessary for lawyers and jurists to carry on their business. He says that historians have different aims and obligations and may properly reject this view of the Constitution. We may ask, however, whether historians should not try to understand the words and deeds of political actors as they themselves understood them. If lawyers and judges, and government officials and the people in general, understood the Constitution to be an objective and intelligible document, are not historians required as a matter of sound historical method to adopt a like perspective?

Many students of the Founding deny that the meaning, purpose, and intent of the Constitution can be historically recovered, or that such knowledge is in any case relevant to contemporary government. The earnestness with which liberal historians disavow the ability to answer the essentially historical question of constitutional original intent is puzzling. According to Wood, it is "wrong to see the Constitution as having timeless and universal meaning embodied in the philosophical aims of the Founders and discoverable through textual analysis." Original intent may be a useful fiction for limiting judicial discretion, he observes, "but historically there can be no real 'original intention' behind the document."[63] Jack Rakove contends that there is no verifiable way of knowing how the Constitution was understood by the nation at the moment of ratification, while Peter S. Onuf says flatly that history is incompatible with original intent.[64] Terence Ball and

J. G. A. Pocock concede that it is possible for historians to reach agreement on statements concerning original intent. They note that such statements are not incontestable, however, and that the decision to follow one or another view of original intent is properly one for the jurist. Originalist scholars would tend to agree. Ball and Pocock argue further, however, that although the Constitution is the kind of text that exercises authority over a long period of time, the appeal to original intent is a conservative strategy which if implemented would require a return to eighteenth-century contexts of discourse and vocabulary. They regard the doctrine of original intent as a "canute-like attempt to turn back the tide of linguistic and conceptual change," which would divorce our constitutional language from the concerns of contemporary life.[65]

The linguistic-ideological view of the Constitution has provoked dissenting opinions. Forceful criticism has come from Straussian-trained political scientists, who though described as "ideologically repellent" and "methodologically incomprehensible" by one historian,[66] are credited by another with having paid closer attention to the words of the Framers than historians have.[67] Among the critics, Ralph Lerner faults the linguistic-ideological school for denying human thought as a central reality and independent variable in history. Arguing that individuals have direct access to ideas through reason and intellect, unmediated by ideology, Lerner urges historians to study the way the Framers reshaped the presuppositions of their age and replaced old intellectual precepts with new ones of their own design.[68] Thomas L. Pangle seeks to understand the Constitution in relation to political philosophy, or the quest for permanent principles. Believing that historical analysis should be open to the view that political ideas are not entirely reducible to ideology, Pangle states that the Founding was dominated by a small number of geniuses who not only reflected common opinion, but saw further into the philosophic roots of the modern liberal republic than other men.[69] John P. Diggins, a non-Straussian, attacks the linguistic-ideological interpretation for its epistemological skepticism. "If all ideas require a linguistic medium for their expression," he points out, "ideas are no longer regarded as purveyors of truth and language is no longer regarded as representative of reality."[70]

Ultimately the logic of the linguistic-ideological approach to the Constitution may threaten constitutionalism and the rule of law. Diggins recognizes this when he says it is necessary for historians to ask not only what political words were used for, but also "whether they are being used correctly and justifiably."[71] Linguistic-ideological analysis denies the nature of political life as individuals experience it. Daniel T. Rodgers, an exponent of linguistic interpretation, illustrates this tendency in asserting that political and constitutional history consists in struggles over—not for or on behalf of—basic political and governmental concepts that he calls "keywords." Rodgers argues that in such controversies "language no longer registers an exogenous change: contest over linguistic legitimacy and control will lie at the heart of the event itself."[72]

A contradiction exists in the linguistic-ideological interpretation of the Founding. Skeptical of the possibility of ascertaining constitutional original intent, its adherents nevertheless believe that classical republican ideology can be recovered and applied as a political theory answering the needs of contemporary American society. While this use of history appeals especially to constitutional law scholars,[73] it is supported by historians and political scientists as well.[74] Michael Lienesch states that the republican tradition in American politics—the fear of corruption, conspiracy, entrenched power, and constitutional decline—has not been merely nostalgic. It has been a continuing source of inspiration for reformers and radicals who resist corporate and public power, and can be a model for the future.[75] The inconsistency of the linguistic-ideological school concerning the use of the past suggests that the basic issue is not whether the purpose and intent of the Constitution can be known, but whether its principles are to be regarded as sound, reasonable, and just.[76]

Scholarly disagreement on the substantive value of the Framers' Constitution points to the central issue in the study of the Reconstruction amendments after the Civil War. The question is whether the Thirteenth, Fourteenth, and Fifteenth Amendments are to be understood as consistent with the original Constitution with respect to the meaning of liberty, or whether these measures introduced new values and transformed the fundamental law, becoming in effect a new Constitution. Early twentieth-century histories written from a progressive point of view sympathetic to the South viewed Reconstruction as a political tragedy and constitutional error which revolutionized the federal system by consolidating power in the national government. Revisionist scholarship in the era of the civil rights movement interpreted the Reconstruction amendments in a positive light as extending the liberal principles of the Founding to blacks who had wrongfully been denied liberty and equality. According to revisionist accounts, the amendments recognized the traditional federal-state balance, while establishing federal guarantees of civil rights requiring the states to extend equal protection of the law to their citizens irrespective of race.[77]

In the past two decades, in the context of affirmative action policy, the legal history of Reconstruction has taken a new turn. Consistent with the expansion of Fourteenth Amendment litigation as an all-purpose reform instrument, radical legal historians have viewed the Reconstruction amendments as effecting a revolution in national citizenship and federal-state relations. According to this interpretation, the Thirteenth and Fourteenth Amendments conferred absolute civil rights on blacks as U.S. citizens, protecting them against state and private discrimination under guarantees of plenary and absolute federal authority.[78] In the OAH bicentennial volume referred to previously, Vincent Harding expresses the radical revisionist view in describing the "transformative force" of the black struggle for freedom on the Constitution. "Obviously the instrument that contained the Thirteenth Amendment . . . was not the same one that had been created at Philadelphia," Harding asserts.[79]

More than is ordinarily the case in constitutional history, the radical account of Reconstruction is a pragmatic response to the litigation strategy of the civil rights lobby. It is fitting therefore that Supreme Court Justice Thurgood Marshall should popularize radical revisionism. In a widely noted bicentennial speech which cautioned against making "a blind pilgrimage to the shrine of the original document," Justice Marshall stated that "while the Union survived the civil war, the Constitution did not," "In its place," he said, "arose a new, more promising basis for justice and equality, the 14th amendment." Observing that the framers of the Reconstruction amendments "refused to acquiesce in outdated notions of 'liberty,' 'justice,' and 'equality,' " he concluded that they conceived of "new constitutional principles" guaranteeing "respect for individual freedoms and human rights . . . we hold as fundamental today."[80]

The pragmatic approach of radical legal history is evident in historical arguments filed in *Patterson v. McLean Credit Union*, the recent Supreme Court case that reconsidered a previous decision declaring private discrimination to be prohibited by the Civil Rights Act of 1866 under the Thirteenth Amendment. Civil rights lawyers argued that the question of congressional intent, as a matter of statutory interpretation, was "an essentially pragmatic one." The meaning of the statute was to be derived more from historical knowledge of the actual situation facing the freedmen in the post-emancipation period, in which private discrimination was rife, than from textual analysis or congressional debate on the Civil Rights Act, which referred frequently to state action and not at all to private discrimination. The means which Congress adopted, civil rights lawyers contended, should be assumed to be commensurate with the evils it perceived.[81]

In response to radical revisionism, the moderate or conservative view of the Reconstruction amendments has been reaffirmed in a number of recent works.[82] In essence the argument is that the Thirteenth and Fourteenth Amendments were intended to remove the exceptions to liberty and equality signified by the recognition of the slavery provisions of the Constitution, and to complete the document by bringing it into conformity with the Declaration of Independence. The Republican framers of the amendments intended neither a revolution in federalism nor a radical transformation in the meaning of liberty and equal rights. Their aim was to extend to the freed people the protection of person and property that delineated the condition of civil liberty under U.S. citizenship. Although the abolition of slavery required amendment of the Constitution restricting state powers, according to Earl Maltz, "substantial changes in constitutional theory inherent in Republican policy were moderated by strong conservative influences."[83] In the view of William E. Nelson, the authors of the Fourteenth Amendment intended to reaffirm their commitment to general principles of equality, individual rights, and local self-government.[84]

The question of continuity versus radical change arises in discussions of the third critical episode in American constitutional history, the New Deal. The perception of radical governmental change that existed in the 1930s was superseded in subsequent historical accounts by an emphasis on the continuity of the New Deal with the constitutional tradition.[85] Recent evaluations tend to underscore the extent to which the New Deal departed from the constitutional tradition.[86] This theme may be pursued in relation to the presidency, the rise of the administrative state, and the party system.[87] Even more important because of its direct relation to the nature and meaning of the Constitution is the development of modern judicial activism as an aspect of New Deal government.

Although President Franklin D. Roosevelt's Court-packing plan threatened judicial independence and revealed the weakness of the Supreme Court, in the aftermath of the crisis the Court's authority was strengthened.[88] In 1937 judicial restraint was a rallying cry for liberals, but the limited scope of the commitment to restraint soon became clear. The problem in constitutional politics, from the liberal standpoint, was to gain acceptance of New Deal policies. One way to do this was through judicial deference to the executive and legislative branches, safely controlled by the liberal governing coalition. The alternative approach was judicial activism, by which courts under the preferred freedoms theory intervened directly to protect the political process and the interests of discrete and insular minority groups. Tension between these alternative liberal strategies continued in the post–New Deal period until it was resolved in the 1960s in favor of judicial activism.[89]

The remarkable expansion of judicial power in the past three dec-

ades has transformed debate about the legitimacy, scope, and effect of
judicial review, a familiar feature of our constitutional history, into
fundamental controversy over the nature of the Constitution and the
tendency of American constitutionalism. The controversy is primarily
one of constitutional and political theory. Yet it implicates constitutional and legal history. Those who would institutionalize judicial activism in a revised theory of constitutionalism, as well as those who
would restore the judicial function to more traditional limits, seek authority in historical knowledge and understanding.

Although the conservative call for a jurisprudence of original intent
in the 1980s is the peg on which the present controversy hangs, conservatives did not start the modern debate over judicial review. Liberals
began it in the 1950s in reaction to the first phase of Warren Court
activism.[90] By the end of the 1970s some liberal scholars were trying to
find a way to retain the benefits of judicial activism, while acknowledging the legitimate restraints of a written constitution.[91] Meanwhile proponents of the theory of a "living Constitution" extended their
argument to the point of claiming that the United States had an unwritten constitution.[92] This signified a readiness to redefine the terms of
the debate. "Interpretivism" versus "noninterpretivism" was the infe-
licitous but accurate nomenclature used to describe the escalation of
the debate into a fundamental controversy over the nature of constitutionalism. The terms indicated that the opponents of activism, called
interpretivists, believed constitutional decision making should depend
on the application and interpretation of the constitutional text, while
supporters of activism, called noninterpretivists, believed constitutional decisions should be based on sources of authority outside the
Constitution.[93]

Critics of activism have attempted to recover the historical understanding of the judicial function intended by the framers of the Constitution. Christopher Wolfe's survey of the history of constitutional
adjudication emphasizes the change from a judicial conception of judicial review, based on the distinction between law and politics, and the
modern legislative conception which assimilates judicial review to the
legislative power as an instrument of will rather than judgment. Observing that the debate over constitutional adjudication concerns basic
issues of republican government and the distribution of political
power, Wolfe asks: "What is—and should be—the meaning and authority of the Constitution in the context of our national political
life?"[94] Gary L. McDowell similarly views the controversy over constitutional adjudication in relation to basic regime principles. As he for-
mulates it, the question is whether the judiciary shall be committed to
moral self-government under a constitution of open texture and evolv-

ing principles, as in the judicial activist approach, or to the morality of government by consent under the principles and forms of the Constitution as defined by the text and intentions of the Framers. To justify judicial activism because of the results it has achieved, McDowell argues, is "to deny the fundamental wisdom of the American founding."[95]

A different version of the originalist-restraint position argues the theory of judicial statesmanship. As discussed by Harry M. Clor, this theory views the Constitution as a vital constituent of the political community. It holds that no sharp dividing line can be drawn between the standards of constitutional law and the principles of the polity or the regime. The Constitution is law, but it is extraordinary law, requiring knowledge of the ends of government and pointing to political fundamentals. Clor says historically it was almost inevitable that courts should seek guidance from political understandings and principles of right and justice that transcend the constitutional text. The indefinite or ambiguous clauses of the Constitution are not, however, according to the theory of judicial statesmanship, merely empty vessels to be filled by whatever morality a judge may think best. "Even the least precise constitutional provisions have substance," Clor writes, "when one considers them in light of the premises and aims of the constitutional polity." The judicial statesmanship school of interpretivists thus calls for a "regime-oriented" jurisprudence that depends on historical and philosophical understanding of the Founding.[96]

Still another historically grounded attempt to address the problem of constitutional adjudication is Sylvia Snowiss's analysis of the origins of judicial review. Snowiss emphasizes that the distinctive feature of American constitutionalism, which provided the basis for repudiating the doctrine of legislative supremacy and for conceiving of a judicial review function, was the concrete reality and explicitness of the Constitution expressed in its documentary character. In its earliest phase the determination of the unconstitutionality of a law, the essence of judicial review, was a public or political act rather than a legal one. In stage two of judicial review judges consulted the first principles of government as identified in the constitutional text, but more importantly grounded in the common assumptions of the social contract. Snowiss contends that the decisive shift to modern judicial review occurred when John Marshall, in the contract and federalism cases from 1810 to 1825, transformed the Constitution from politically binding fundamental law into legally binding supreme ordinary law. Marshall effected this change by applying the rules for statutory interpretation to the Constitution, thereby enabling policy considerations appropriate to legislation to enter constitutional adjudication. Intellectually and theoretically the way was clear to the "fundamental values" jurisprudence of modern judicial activism. Although Snowiss's account suggests the inevitability of this development, she recognizes the problematic character of contemporary activism. She proposes therefore to recapture and strengthen the inescapable political component of constitutional law, derived from the principle of republican government, as a restraint on the legislative character of modern activism.[97]

The conservative appeal for a jurisprudence of original intent in the 1980s has provoked historical investigation by liberal scholars. Widely accepted is H. Jefferson Powell's contention that the Founding Fathers intended the Constitution to be interpreted according to the common law rules of statutory interpretation, unassisted by reference to extrinsic aids such as speeches in the Constitutional Convention. Powell thus argues that the conservative notion of original intent, relying on extrinsic aids, disregards the Framers' true intent.[98] Paul W. Kahn further denies a privileged place to original intent by presenting it as a nineteenth-century development divorced from the approach to constitutionalism taken by the founders. He argues that originalism, first fully realized in the *Dred Scott* decision, was a mythical construct that developed in the post-founding generation as constitutional interpreters rejected rationally based political and moral theory and turned to the intentions of the Framers for authority.[99]

Leonard W. Levy has written the strongest liberal attack on the idea of constitutional original intent. Levy rejects originalism as a jurisprudential approach on the ground that the documentary basis for it is insufficient. More importantly he contends that the nature of the Constitution as a written document containing ambiguous words does not allow original-intent analysis to be dispositive or even meaningful. Levy does not deny that original intent, as a matter of historical fact, can be ascertained. In his own writings he claims to have discovered the original understanding of the religion clauses and other constitutional provisions. He argues, however, that the Supreme Court is incapable of the historical research and analysis that original intent requires. While condemning politically motivated, result-oriented jurisprudence, Levy believes judicial activism has dominated constitutional adjudication from the outset. The inconsistency between Levy's historical finding of a thoroughgoing political jurisprudence, and his constitutionalist demand for a nonpolitical judicial function, is resolved only by his conclusion that modern liberal judges like Chief Justice Warren have served the public interest and followed the Constitution.[100]

Although liberals presently reject the notion, original-intent jurisprudence has appealed to progressive scholars in the past.[101] There are indications of liberal reconsideration of the issue in the present debate. Constitutional law scholar Robert N. Clinton, for example, seeks to reclaim original intent from the conservatives. Acknowledging the fact of a written Constitution and a body of historical data on the Framers' intent, Clinton defines a middle position that recognizes originalism as a legitimate concern in constitutional adjudication, while reconciling it with post-realist legal thought. His approach to original intent, however, is pragmatic and instrumental. Believing the public would look unfavorably on a general repudiation of the idea that original intent has constitutional significance, Clinton adopts an originalist position for the pragmatic reason that it will promote constitutional stability.[102]

The call for original-intent jurisprudence in the 1980s emanated from a conservative administration that was arguably effecting a realignment of American politics. While party lines may be too evanescent to permit a clear judgment of the success of this project, it seems reasonable to view the original-intent appeal as part of a movement aimed at reasserting constitutional forms and principles deemed in jeopardy. Conservatives might be seen as seeking a constitutionalist realignment in their recurrence to federalism, deregulation or market freedom, equal rights for individuals, and a strong national defense.[103] The attempt to curb judicial discretion through revival of an original intent standard was yet another expression of the desire to return to first principles: the concept of limited government under a written constitution. Intruding upon an academic and political establishment that had long since concluded that the Constitution did not refer to anything objective and was only to be understood as expressing the subjective preferences of judges or other officials, the original-intent idea was deeply offensive.[104] Yet it was part of a broader reaction against intellectual modernism, of which legal realism and liberal activism were particular expressions. In law as in culture and society generally there has been a search for a stable reference point from which to ground otherwise subjective values.[105]

Some liberal scholars share the concern for constitutional and legal stability. In a diagnosis which many originalists would accept, H. Jefferson Powell says the perception that the Constitution has no objective reference results in "a cynicism about constitutional discussion that is personally and socially corrosive."[106] Ronald L. K. Collins makes a similar point in criticizing Levy's conclusion that constitutional adjudication has been overwhelmingly result-oriented. According to Collins, Levy insists on the open ended nature of constitutional interpretation to the point where "one is tempted to deny what any constitution-*maker* would unquestionably affirm; namely, that written words do matter. . . ." Collins fears the extremes to which constitutional law could be taken in the absence of any common ground or objective reference of textual, historical, and analytical judgment in constitutional decision making.[107]

"Constitutional objectivism" has been suggested as a liberal answer to the problem of stability in constitutional development. H. Jefferson Powell uses this term to describe the concept of constitutional interpretation adopted by Walter F. Murphy and his associates.[108] The approach is apparently traditional in its emphasis on the Constitution as a text. Yet the notion of a text is to be understood in a deconstructivist way. The Constitution as a text consists in the document, plus the polity or the institutions surrounding it. According to Powell, constitutional objectivism "approaches the 'text' to be interpreted—document plus polity—as itself the source of the interpreter's methodology." Interpretation of the Constitution as a normative text is "determined methodologically by the text and the structure of the institutions it creates." Powell concludes that the Constitution, "both the historical document and its polity," creates a bounded yet somewhat indeterminate sphere of discourse.[109]

Encouraging as liberal reconsiderations of judicial activism may be, the theory of constitutional objectivism is but an updated version of the legal realist preference for defining the Constitution as the existing institutions and practices of government.[110] It is difficult to see where limits would be established by a Constitution consisting of documentary and institutional texts. Reading the text of institutional development would seem to yield a variety of contestable meanings, more so than reading the written constitutional text. Interpretive uncertainty would be compounded by divorcing the documentary text from the intent of the Framers, as the objectivist theory proposes.[111]

The theory of constitutional objectivism recalls Edward S. Corwin's 1934 prediction that the United States would soon be governed by an unwritten constitution. Corwin saw in New Deal reform measures a constitutional revolution that would bring about cooperation and a fusion of powers, in place of the tension and competition produced by the separation of powers in the original Constitution. The documentary Constitution would be retained, but it would become more political and less legalistic, valued for instrumental social purposes rather than as a lawyers' document. Corwin believed the Constitution would become merely a part of the actual constitution. Like Magna Carta in relation to the English constitution, the Constitution would be absorbed into a vast complex of political institutions.[112] Gordon Wood echoes Corwin in his recent assertion that "our Constitution is no more important to the longevity and workability of our government than

Magna Carta is to the longevity and workability of the British government. Our Constitution is as unwritten as theirs."[113]

Despite repeated discovery of this realist "insight," we have not yet had a constitutional history written from a perspective which views American government as resting on an unwritten constitution. In fact a recent constitutional history based on legal realist-instrumentalist assumptions gives a great deal of attention to the analysis of formal constitutional doctrines in Supreme Court decisions. It is not clear why a realist should be concerned with legal logic.[114] The concern may reflect the fact that legal and constitutional reasoning, a vestige of formalism and declaratory jurisprudence, is a basic reality of American constitutionalism.

III

The controversy over original intent is an extension and escalation of the debate over modern judicial review that was precipitated by judicial activism in the era of New Deal and post–New Deal liberalism. The scholarship it has produced, like that on the Founding and the Reconstruction amendments, reveals sharp disagreement concerning the nature, meaning, effect, and significance of the Constitution in American politics. Liberal scholars concede on the one hand that it may be useful and necessary to treat the Constitution as "fundamental scripture" or to tolerate myths or legal fictions about original intent.[115] They believe on the other hand that historians should penetrate these fictions and describe the past in realist, instrumentalist, and historicist terms. There seems to be something politically and constitutionally unsound in a situation where government is conducted under a Constitution that is thought to be objective, intelligible, and reasonably clear in meaning from the standpoint of those participating in it, but which is perceived by at least a substantial part of the scholarly community as mythical, meaningless, or nonexistent. One wonders what the consequence of such scholarship might be for constitutionalism. Yet such a situation appears to characterize constitutional and legal history in the 1980s.

Wood observes that the conservative view of the Constitution as the product of reason, and the Founding as a monumental event in American history, rests on "a deep and longstanding popular belief in the sanctity of the Constitution and the uniqueness of the Founding Fathers."[116] This belief has been a basic feature of American constitutionalism. Whether it is accurate or inaccurate might be said to be the ultimate question which our constitutional history addresses.

A survey of constitutional and legal history in the 1980s suggests that no generally agreed upon answer to this question will be forthcoming because of the significant differences in the way scholars conceive of the Constitution and in their use of history. Consider, for example, Bruce A. Ackerman's "discovery" of the Constitution. A constitutional law scholar, Ackerman seeks to overcome the stalemate in the present debate between interpretivists and noninterpretivists and to affirm the democratic character of judicial review. Philosophical and economic analysis and common law techniques having been found inadequate to the task, he turns to history. He argues from *The Federalist* that judicial review is democratic insofar as it upholds the Constitution, an expression of popular sovereignty. He posits a distinction between normal politics, which must be tolerated in the name of individual liberty, and the "politics of public virtue associated with moments of constitutional creation." In order to multiply the number of creative constitutional moments that may provide a source of higher law principles that the courts can apply, he advances the theory of structural amendment of the Constitution.

Based on what Ackerman calls a nonformalist reading of Article V, the theory contends that the Constitution has actually been amended by the convention method on several occasions, beyond the Philadelphia Convention of 1787. The "best interpretation of our constitutional history," he writes, "requires the conclusion that We the People . . . have indeed amended our Constitution through 'conventional' means."[117] Asserting that Article V is the beginning, not the end, of constitutional transformation, Ackerman declares: "Only after we have reflected on this history can we hope to do justice to our constitutional future."[118] Ackerman offers the theory of structural amendment as a means by which interpretivists can avoid "clause fetishism," respond to the "nihilist critique" that sees all judicial value imposition as arbitrary, and "elaborate the nature of our existing constitution in a legally compelling way."[119] He takes such extraordinary license with the historical record, however, as to discredit his entire effort.[120]

A more sober use of history to illuminate a constitutional problem is found in Russell L. Caplan's study of the Article V amendment process. Concerning a subject about which constitutional scholars have said text and history offer no guidance, Caplan traces text and practice historically to provide guidance on the question of whether a state-inspired constitutional convention could be confined to specific subjects. As important as his conclusion—that a convention can be limited and that Congress has obscured this fact in order to maintain its own power over the amendment process—is the premise of his study. It is that "the Convention clause, like every other in the Constitution, has a historical meaning that can be successfully retrieved." Caplan provides us with a valuable example of original-intent history.[121]

Notwithstanding scholarly uncertainty concerning the nature and meaning of the Constitution as seen in the debate over constitutional adjudication, it is likely that historians who actually write about the Constitution, like most lawyers and the people in general, regard it as the original text and the twenty-six amendments subsequently added to it. There are indications that this conventional view is still widespread. Constitutional law scholar Gary C. Leedes writes about conventional theory, which explains the beliefs of law-abiding citizens and the content of case law. The conventional specialist, says Leedes, unlike radicals and skeptics considers the Supreme Court competent to decide cases in accordance with the written Constitution. This is the basic norm of the legal system which represents definable limits on power that officials respect. "The Constitution itself, and not the theory which explains it, is the basic norm," Leedes observes.[122] In an account of Supreme Court history intended to illuminate the present controversy over constitutional adjudication, William M. Wiecek views the Constitution in the conventional way. He identifies as criteria for constitutional decision making text, intent, the structure and relationship of constitutional forms and procedures, and history.[123] David P. Currie's history of the Supreme Court is similarly based on the conventional view that the Constitution is a law binding on judges no less than on other officials. He concludes that judges were expected to base their decisions on the law as found in the Constitution, and that very few important decisions in the first century of the Supreme Court clearly distorted the Constitution. Eschewing theory, Currie says his aim is "not to defend the rule of law but to apply its methodology to the cases."[124] Finally, a British scholar observes that despite sharp controversy over original intent and constitutional reform, the Constitution itself is not under challenge.[125]

In his study of popular attitudes toward the Constitution, Michael Kammen contrasts reverence for the document with what he finds to be general ignorance, neglect, and lack of understanding of its specific provisions. Claiming that "realism" rather than "mindless reverence" has been the bulwark of liberty, Kammen says Americans have been more likely "to read and understand the Constitution" when it has been controversial and there has been argument about its misuse, than in moments when it was venerated.[126] Yet might not the success of the Constitution in time of controversy or crisis be related to an attitude of veneration, reverence, or conviction? And does not this conviction ultimately rest on historical fact?

In *Federalist* No. 49 Publius cautions against a too frequent recurrence to the people in convention to resolve constitutional decisions, on the ground that it would carry an implication of some defect in the government. It would "deprive the government of that veneration which time bestows on everything, and without which perhaps the wisest and freest governments would not possess the requisite stability." In a nation of philosophers, Publius argues, a reverence for the laws would be sufficiently inculcated by the voice of an enlightened reason. But a nation of philosophers can never exist, he observes, and "in every other nation, the most rational government will not find it a superfluous advantage to have the prejudices of the community on its side."[127]

It would be unsound to argue that the essence of constitutionalism is legalism, or the belief that right conduct consists in following rules. Yet it seems unwise to deny the importance of the high public status that the rule of law has had in American history, and especially the law of the Constitution.[128] Like positive legal rules, the Constitution may be used instrumentally by groups and individuals. In order to be effective in shaping political life for its declared objects, however, a constitution must be upheld for intrinsic rather than instrumental reasons, at least by some people some of the time. Those in our polity who most significantly and decisively tend to regard the Constitution as a real thing possessing intrinsic validity and intelligible meaning are the people. Their view of the Constitution is the basis of the constitutionalist conviction which Lincoln and other statesmen have seen as essential to the preservation of American institutions. This conviction of intrinsic constitutional validity is not mythical, however. It is grounded in historical fact and understanding.

The nature of the Constitution as a written charter of first principles, adopted at a single moment to establish the ends and purposes of a new political society, necessarily makes original intent pertinent to the conduct of political life. It necessarily implicates history in the preservation of constitutional government. Critics of traditional constitutionalism are impatient with, if they do not scorn, the enduring appeal to historical original intent. Yet this appeal is not based on mere symbolism or social mythology. It rests on the historical fact that in a nation where political legitimacy derives from the act of foundation, where nationality itself is defined by political principles and institutions written into the Constitution, the founders possess lasting authority. The written Constitution, a thing subject to varying interpretation in certain respects but not ultimately a subjective state of mind, expresses the wisdom and justice of the act of foundation. The constitutional history which tells this story provides an essential basis of American constitutionalism.

Notes

1. "One of the interesting things about communism," a former Secretary of State observes, "is that when the reign of terror stops, there seems to be almost no way they can achieve regular political legitimacy." Washington Times, June 7, 1989, p. A10, quoting Henry Kissinger. Concerning the revival of interest in constitutionalism in recent years, see Vernon Bogdanor, ed., Constitutions in Democratic Politics (Gower, Eng., 1988).

2. Donald S. Lutz, The Origins of American Constitutionalism (Baton Rouge, 1988).

3. Hannah Arendt, On Revolution 139–178 (New York, 1963).

4. For enumeration of current constitutional problems, see 1 this Constitution: A Bicentennial Chronicle 4–8 (1983) and 18 this Constitution 66–69 (1988).

5. Harry N. Scheiber, *Introduction: The Bicentennial and the Rediscovery of Constitutional History,* 74 Journal of American History 668–670 (1987).

6. Stanley C. Brubaker, *Constitutional Scholarship: What Next?* 5 Constitutional Commentary 48 (1988).

7. Robert N. Clinton, *Original Understanding, Legal Realism, and the Interpretation of 'This Constitution,'* 72 Iowa L.R. 1179, 1243 (1987).

8. Michael Kammen, A Machine That Would Go of Itself: The Constitution in American Culture xviii–xix (New York, 1986).

9. William H. McNeill, *Modern European History,* in Michael Kammen, ed., The Past Before Us: Contemporary Historical Writing in the United States 107–109 (Ithaca, 1980); William H. McNeill, *World Civ as an Alternative,* 12 Continuity 25–27 (1988).

10. Herman Belz, *The Constitution in the Gilded Age: The Beginnings of Constitutional Realism in American Scholarship,* 13 Amer. J. Legal Hist. 110 (1969).

11. Kammen, *supra* note 8, at 22–23.

12. Herman Belz, *The Realist Critique of Constitutionalsim in the Era of Reform,* 15 Amer. J. Legal Hist. 288 (1971); Herman Belz, *Changing Conceptions of Constitutionalism in the Era of World War II and the Cold War,* 59 J. American Hist. 640 (1972); Edward A. Purcell, *American Jurisprudence Between the Wars: Legal Realism and the Crisis of Democratic Theory,* 75 Amer. Hist. Rev. 424 (1969).

13. Paul L. Murphy, *Time to Reclaim: The Current Challenge of American Constitutional History,* 69 Amer. Hist. Rev. 64, 74–77 (1963).

14. Hurst's followers later acknowledged this fact. See Harry N. Scheiber, *American Constitutional History and the New Legal History: Complementary Themes in Two Modes,* 68 J. Amer. Hist. 343 (1981), and Lawrence M. Friedman, *American Legal History: Past and Present,* 34 J. Legal Ed. (1984), reprinted in L. Friedman and H. Scheiber, eds., American Law and the Constitutional Order, 2 ed. 466 (Cambridge, 1988).

15. James Willard Hurst, *Legal Elements in United States History,* 5 Perspectives in American History 28, 91 (1971). Cf. Willard Hurst, *Legal History: A Research Program,* 1942 Wisconsin L.R. 323; Hurst, The Growth of American Law: The Law Makers (Boston, 1950); Hurst, Law and Social Process in United

States History (Ann Arbor, 1960); Hurst, Law and the Conditions of Freedom in the Nineteenth Century United States (Madison, 1956); Hurst, *The Law in United States History,* 104 Proceedings of the Amer. Philosophical Soc. 521 (1960); Harry N. Scheiber, *At the Borderland of Law and Economic History: The Contributions of Willard Hurst,* 75 Amer. Hist. Rev. 744 (1970).

16. Lawrence M. Friedman, A History of American Law 10 (New York, 1973).

17. Lawrence M. Friedman, "Some Problems and Possibilities of American Legal History," unpublished MS, 1969, p. 13.

18. Friedman, *supra* note 16, at 14–15, 102–103, 570, 595.

19. Friedman wrote: "I have surrendered myself wholeheartedly to some of the central insights of social science." *Id.* at 10.

20. Robert W. Gordon, *J. Willard Hurst and the Common Law Tradition in American Legal Historiography,* 10 Law and Society Rev. 34 (1975); Daniel J. Boorstin, *Tradition and Method in Legal History,* 54 Harvard L.R. 424 (1941); William E. Nelson and John Phillip Reid, The Literature of American Legal History 2–5 (New York, 1985).

21. Morton J. Horwitz, The Transformation of American Law 1780–1860 (Cambridge, 1977).

22. Morton J. Horwitz, *The Conservative Tradition in the Writing of American Legal History,* 17 Amer. J. Legal Hist. 281 (1973).

23. Morton J. Horwitz, *The Rule of Law: An Unqualified Human Good?* 86 Yale L.J. 561–566 (1977).

24. *Id.* at 565.

25. Morton J. Horwitz, *History and Theory,* 96 Yale L.J. 1825 (1987).

26. Robert W. Gordon, *An Exchange on Critical Legal Studies,* 6 Law and History Rev. 145, 170–171 (1988).

27. *Id.* at 171.

28. *Id.* at 145, 153, 170–171, 182

29. Walter LaFeber, *The Constitution and United States Foreign Policy: An Interpretation,* 74 J. Amer. Hist. 696 (1987); R. Kent Newmyer, *Harvard Law School, New England Culture, and the Antebellum Origins of American Jurisprudence,* 74 J. Amer. Hist. 825 (1987); Donald J. Pisani, *Promotion and Regulation: Constitutionalism and the American Economy,* 74 J. Amer. Hist. 767 (1987).

30. Hendrik Hartog, *The Constitution of Aspiration and 'The Rights That Belong to Us All,'* 74 J. Amer. Hist. 1029–1030 (1987).

31. *Id.* 1024, 1029.

32. *Id.* at 1031.

33. *Id.* at 1013, 1020, 1024, 1029–1033.

34. For an example of an historian seeking to escape the Constitution, see the comment of Norman Rosenberg in the symposium, *Constitutional Scholarship: What Next?,* 5 Constitutional Commentary 46 (1988). Rosenberg urges a moratorium on writing about the Constitution. He states: "Free from the grasp of IT [i.e. the Constitution], writers could delve into all those very human stories about powers and knowledge, about the reach of social institutions and groups, and about the popular needs and aspirations that actually bring into play . . . the specialized rhetoric of constitutional lawyers and judges."

35. For the testimony of a believing practitioner, see Gregory Leyh, *Toward a Constitutional Hermeneutics*, 32 Amer. J. of Pol. Sci. 369 (1988). For criticism of deconstruction theory, see R. V. Young, Jr., *Constitutional Interpretation and Literary Theory*, 23 The Intercollegiate Review 49 (1987), and Ewa Thompson, *Body, Mind, and Deconstruction*, 23 The Intercollegiate Review 25 (1987).

36. Joyce Appleby, *The American Heritage: The Heirs and the Disinherited*, 74 J. Amer. Hist. 798–813 (1987).

37. Scheiber, *supra* note 14, at 338.

38. Harry N. Scheiber, *The Constitution in the School Curriculum: A Proposal for the 1987 Bicentennial*, in B. R. Gifford, ed., History in the Schools 165–166 (New York, 1988). See also Scheiber, *supra* note 5. It should be noted that Scheiber is out of place among the radicals who dominate the OAH bicentennial volume. The same may be said of liberal historian Morton Keller. See his essay, *Powers and Rights: Two Centuries of American Constitutionalism*, 74 J. Amer. Hist. 675 (1987).

39. Friedman, *supra* note 14, at 467, 469, 471–472.

40. Nelson and Reid, *supra* note 20, at 193.

41. *Id.* at 194. The conservative scholar whom Nelson quotes is James McClellan.

42. *Id.* at 197.

43. William E. Nelson, *An Exchange on Critical Legal Studies*, 6 Law and History Rev. 161 (1988); Nelson and Reid, *supra* note 20, at 262.

44. Nelson, *supra* note 43, at 162.

45. William E. Nelson, *Reason and Compromise in the Establishment of the Constitution, 1787–1801*, 44 William and Mary Q. 458 (1987).

46. Nelson and Reid, *supra* note 20, at 288, 296, 302.

47. William T. Hutchinson, *The significance of the Constitution of the United States in the Teaching of American History*, 13 The Historian 3 (1950); Shirley A. Bill, *The Really Crucial Matter: Prosper Constitutional History*, 48 Mid-America 126 (1966); Calvin Woodard, *History, Legal History and Legal Education*, 53 Virginia L.R. 89 (1967); Calvin Woodard, *The Limits of Legal Realism*, 54 Virginia L.R. 689 (1968).

48. Alfred de Grazia, The Elements of Political Science 305 (New York, 1952).

49. Cf. Michael S. Moore, *The Constitution as Hard Law*, 6 Constitutional Commentary 51 (1989).

50. For illustrative purposes, consider: Clinton Rossiter, The American Quest 1790–1860 (New York, 1970); Donald G. Morgan, Congress and the Constitution: A Study in Responsibility (Cambridge, 1966); Raoul Berger, Congress v. The Supreme Court (Cambridge, 1969); Raoul Berger, Government by Judiciary: The Transformation of the Fourteenth Amendment (Cambridge, 1977); Charles Fairman, Reconstruction and Reunion: 1864–88 Part One (New York, 1971); Don E. Fehrenbacher, The Dred Scott Case: Its Significance in American Law and Politics (New York, 1978); Robert C. Palmer, *Liberties as Constitutional Provisions, 1776–1791*, in Robert C. Palmer and William E. Nelson, Liberty and Community: Constitution and Rights in the Early American Republic (New York, 1987); Forrest McDonald, Novus Ordo Seclorum: The Intellectual Origins

of the Constitution (Lawrence, 1985); G. Edward White, The American Judicial Tradition, 2 ed. (New York, 1988); Christopher Wolfe, The Rise of Modern Judicial Review (New York, 1986); Donald S. Lutz, The Origins of American Constitutionalism (Baton Rouge, 1988); Gary J. Jacobsohn, The Supreme Court and the Decline of Constitutional Aspiration (Totowa, 1985); Walter Berns, Taking the Constitution Seriously (New York, 1987).

51. Charles A. Lofgren, *Constitutional Scholarship: What Next?* 5 Constitutional Commentary 34 (1988).

52. Robert Faulkner, *Constitutional Scholarship: What Next?* 5 Constitutional Commentary 42–43 (1988).

53. Edward J. Erler, *Constitutional Scholarship: What Next?* 5 Constitutional Commentary 53 (1988).

54. Michael Zuckert, *Constitutional Scholarship: What Next?* 5 Constitutional Commentary 37 (1988).

55. Philip B. Kurland and Ralph Lerner, eds., 1 The Founders' Constitution xi (Chicago, 1987).

56. James H. Hutson, *The Constitution: An Economic Document?* in Leonard W. Levy and Dennis J. Mahoney, eds., The Framing and Ratification of the Constitution 259–270 (New York, 1987).

57. See Lance Banning, *Jeffersonian Ideology Revisited: Liberal and Classical Ideas in the New American Republic,* 43 William and Mary Q. 3 (1986).

58. Gordon S. Wood, The Creation of the American Republic 1776–1787 (Chapel Hill, 1969); Gordon S. Wood, *Rhetoric and Reality in the American Revolution,* 23 William and Mary Q. 20 (1966).

59. Peter S. Onuf, *Reflections on the Founding: Constitutional Historiography in Bicentennial Perspective,* 46 William and Mary Q. 347 (1989).

60. Gordon S. Wood, *Ideology and the Origins of Liberal America,* 44 William and Mary Q. 628, 631 (1987).

61. Cf. Thompson, *supra* note 35, at 25.

62. Gordon S. Wood, *Democracy and the Constitution,* in Robert A. Goldwin and William A. Schambra, eds., How Democratic Is the Constitution? 3–4 (Washington, 1980).

63. Gordon S. Wood, *The Fundamentalists and the Constitution,* New York Review of Books 39 (Feb. 18, 1988).

64. Jack N. Rakove, *The Madisonian Moment,* 55 Univ. of Chicago L.R. 302 (1988); Onuf, *supra* note 59, at 343.

65. Terence Ball and J. G. A. Pocock, eds., Conceptual Change and the Constitution 8–11 (Lawrence, 1988).

66. Onuf, *supra* note 59, at 343.

67. Wood, *supra* note 63, at 36. Wood says that although the Straussians do not understand "the process of history," their close textual readings have recovered meanings not seen by historians and have yielded historical insight.

68. Ralph Lerner, *The Constitution of the Thinking Revolutionary,* in Richard Beeman, Stephen Botein, and Edward C. Carter II, eds., Beyond Confederation: Origins of the Constitution and American National Identity 44–50 (Chapel Hill, 1987).

69. Thomas L. Pangle, The Spirit of Modern Republicanism: The Moral Vision of the American Founders and the Philosophy of Locke 1–4, 38 (Chicago, 1988).

70. John Patrick Diggins, *Language and History*, 17 Reviews in American History 1 (1989).

71. *Id.* at 5.

72. Daniel T. Rodgers, *Keywords: A Reply*, 49 J. of the History of Ideas 671 (1988). See Mark Olsen and Louis-Georges Harvey, *Contested Methods: Daniel T. Rodgers's 'Contested Truths,'* 49 J. of the History of Ideas 653 (1988).

73. Cf. Morton J. Horwitz, *Republicanism and Liberalism in American Constitutional Thought*, 29 William and Mary L.R. 57 (1987); Bruce A. Ackerman, *Discovering the Constitution*, 93 Yale L.J. 1013 (1984); Paul W. Kahn, *Reason and Will in the Origins of American Constitutionalism*, 98 Yale L.J. 449 (1989). Kahn says the communitarian ethos of republican political ideology "has swept constitutional theory." *Id.* at 511.

74. Cf. Appleby, *supra* note 36, at 811; James T. Kloppenberg, *The Virtues of Liberalism: Christianity, Republicanism, and Ethics in Early American Political Discourse*, 74 J. Amer. Hist. 32–33 (1987).

75. Michael Lienesch, New Order of the Ages: Time, the Constitution, and the Making of Modern American Political Thought 206–214 (Princeton, 1988).

76. Glen E. Thurow, *Judicial Review, Democracy, and the Rule of Law*, in Sarah B. Thurow, ed., Constitutionalism in America: The Constitution in Twentieth Century Politics 216–219 (Lanham, 1988); Thomas G. West, *Conservatives, Liberals, and the Founding: The Meaning of the Debate Over Natural Rights*, The Heritage Lectures No. 184, p. 7 (1989).

77. Herman Belz, *The Constitution and Reconstruction*, in Eric D. Anderson, and Alfred Moss, eds., The Facts of Reconstruction: Essays in Honor of John Hope Franklin (forthcoming, Baton Rouge).

78. Cf. Arthur Kinoy, *The Constitutional Right of Negro Freedom*, 21 Rutgers L.R. 387 (1967); G. Sidney Buchanan, The Quest for Freedom: A Legal History of the Thirteenth Amendment (Houston, 1976; reprinted from Houston L.R.); Robert J. Kaczorowski, The Politics of Judicial Interpretation: The Federal Courts, Department of Justice and Civil Rights 1866–1876 (New York, 1985); Robert J. Kaczorowski, *To Begin the Nation Anew: Congress, Citizenship, and Civil Rights After the Civil War*, 92 Amer. Hist. Rev. 45 (1987).

79. Vincent Gordon Harding, *Wrestling toward the Dawn: The Afro-American Freedom Movement and the Changing Constitution*, 74 J. Amer. Hist. 724 (1987). See also Stanley N. Katz, *The Strange Birth and Unlikely History of Constitutional Equality*, 75 J. Amer. Hist. 747 (1988).

80. Thurgood Marshall, *Reflections on the Bicentennial of the United States Constitution*, 101 Harvard L.R. 2–4 (1987).

81. Brief for Petitioner on Reargument, Patterson v. McLean Credit Union, No. 87–108, in the Supreme Court of the United States, October Term, 1987, p. 40; Barry Sullivan, *Historical Reconstruction, Reconstruction History, and the Proper Scope of Section 1981*, 98 Yale L.J. 547 (1989); Robert J. Kaczorowski, *The Enforcement Provisions of the Civil Rights Act of 1866: A Legislative History in*

Light of Runyon v. McCrary, 98 Yale L.J. 565 (1989). The argument against the latitudinarian reading of the Civil Rights Act of 1866 is presented in Brief for Respondent on Reargument, Patterson v. McLean Credit Union, No. 87–108, in the Supreme Court of the United States, October Term 1987, and in James McClellan, *The New Liberty of Contract Under the 13th Amendment: The Case Against Runyon v. McCrary*, 3 Benchmark 279 (1987).

82. Cf. Michael P. Zuckert, *Completing the Constitution: The Thirteenth Amendment*, 4 Constitutional Commentary 259 (1987); Michael P. Zuckert, *Congressional Power Under the Fourteenth Amendment—The Original Understanding of Section Five*, 3 Constitutional Commentary 123 (1986); Earl Maltz, *Reconstruction Without Revolution: Republican Civil Rights Theory in the Era of the Fourteenth Amendment*, 24 Houston L.R. 221 (1986); Earl Maltz, *Fourteenth Amendment Concepts in the Antebellum Era*, 32 Amer. J. Legal Hist. 305 (1988); Herman Belz, *The Civil War Amendments to the Constitution: The Relevance of Original Intent*, 5 Constitutional Commentary 115 (1988); Michael Les Benedict, Civil Rights and Civil Liberties (Washington, 1987); William E. Nelson, The Fourteenth Amendment: From Political Principle to Judicial Doctrine (Cambridge, 1988).

83. Maltz, *Reconstruction Without Revolution, supra* note 82, at 278.

84. Nelson, *supra* note 82, at 8.

85. Cf. Alfred H. Kelly and Winfred A. Harbison, The American Constitution: Its Origins and Development (New York, 1948).

86. Cf. Michael E. Parrish, *The Great Depression, the New Deal, and the American Legal Order*, 59 Washington L.R. 723 (1984); Robert Eden, ed., The New Deal and Its Legacy: Critique and Reappraisal (Westport, 1989); Richard A. Harris and Sidney M. Milkis, eds., Remaking American Politics (Boulder, 1989).

87. Cf. Theodore M. Lowi, The Personal President: Power Invested, Promise Unfulfilled (Ithaca, 1985); Sidney M. Milkis, *The Presidency, Policy Reform, and the Rise of Administrative Politics*, in Harris and Milkis, *supra* note 86, at 146; John A. Rohr, To Run a Constitution: The Legitimacy of the Administrative State (Lawrence, 1986).

88. William Lasser, The Limits of Judicial Power: The Supreme Court in American Politics 254–259 (Chapel Hill, 1988). Lasser argues that criticism of Supreme Court decisions in times of crisis, as in the Court-packing episode, implies that the cases in question would have been decided correctly by other judges. The criticism thus assumes that there is a mode of constitutional interpretation which if practiced by honest judges with an understanding of the Constitution is legitimate and appropriate. Lasser regards this as a permanent basis for the power of the Supreme Court.

89. Martin Shapiro, *The Supreme Court from Warren to Burger*, in Anthony King, ed., The New American Political System 179–211 (Washington, 1978); Martin Shapiro, *Fathers and Sons: The Court, The Commentators, and the Search for Values*, in Vincent Blasi, ed., The Burger Court: The Counter-Revolution That Wasn't 218–240 (New Haven, 1983); Martin Shapiro, *The Supreme Court's "Return" to Economic Regulation*, 1 Studies in American Political Development 91–94 (1986).

90. Cf. Herbert Wechsler, *Toward Neutral Principles of Constitutional Law*, 73

Harvard L.R. 1 (1959); Alexander M. Bickel, The Least Dangerous Branch (Indianapolis, 1962).

91. John Hart Ely, Democracy and Distrust: A Theory of Judicial Review (Cambridge, 1980); Jesse Choper, Judicial Review and the National Political Process (Chicago, 1980).

92. Thomas C. Grey, *Do We Have an Unwritten Constitution?* 27 Stanford L.R. 703 (1975); Thomas C. Grey, *Origins of the Unwritten Constitution: Fundamental Law in American Revolutionary Thought*, 30 Stanford L.R. 843 (1978).

93. The nomenclature is provided in Ely, *supra* note 91.

94. Wolfe, *supra* note 50, at 11.

95. Gary L. McDowell, Curbing the Courts: The Constitution and the Limits of Judicial Power 13–48 (Baton Rouge, 1988), The quoted material is at p. 27.

96. Harry M. Clor, *Judicial Statesmanship and Constitutional Interpretation*, 26 South Texas L.J. 397, 400–406, 416, 432–433 (1985). See also John Agresto, The Supreme Court and Constitutional Democracy (Ithaca, 1984); Gary L. Jacobsohn, Pragmatism, Statesmanship, and the Supreme Court (Ithaca, 1977); Gary L. Jacobsohn, The Supreme Court and the Decline of Constitutional Aspiration (Totowa, 1986); Sotirios A. Barber, On What the Constitution Means (Baltimore 1984). The judicial statesmanship argument is criticized in Matthew J. Franck, *Statesmanship and the Judiciary*, 51 Review of Politics 510 (1989).

97. Sylvia Snowiss, *From Fundamental Law to Supreme Law of the Land: A Reinterpretation of the Origin of Judicial Review*, 2 Studies in American Political Development 1–67 (1987).

98. H. Jefferson Powell, *The Original Understanding of Original Intent*, 98 Harvard L.R. 885 (1985). For a contrary view, see Charles A. Lofgren, *The Original Understanding of Original Intent?* 5 Constitutional Commentary 77 (1988), and Clinton, *supra* note 7, at 1186–1197.

99. Kahn, *supra* note 73, at 449.

100. Leonard W. Levy, Original Intent and the Framers' Constitution xiv, 310, 398 (New York, 1988). Levy's interpretation of judicial review is reflected in Melvin I. Urofsky, A March of Liberty: A Constitutional History of the United States (New York, 1988).

Although condemning original-intent jurisprudence, Levy himself fashions a civil libertarianism of original intent. Insofar as his constitutional interpretation is guided by consistent principle, it is a Bill-of-Rights libertarianism based on the constitutional text, which he believes was intended by the Framers to be interpreted expansively in favor of the natural rights of individuals. He employs a theory of original intent in arguing, for example, that the Framers left crucial terms undefined so they could be given the widest possible interpretation, and in asserting that in the Ninth Amendment they put their "thumbs down on the 'rights' side of the scales that weigh rights against powers." (p. 392).

101. Belz, *supra* note 82.

102. Clinton, *supra* note 7.

103. Robert Eden, *Tocqueville on Political Realignment and Constitutional Forms*, 48 Review of Politics 349 (1986).

104. H. Jefferson Powell, *Constitutional Law as Though the Constitution Mattered*, 1986 Duke L.J. 915.

105. G. Edward White, *Recapturing New Deal Lawyers*, 102 Harvard L.R. 518 (1988).

106. Powell, *supra* note 104, at 915.

107. Ronald L. K. Collins, *The Historian as Judge*, 15 Reviews in Amer. Hist. 193, 196 (1987).

108. Walter F. Murphy, James E. Fleming, and William F. Harris, II, American Constitutional Interpretation (Mineola, 1986).

109. Powell, *supra* note 104, at 925–926.

110. Karl Llewellyn, *The Constitution as an Institution*, 74 Columbia L.R. 1 (1934).

111. William F. Harris, II, *Bonding Word and Polity: The Logic of American Constitutionalism*, 76 Amer. Pol. Sci. Rev. 34 (1982).

112. Edward S. Corwin, *Some Probable Repercussions of 'Nira' on Our Constitutional System*, 72 Annals of the American Academy of Pol. and Soc. Science 139–144 (1934). See also Corwin, *Standpoint in Constitutional Law*, Bacon Lectures on the Constitution of the United States 1928–1938 (Boston, 1939).

113. Wood, *supra* note 63, at 40.

114. Urofsky, *supra* note 100. Urofsky does not appear to regard legal logic and constitutional doctrine as a mystification or glossing of power, according to the radical history rationale.

115. Wood, *supra* note 63, at 39–40.

116. *Id.* at 37.

117. Ackerman, *supra* note 73, at 1062. Ackerman defines a convention in the sense of Article V as "an assembly whose right to propose a new constitutional solution is open to substantial good-faith legal doubt," but which nevertheless "proposes to ratify these proposals by a procedure that plainly departs from preexisting constitutional understandings." *Id.* at 1018. The Reconstruction amendments are seen as the result of the Thirty-ninth Congress acting as a constitutional convention, and the election of 1936 and New Deal legislation are counted as a constitutional amendment that repudiated laissez-faire capitalism.

118. *Id.* at 1013, 1022–1023, 1062, 1065, 1071.

119. *Id.* at 1070.

120. See the criticism in David Chang, *Conflict, Coherence, and Constitutional Intent*, 72 Iowa L.R. 753 (1987).

121. Russell L. Caplan, Constitutional Brinkmanship: Amending the Constitution by National Convention vii–xi (New York, 1988).

122 Gary C. Leedes, The Meaning of the Constitution: An Interdisciplinary Study of Legal Theory ix, 14 (Millwood, 1986).

123. William M. Wiecek, Liberty Under Law: The Supreme Court in American Life 185–186 (Baltimore, 1988).

124. David P. Currie, The Constitution in the Supreme Court: The First Hundred Years 1789–1888 xi–xiii, 455 (Chicago, 1985).

125. Richard Hodder-Williams, *The Constitution (1787) and Modern American*

Government, in Vernon Bogdanor, ed., Constitutions in Democratic Politics 100 (Gower, Eng., 1988).

126. Kammen, *supra* note 8, at 24, 38.
127. The Federalist, Edward Mead Earle Ed. 328–329 (New York, 1938).
128. Martin Spencer, *Rule of Law in America,* 14 Southern Q. 333 (1976).

9

History, Theory, and the Constitution

On the occasion of this journal's tenth anniversary, readers may find profit in recalling two seminal essays on the American Constitution that may be thought of as providing an intellectual provenance for the kind of scholarship that *Constitutional Commentary* seeks to encourage. In 1934, in the midst of the Great Depression, Karl Llewellyn and Edward S. Corwin, two leading representatives of legal liberalism, assayed the nature and tendency of American constitutionalism. Llewellyn, writing with the explicit intent of laying "the foundation for an intelligent reconstruction of our constitutional law theory," offered an empirical description of the Constitution that can be regarded as a possible model for the study of constitutional history.[1] Corwin, writing as a historian of the Supreme Court and constitutional law, relied on theory to explain the significance of the New Deal for the constitutional order. Although approaching their subject from the differing standpoints of theory and history respectively, each scholar's account implicated the other's discipline.

The purpose of the present essay is to consider historical and theoretical perspectives in writing about the Constitution. It is intended to be exploratory and suggestive, continuing in a modest way a scholarly inquiry begun over two decades ago by Charles A. Miller in his illuminating study, *The Supreme Court and the Uses of History*.[2] To rely on history in constitutional adjudication raises a question about historiographical method. As Miller noted, it also poses a problem in legal theory.[3] Miller's interest in the problem was provoked in part by changes in race relations in the 1960s, which constituted a chasm in history and required major revision in constitutional law and theory.[4] Since then a revival of interest in original-intent jurisprudence has occurred that has stimulated further consideration of the role of history in constitutional and legal theory. At the same time, the historical profession has responded to political and social change, including specific developments in constitutional law, by becoming increasingly sensitive to normative and theoretical concerns.[5]

Part I of this essay will briefly review Llewellyn's and Corwin's analyses of the Constitution, which have intrinsic historical importance and are worthy of reflection and contemplation. Parts II and III of the essay will then examine some recent writing in constitutional history and theory, illustrating the tendency toward reciprocal involvement of each field in the other's disciplinary metier. While the inquiry seeks to clarify the nature of the knowledge and understanding of the Constitution which Americans require to carry on their political life, its approach is mainly that of historical description.

I

Rejecting the orthodox view that written and unwritten constitutions were fundamentally different in nature, Karl Llewellyn argued that the United States Constitution was "in essence not a document, but a living institution built (historically, genetically) in first instance *around* a particular Document."[6] The United States, he said, had "the sort of constitution loosely designated as 'unwritten.' "[7] It consisted of existing political, governmental, and legal institutions and practices, and operated through the agency of "specialists in governing," "interested groups," and the "general public."[8] Llewellyn acknowledged that the constitutional text had "a little influence," but only "*[w]here it makes no important difference which way the decision goes.*"[9] The "first principle of a sane theory of our constitutional law," he asserted, was that "[w]herever there are today established practices 'under' or 'in accordance with' the Document, *it is only the practice which can legitimize the words as still being part of our going Constitution. It is not the words which legitimize the practice.*"[10]

If governmental practice without reference to the document was the standard of constitutional legitimacy, what then became of the Constitution as a fundamental law limiting government? Where was the line to be drawn defining principles and institutions basic to the whole? Llewellyn recognized the problem, but it is hard to see how he provided a satisfactory answer. Neither in his empirical description nor in his theory were there clear lines, limits, or boundaries distinguishing the "working constitution" from "mere working government." Llewellyn wrote: "[w]hatever one takes as being this working Constitution, he will find the edges of his chosen material not sharp, but penumbra-like. And the penumbra will of necessity be in constant flux."[11] When questions arose in "the penumbra-border of the Constitution" as to whether a change should be approved, recourse could not be had to a definite institution because none was definite on the point at issue. "The appeal must therefore be . . . to a normative *ideal* of what the institution in question *should* be and do," Llewellyn reasoned.[12] In like manner, explaining how the Constitution restrained the power of government officials, he said it was "the job of the [Supreme] Court . . . to *control* the course of governmental practice by reference to an ideal not found in that practice, but in the nature of what our government should be."[13] To rely on "the language of the Document and its 'intent' " as a standard for constitutional interpretation, Llewellyn concluded, in contrast to the "development-tendency of existing and formative practice," was to "offer a basis utterly self-inconsistent, unworkable, and heavy with the fragrance of a charnel-house."[14]

Edward S. Corwin presented a similar assessment of the tendency of American constitutionalism. Analyzing the National Industrial Recovery Act as the cynosure of the New Deal, Corwin described the Act as "declaratory . . . of certain legal principles which it is hoped will prove to be adapted to the present economic situation of the United States." But the principles in this "declaratory statute" were not in the Constitution, or at least they received little illumination from the twenty or so words in the text that Corwin said had any bearing on the subject. "The problem," he observed, "is one rather of Constitutional law and theory."[15]

Corwin stated that the N.I.R.A. rested on the theory of "the solidarity of American business" and the power of Congress to regulate "the whole business structure." It was not based on the Commerce Clause, which limited congressional power to commerce among the states, nor on the traditional theory that the national government had only the powers clearly delegated to it. To justify the statute in constitutional theory, Corwin invoked history. He argued that the commerce power in fact had never been confined to regulating acts of commerce among the states, but extended to noncommercial matters insofar as it included the safeguarding of commerce. A major effect of the N.I.R.A., a form of centralized economic regulation, was to destroy the federal system by driving the states from the field of economic regulation or subordinating their powers to the supreme power of Congress. Again Corwin's justification of this doctrinal development was historical: "in the field of business relations state power has long been moribund, so that the N.I.R.A. simply recognizes and gives effect to a Constitutional theory which is the counterpart of a condition already long established in the facts of our everyday economic life."[16]

In Corwin's view, the New Deal signified a revolution in the understanding of the basic constitutional principles of federalism, judicial review, and the separation of powers.[17] Underlying these theoretical changes, and linking his analysis both to Llewellyn's assessment and to constitutional theory a half century later, was Corwin's untroubled assumption that "the Constitution of the United States can accommodate itself to the revolution which the N.I.R.A. undoubtedly does spell." Ultimately Corwin perceived "a change in the character of the Constitution itself." In this he saw a historical parallel between English and American constitutionalism. In 1400 Magna Carta was the English Constitution in great part, yet by 1700 that document "had been absorbed into a vast complexus of environing institutions." The same thing was now happening to the American Constitution. The Constitution, Corwin reasoned, would become absorbed into the governmental revolution that the New Deal augured, and Americans' attitude toward the Constitution "will consequently become less legalistic and more political. We shall value it for the aid it lends to considered social purpose, not as a lawyers' document." Corwin thus described a transforming historical development with far-reaching theoretical consequences.[18]

Corwin and Llewellyn implicate history in the broadest sense in their view of momentous political and social change signaling the decline of legal-formalist constitutionalism and the advent of the unwritten constitution as a conceptual framework of American government. Consisting of existing governmental institutions and practices shaped by social forces, the unwritten constitution represented the historicization of the constitutional text. As a theoretical construct, it explained what happens to a charter of fundamental law under the ravages of time. The Constitution becomes, in the characterization later employed by Supreme Court Justice Felix Frankfurter, "a stream of history."[19] To know and understand what the Constitution is, therefore, requires historical inquiry, and a different type of inquiry from that associated with a written constitution. The latter entails an understanding of history as discrete events and the objective, immanent meaning and intent of specific actions and decisions. Unwritten, political constitutionalism, in contrast, depends upon a concept of history as ongoing process, growth, and development.[20]

As constitutional theory implicates history, so any account of constitutional history rests on certain theoretical assumptions. In order to decide what kind of evidence to consult, it is necessary to have in mind an idea of the nature and scope of the Constitution, or what constitutes it. Furthermore, the purpose of constitutional history, like any other historical inquiry, may involve normative concerns raising questions of political theory and moral philosophy. Concerned as it is with knowledge of past decisions and actions that may have a direct bearing on questions of policy, constitutional history may be more subject to normative-theoretical demands than scholarship in fields that have less immediate practical import.

Rereading the essays of Llewellyn and Corwin half a century later naturally invites reflection on the accuracy of their assessment of American constitutionalism. Do they offer, in essence, a prolegomenon to contemporary constitutional scholarship?

In many respects Corwin and Llewellyn appear as far-sighted, perspicacious observers. A generation after they described the triumph of political constitutionalism over declaratory jurisprudence and legal formalism, public law scholars generally accepted political jurisprudence in theoretical and empirical terms.[21] Even the process jurisprudence of the 1940s and 1950s, which was a reaction to legal realism, conceded the substantially political nature of constitutional adjudication.[22] Since Corwin and Llewellyn wrote, moreover, several scholars have elaborated the concept of an unwritten constitution in explaining the nature of American constitutionalism.[23] And it seems unnecessary to add that the project of reconstructing constitutional theory, initiated especially by Llewellyn with his prescient reference to penumbras in constant flux, has flourished in recent years as legal commentators try to rationalize the expansion of judicial policy making.[24]

Yet there is evidence that legal-formalist constitutionalism, which Llewellyn and Corwin considered to be historically exhausted, has not only persisted in the post-New Deal era, but has experienced something of a revival.[25] Perhaps the clearest indication of formalist survival is the aggrandizement of constitutional law as an instrument of judicial governance. One can assume of course that despite formal appearances all constitutional adjudication is politically willful and subjective. But then it becomes necessary to ask why legal-juridical forms must be maintained. Why does not the Supreme Court candidly acknowledge, for example, that its decisions are based on an unwritten constitution and laws when, in the opinion of many scholars, this is so obviously the case?[26] Perhaps the reason is that principles, forms, and procedures are essential elements of constitutionalism. Accordingly the formal, written Constitution continues to have great practical importance in shaping the course of American political life.[27]

The resuscitation of original-intent thinking, which began in the 1970s, occurred *when* it did because of substantive objections in the society to many Supreme Court decisions in the previous decade. The reasons *why* it occurred, however, concern the very nature of constitutional government in the United States. In the deepest sense the concept of Framers' intent as an approach to constitutional adjudication, and the corollary interpretive method of textualism, reflects the fact that the American Constitution is not simply or primarily an ongoing historical process. It is a written document, adopted at a particular point in history (and subsequently amended), that signifies political action and purpose of the most fundamental sort, namely, the founding of a regime. Critics of original intent, citing epistemological and other difficulties, labor mightily to discount if not dismiss the solid grounding in empirical fact on which this approach to constitutional decision making rests. They labor in vain, however, because the history of the making of the Constitution, abundantly documented despite inevitable lacunae, prevents it from being dissolved into some immemorial past—or transformed into an assemblage of existing political institutions and practices.

Writing before the revival of original-intent jurisprudence, Charles Miller observed:

> Neither the clinical destruction of the Court's use of history through legal scholarship nor outright advocacy of forward-looking decisions has been able to tear up traditions of constitutional and judicial thinking deeply rooted in the American political culture. The ties of the Constitution are to the past, and when history calls the justices strain to listen.[28]

A generation later Paul Kahn, surveying the history of constitutional theory, made the same point in stating that constitutional law is a historical enterprise: "In recognizing its authority, citizens recognize the continuity of the past with the present. In respecting the Constitution as law, they respect the authority of past political acts over present community preferences."[29]

If Llewellyn and Corwin failed to appreciate the necessity and enduring appeal of legal-formalist elements in the regime, their analyses are nevertheless instructive for the reflection they provoke on history and theory in constitutional interpretation. Both historical knowledge of the purpose of the Constitution, and theoretical understanding of basic constitutional principles, are essential to maintaining the American regime as a lawful system of government. History and theory as separate disciplines contribute to constitutional maintenance. Yet the question of the scope and precise limits of the two fields warrants further investigation. A review of some recent writings on the Constitution suggests a more complicated interdisciplinary tendency in which practitioners in each field employ the methods and engage some of the concerns of the other.

II

History is usually thought of as a nontheoretical inquiry, in comparison with philosophy, law, and political science, all of which it is allied with in constitutional scholarship. Historians like to talk about evidence and methods; they regard theory as speculative and hypothetical. This restraint is warranted, for theory is difficult to define and hard to know how to use in a disciplined way. Theory can refer to systematically organized knowledge that is applicable in a variety of circumstances, to a set of assumptions, principles, and rules of procedure devised to analyze, predict, or explain the nature or behavior of a set of phenomena, or simply to abstract reasoning and speculation. As used in public law scholarship, theory has a decidedly normative connotation. It expresses opinion and belief about what the Constitution and the laws ought to be, rather than empirical description of what they are or were in the past. Indeed, contemporary legal commentary has been described as pervasively normative in the sense of being grounded in various conceptions of justice.[30]

History that aims at an objective factual account of past events is often considered to be untheoretical antiquarianism.[31] Yet in a strict sense any type of historical inquiry rests on theoretical assumptions. In his attack on original-intent historicism, Jacobus ten Broek noted that the historical approach rests on logic, or theory. It assumes that the intent of a constitutional provision can be discovered by identifying matters that demanded treatment by constitution makers, on the theory that ideas which were part of the climate of opinion or which resulted from current problems must have been in the minds of the authors of the text.[32] The purpose of inquiries into legal history, moreover, is often to resolve contemporary legal controversies.

William Nelson, a liberal legal historian, has argued that conservative original-intent scholars on the one hand and radical devotees of critical legal studies on the other use history to resolve present problems.[33] Yet if liberal historians have been unsuccessful in illuminating legal policy questions, it has not been for want of trying. A glance at recent legal historiography suggests that liberal scholars, no less than other historians, have been theoretically inclined in the sense of joining history with normative philosophical considerations to help solve current problems.

The tradition of external legal history, defined in relation to social and economic forces rather than the formal doctrines of internal legal history, is self-consciously instrumental. James Willard Hurst, the founder of law-and-society historiography, took for granted the reformist ends of social science and legal realism in the 1930s in his effort to re-direct legal history away from technical professional concerns. Hurst viewed law as a social institution, an instrument of individual, group, and community purpose rather than a self-contained body of autonomous principles and rules. Hurstian legal history aimed at measuring the actual past performance of government against man's potential for rational control of his environment and decision making. It provided a standard by which the present generation of lawyers could determine the circumstances that best promoted the intelligent direction of society in favor of growth.[34]

Normative moral ends were more explicitly avowed in Paul Murphy's appeal in the early 1960s to historians to reclaim the field of constitutional history from lawyers and political scientists. Issuing a kind of liberal manifesto for the era of judicial activism that was then beginning, Murphy advocated the use of history to promote social change. The theoretical basis of the project he envisioned was the assumption that the judicial function tends naturally to historical study to discover the precise locus of constitutional language, and to ascertain its thrust, implications, and overall justification. Murphy proposed a "new role" for constitutional history "as an auxiliary tool for the jurist, not for 'the consecration of an already established order of things,' but for a new order seeking a new level of equal rights and social justice through law."[35]

In the 1970s radical historians, updating the theory of legal realism, began to challenge the normative perspective of liberal legal history. To proponents of critical legal studies, the work of the Hurst school appeared as pragmatic functionalism signifying political acceptance of the existing order. In an early statement of the radical argument, Morton Horwitz asserted that legal history should no longer be content with justifying the world as it is, but should penetrate the distinction between law and politics. It should view jurisprudential change as the product of social forces and political struggle.[36] In more mature form this argument became an explicit plea for historians to take up questions of legal and political theory. According to Horwitz, legal theory inevitably uses history to show how existing arrangements were created and legitimized. By the same token, historical interpretation serves as a proxy for more general controversies over political theory. When, for example, historians argue over whether liberalism or republicanism was the ideology of the American Revolution, they are really debating the primacy of politics and substantive visions of the good society. "It is time for us to bridge the chasm between legal theory and legal history," Horwitz urges.[37]

Robert Gordon contends that history in general liberates the political imagination by revealing suppressed alternatives, and radical history discloses the fact that the rule of law is really "a teeming jungle of plural, contradictory, orders struggling for recognition and dominance." In the politics of radical reformation, the role of history is "to describe as concretely as possible how constraints upon freedom get socially manufactured and how people acting collectively through politics sometimes succeed and sometimes fail in breaking through the constraints."[38] According to Gordon, radical legal history teaches the "political lesson" that there exist, "immanent in such familiar ideals and institutions as private property and free contract, possibilities for transforming the society and economy in more democratic and egalitarian . . . directions."[39]

The result of uniting history and theory can be seen in the bicentennial symposium of the Organization of American Historians. Repudiating the traditional concern of constitutional history with constitutional maintenance, the symposium authors build their accounts around the idea of constitutional aspiration popular among legal theorists. Undertaking "the social construction of constitutional history," they describe how "disinherited groups" "have made aspirations to a life free from legally recognized hierarchies—to a life without the badges and incidents of slavery—into a superconstitution that has taken precedence over any merely transitory determination of constitutional meaning." The effect of this reconstruction of constitutional history, speculates Hendrik Hartog, may be the rejection of "notions of a distinctly legal or constitutional history, abandoning a perspective founded on the American Constitution's separation from the indeterminacies of American social and political history."[40]

Despite its growing professional acceptance, the trend toward explicitly normative historiography has provoked dissent. The constitutional historian Alfred Kelly, after first-hand experience using history to promote legal reform in the school desegregation cases, condemned the types of history found in constitutional adjudication. This consisted of a priori history, created by judicial fiat, and law-office history aimed at selection of data favorable to a position. Questioning whether court-oriented history and scholarly history were reconcilable, Kelly held that truth in history was independent of its usefulness.[41] Similarly Charles Miller, though fully sensitive to the normative use of history to transmit values, cautioned against reliance on ideologically charged "ongoing" history by the Supreme Court. Miller declared: "The Supreme Court as a whole cannot indulge in historical fabrication without thereby appearing to approve the deterioration of truth as a criterion for communication in public affairs. . . . where it matters most to society, it matters most that the story be a true one."[42]

A recent convert to nontheoretical, objective history is William Nelson, who concedes the failure of his own efforts to show the utility of legal history in contemporary legal analysis. Criticizing the normative-theoretical bent of both the original-intent school and the critical legal studies movement, he appeals to a pure, genuinely historical inquiry that studies the past for its own sake.[43] Michael Les Benedict similarly sees a clear distinction between genuine historical inquiry and legal scholarship that uses historical materials. The legal scholar is committed to settling a policy question and uses judicially tested rules of evidence to evaluate evidence. The historian seeks to explain change over time, showing how events occurred to produce the present state of affairs. Benedict observes further that legal scholarship using history tends toward advocacy, while historical inquiry eschews judgment and accepts ambiguities in the evidence. It does not force the evidence to yield a definite conclusion.[44]

Benedict's historiographical analysis may be more heuristic than empirical. While disavowing a normative task for history, he himself employs theoretical premises. Historians assume, he tells us, that historical actors do not have firm intentions and clear understandings about events they are involved in. Historians assume further that understandings will change over time and intentions will go awry.[45] Benedict's "historical principles of analysis" implicate a philosophy of history that is no less important for being presented in a theoretically modest way.

III

If it is hard to disentangle history from philosophy, it is equally difficult to extricate theory from the toils of history. At first glance the pursuit of legal theory, in its eager embrace of moral philosophy, seems remote from the pedestrian factuality of history. History must nevertheless be taken into account, for constitutional and legal theorists recognize that their normative arguments will gain in persuasiveness if supported by evidence of the actual experience of human thought and action in the past.

Theory, including political science, is integral to American constitutionalism. At the start of the twentieth century constitutional theory became preoccupied with the justification of judicial review, the famous "countermajoritarian difficulty" which inspired a rich body of criticism through the 1960s.[46] In the past two decades constitutional theorizing has assumed a new level of urgency. This is in large part a response to the historicist challenge to judicial activism thrown down by the proponents of original-intent jurisprudence. William Wiecek notes that the coherence of constitutional theory disintegrated in the 1980s as debate focused on the Framers' intent and the use of history in constitutional adjudication.[47] The fight over the Bork nomination in 1987 signified fundamental conflict over constitutional philosophy and theory.[48]

The varieties of constitutional theory can be bewildering.[49] For present purposes it is sufficient to note the basic distinction between those who appeal to the Constitution as an authoritative historical document having a substantially fixed, objective meaning, and those who conceive of the Constitution as a text of largely symbolic import that enables interpreters to appeal elsewhere for authority to decide constitutional questions. We shall note the response of representative theorists on both sides of this distinction to the fundamental requirement that history be taken into account in constitutional interpretation.

Radical historicism figures prominently in the writing of several theorists who adopt the second of these views, and who can be considered in the "fundamental values" school. The defining feature of radical historicism is the idea that the Constitution, although it has a history, never has a historical meaning, but always and only a current meaning.

In the theory of Ronald Dworkin, for example, law is the rights and duties that flow from past collective decisions. Judges are not required, however, to understand the law they enforce as continuous and consistent in principle with the law of the past. "Law as integrity," he explains, "begins in the present and pursues the past only so far as and in the way its contemporary focus dictates." It does not aim to recapture the ideals or practical purposes of those who created it.[50] Hercules, Dworkin's fabled judge-interpreter, seeks in statutory and constitutional construction "to make the best he can of this continuing story [i.e. the life of the statute or constitution], and his interpretation therefore changes as the story develops." Making the story the best it can be, Hercules "interprets history in motion."[51] Dworkin rejects the historical approach of original-intent interpretivism because it makes the Framers' mental state decisive in reading the abstract language of the Constitution. It thus denies that the Constitution expresses principles. Asserting that constitutional principles do not stop "where some historical statesman's time, imagination, and interest stopped," Dworkin avows a "thoughtful" historicism that retrieves the Framers' abstract convictions and asks how they can be best understood in contemporary terms.[52]

David Richards argues similarly that legal interpretation is a form of historical reconstruction by which a community understands itself as a legal tradition. According to Richards, sound legal interpretation requires critical historiography, in contrast to the providential and mythical history often found in legal arguments. Richards attacks Raoul Berger's original-intent historicism as an abuse of critical historiography because it does not fit the available data. Berger's history is flawed as a theory of interpretation because it identifies the meaning of the Constitution with the Framers' subjective intent. It is also inadequate as political theory because it rests on an indefensible notion of popular sovereignty.[53] Richards advocates a type of historical reconstruction in which the facts bearing on the central texts of the legal tradition are used to provide the best theory of the values constituting the tradition.[54] "[G]ood legal interpretation," he declares, "requires that history and moral philosophy be practiced together."[55] But in Richards's scheme the meaning of a political theory or constitutional principle is never something objective to be discovered in the past; it is a contemporary philosophical conception. He concludes that constitutional interpretation is best understood "as the imputation of reasonable purposes to the text and history of the Constitution."[56]

A different concept of history operates in the theory of constitutional aspiration. As seen in the writings of Sotirios Barber and Walter F. Murphy, this historical understanding is substantially different from radical historicism in a philosophical sense, although in programmatic terms the difference may be only slight. Barber's theory of aspirational constitutionalism rests on the proposition that the Constitution has a meaning—in the past, presumably, as well as in the present—that is independent of what any interpreter might want it to mean.[57] Affirming natural law principles, Barber rejects the relativist position, which denies this independent meaning and holds that a constitutional principle means different things at different times. Historical relativism cannot comprehend the Constitution as supreme law, a concept that assumes some values are fundamental and transhistorical.[58] At the same time, Barber avoids the pole of positivistic conventionalism. He argues that the Constitution embodies the nation's traditions, not simply its history in the sense of the indiscriminate past. Tradition in this view is different from the past. It is a normative theory of what we stand for and what has been best in us as a people.[59]

Aspirational historicism rejects original-intent historicism, with its focus on a single, discoverable intent and the specific ideas of the Framers as the key to understanding the meaning of constitutional principles.[60] Aspirational theorists nevertheless recognize the significance of empirical research and find examples of constitutional aspiration in history.[61] The work of Walter F. Murphy has been described as a natural law theory, built largely out of historical materials of law and politics in action, that finds a coherent vision of the lessons of constitutional history.[62]

A more astringent theory of constitutional aspiration seeks to recover the meaning of constitutional principles as the Framers understood them. In this historical outlook, constitutional concepts are not
merely symbolic abstractions that permit boundless interpretive possibilities for those who would improve on the work of the Founders.[63]
Gary Jacobsohn, for example, holds that the Constitution embodies our
aspirations, but he rejects the idea that to be supreme it must always
be "reaffirmed as descriptive of our best current conception of an ideal
state of affairs."[64] Analyzing Lincoln's statesmanship as the preeminent example of constitutional aspiration, Jacobsohn emphasizes Lincoln's interpretation of the Constitution in relation to the moral theory
of the Founders. "Only in the framework of this particular association," he reasons, "may the Constitution be understood to embody the
nation's aspirations."[65] Rejecting both the undisciplined subjectivism
of unwritten constitutionalism and the parsimonious positivism of
original-intent historicism, Jacobsohn understands the Constitution as
"flow[ing] out of a coherent and knowable, not arbitrary or ever-muta-
ble, set of philosophic presuppositions."[66]

The theoretical writing of Hadley Arkes further illustrates what we
may refer to as a nonhistoricist historical inquiry aimed at understanding constitutional principles as the Framers understood them.[67] According to Arkes, in order to defend, justify, and preserve the
Constitution it is necessary to establish its essential character or meaning. This is not a historicist meaning that changes with the passing
generations; it is a philosophical meaning and moral understanding,
grounded in modern natural rights theory, that can be grasped again.
"To restore those understandings is not to engage in a quaint project in
'historical' reconstruction," Arkes observes. It is a task of philosophical
recovery and reflection on principles that have a timeless historical existence. The purpose of this type of inquiry, Arkes writes, is "to recall
the arguments of the Founders themselves in order to restore" their
original understanding that "it was necessary to move . . . beyond the
text of the Constitution to the principles of right and wrong that stood
antecedent to the Constitution."[68] Arkes proposes "to state anew, and
perhaps state more fully, the issues that were raised" in the debate
over the Constitution and the Bill of Rights. In order to apply the Constitution in practical cases and preserve and perfect constitutional government, he declares, "[t]here is a need to know again what was
known by these men."[69]

It is generally agreed that the Framers were natural law thinkers
who relied on modern natural rights theory. Sound historical method,
in order to understand the Framers as they understood themselves,
should therefore be open to the possibility that philosophical truth or

moral reality exists.[70] This historical attitude is disputed by radical historicism on the left (informed by pragmatism and cognitive relativism), and by original-intent historicism on the right (informed by legal positivism).

It is ironic that while originalist scholars have forced legal theorists to take history into account, they have been somewhat reticent about the type of historical thinking that original-intent jurisprudence requires. The writings of Raoul Berger, the most prolific originalist legal historian, appear to rest on the assumption that historical facts are objectively knowable, that the past exists independently of the way it is interpreted and does not change, and that applying the past to the present is simply a matter of getting the historical facts straight.[71] Whether this approach to history is sound is not the issue, or at least it is not an issue that originalist scholars feel obliged to discuss.[72] Their task rather has been to explain in normative terms why constitutional original intent, which they assume can be ascertained as readily as the purpose or intent of any other historical event or idea, should be relied on in constitutional adjudication.

The reasons for employing original intent include considerations of democratic political theory, the rule of law, neutrality in judicial decision making, and governmental flexibility and responsiveness. According to Earl Maltz, originalism and original intent are labels for a set of conventions reflecting a political theory about the judicial function. Maltz argues that modern theory, not traditionalism or an obligation to the past, requires fidelity to Framer intent.[73] Thus, although original-intent thinking is in some sense historical by definition, there is an element of truth in John Phillip Reid's assertion that original-intent jurisprudence is more accurately seen as a rejection of judicial activism, rather than "a respect for constitutional meaning discovered through the discipline of history."[74]

The best known recent work of originalist scholarship, Robert H. Bork's *The Tempting of America*,[75] presents very little, if any, historical evidence that original intent was ever a practical and effective method of constitutional adjudication. Bork's theory of judging is not supported by his history, which is a tale of judicial legislation from John Marshall to Thurgood Marshall.[76] A more illuminating account written from an original-intent point of view is Christopher Wolfe's *The Rise of Modern Judicial Review*.[77]

Wolfe attempts to show that interpretivism, or constitutional interpretation in accordance with the Framers' purpose and intent, was standard judicial practice in the nineteenth century. He argues that John Marshall, for example, relied on intrinsic and extrinsic sources of intent, with a view toward discovering what the Framers meant by the principles they embodied in the Constitution.[78] Wolfe's concept of original intent recognizes the role of prudence in the performance of the judicial function and is different from Berger's and Bork's positivist conception.[79] A more philosophically precise description would say Wolfe seeks to determine the real or intrinsic meaning—as opposed to either original or current meaning—of the Constitution.[80] In the context of the present analysis, however, the important point is Wolfe's attempt to demonstrate the possibility of objective constitutional interpretation, as a theoretical matter, by making a good-faith effort to be faithful to the Constitution through historical reenactment of the process of interpretation.[81]

To conclude this brief survey we consider a different kind of historical reenactment, tending toward radical historicism and recalling the legal realism with which we began, that has been proposed by the constitutional theorist Bruce Ackerman. Criticizing the ahistorical character of much constitutional theory, Ackerman urges "a reflective study of the past" to determine "the concrete historical processes" that allowed Americans to transform moments of passionate political mobilization into lasting legal achievement.[82] The result of his historical inquiry is the theory of dualist democracy, describing how the people at decisive historical moments amend the Constitution through the practice of constitutional—as opposed to normal—politics. Ackerman claims the authority of the Framers for this theory. As they made the original Constitution by acting illegally outside the Articles of Confederation, so later generations properly emulate them by creatively altering the regime (in reality creating new regimes as in Reconstruction and the New Deal), through the exercise of the de facto amending power inherent in popular sovereignty. In the legal realist spirit of Llewellyn and Corwin, Ackerman views the Constitution as "a historically rooted tradition of theory and practice—an evolving language of politics" and "historical practice." He evokes their unwritten, political constitutionalism in asserting that the basic reality is the radically different government Americans have made for themselves, to which the paper or ceremonial Constitution is adapted.[83] Ackerman's radical historicism convinces him that we are not "rootless epigones of bygone eras of constitutional creativity." By rewriting history, the constitutional theorist can recover "the distinctive aspirations of the American Republic."[84]

History and theory are reciprocally related in American constitutionalism. To assist in realizing the ends of constitutional government in the United States, theory must take account of history.[85] At the same time, the historical knowledge that is essential for maintaining the Constitution has a normative dimension. This is not to endorse partisan or ideological history, any more than to say the purpose of liberal education is political is to approve the politicization of the university.[86] As education is political in aiming to produce good citizens, so history—like its sister discipline political science—has reason to be partial to the regime of liberal democracy.[87] Of course there is always the risk that history and theory will be abused in the service of ideology. In constitutional scholarship, no less than in political life generally, prudence is required in applying the principles and rules that constitute and define inquiry in the respective fields. When pursued according to rational and objective scholarly standards, however, the disciplines of history and theory can enrich each other and contribute much to the discipline of constitutionalism.

Notes

1. Karl Llewellyn, *The Constitution As An Institution*, 34 Colum. L. Rev. 1, 3 (1934).

2. Charles A. Miller, *The Supreme Court and the Uses of History* (Harv. U. Press, 1969).

3. Id. at 1–2.

4. Id. at 115–16.

5. Michael Kammen, ed., *The Past Before Us: Contemporary Historical Writing in the United States* 19–46 (Cornell U. Press, 1980), and Peter Novick, *That Noble Dream: The "Objectivity Question" and the American Historical Profession* (Cambridge U. Press, 1988).

6. Llewellyn, 34 Colum. L. Rev. at 3 (cited in note 1).

7. Id. at 2 n.5. Llewellyn acknowledged earlier writers who questioned the theory of the written Constitution, including Arthur F. Bentley and Howard L. McBain. For discussion, see Herman Belz, *The Realist Critique of Constitutionalism in the Era of Reform*, 15 Am. J. Legal Hist. 288 (1971).

8. Llewellyn, 34 Colum. L. Rev. at 19 (cited in note 1).

9. Id. at 39 (emphasis in original).

10. Id. at 12 (emphasis in original).

11. Id. at 26.

12. Id. at 28 (emphasis in original).

13. Id. at 39 (emphasis in original).

14. Id. at 28.

15. Edward S. Corwin, *Some Probable Repercussions of "Nira" on Our Constitutional System*, 172 Annals Am. Acad. Pol. & Soc. Sci. 139, 139–40 (1934).

16. Id. at 140–41.

17. Corwin said that although the end of the federal-state balance removed a major rationale for judicial intervention in national policy making, judicial review would continue "in behalf of the helpless and oppressed against local injustice and prejudice." He also predicted that fusion of powers and coopera-

tion among the branches of government would supersede the ideas of separation and competition on which the constitutional system was originally based. Id. at 142.

18. Id. at 144.

19. Quoted in Sanford Levinson, *Constitutional Faith* 33 (Princeton U. Press, 1988).

20. Miller, *The Supreme Court and the Uses of History* at 25–26, 191–92 (cited in note 2).

21. Sotirios A. Barber, *Normative Theory, the 'New Institutionalism,' and the Future of Public Law*, 3 Stud. Amer. Pol. Dev. 56, 57 (1989).

22. G. Edward White, *The American Judicial Tradition* (Oxford U. Press, 1976).

23. Thomas C. Grey, *Do We Have an Unwritten Constitution?*, 27 Stan. L. Rev. 703 (1975); Thomas C. Grey, *Origins of the Unwritten Constitution: Fundamental Law in American Revolutionary Thought*, 30 Stan. L. Rev. 843 (1978); Stephen R. Munzer and James W. Nickel, *Does the Constitution Mean What It Always Meant?*, 77 Colum. L. Rev. 1029 (1977); Suzanna Sherry, *The Founders' Unwritten Constitution*, 54 U. Chi. L. Rev. 1127 (1987); Michael Zuckert, *Epistemology and Hermeneutics in the Constitutional Jurisprudence of John Marshall*, in Thomas C. Shevory, ed., *John Marshall's Achievement: Law, Politics, and Constitutional Interpretations* 202–15 (Greenwood Press, 1989); Robert F. Nagel, *Constitutional Cultures: The Mentality and Consequences of Judicial Review* 1–26 (U. of Cal. Press, 1989) (*"Constitutional Cultures"*).

24. See, for example, Philip Bobbitt, *Constitutional Fate* (Oxford U. Press, 1982); Sotirios A. Barber, *On What The Constitution Means* (Johns Hopkins U. Press, 1984); Ronald Dworkin, *Law's Empire* (Belknap Press, 1986); Cass R. Sunstein, *The Partial Constitution* (Harv. U. Press, 1993).

25. See Nagel, *Constitutional Cultures* at 121–55 (cited in note 23).

26. Leslie Friedman Goldstein, *In Defense of the Text: Democracy and Constitutional Theory* 67 (Rowman & Littlefield, 1991) (*"In Defense of the Text"*).

27. Harvey C. Mansfield, Jr., *America's Constitutional Soul* (Johns Hopkins U. Press, 1991).

28. Miller, *The Supreme Court and the Uses of History* at 51 (cited in note 2). Miller's reference to an attempted destruction of judicial reliance on history is a reference to Jacobus ten Broek, *Use by the United States Supreme Court of Extrinsic Aids in Constitutional Construction*, 26 and 27 Cal. L. Rev. 437, 664 (1938) and 157, 399 (1939).

29. Paul W. Kahn, *Legitimacy and History: Self-Government in American Constitutional Theory* 189 (Yale U. Press, 1992) (*"Legitimacy and History"*).

30. Peter H. Schuck, *Public Law Litigation and Social Reform*, 102 Yale L.J. 1763, 1764 (1993) (book review).

31. William M. Wiecek, *The Constitutional Snipe Hunt*, 23 Rutgers L.J. 253, 254 (1992).

32. ten Broek, 26 Cal. L. Rev. at 677 (cited in note 28). ten Broek denied that facts now apparent can be assumed to have presented themselves to the framers of a constitution in the same light and with the same force as they now appear to a historical observer.

33. William E. Nelson, *New Directions in American Legal History*, 4 Benchmark 283, 284–86 (1990).

34. James Willard Hurst, *Legal History: A Research Program*, 1942 Wis. L. Rev. 323, 323–33; James Willard Hurst, *Law and Social Process in United States History* 1–15 (U. of Mich. Law School, 1960); Robert W. Gordon, *J. Willard Hurst and the Common Law Tradition in American Legal Historiography*, 10 Law & Soc. Rev. 9, 48 (1975).

35. Paul L. Murphy, *Time to Reclaim: The Current Challenge of American Constitutional History*, 69 Am. Hist. Rev. 64, 74–77 (1963).

36. Morton J. Horwitz, *The Conservative Tradition in the Writing of American Legal History*, 17 Am. J. Legal Hist. 275, 281 (1973).

37. Morton J. Horwitz, *History and Theory*, 96 Yale L.J. 1825, 1830, 1832, 1835 (1987).

38. Robert W. Gordon, *An Exchange on Critical Legal Studies between Robert W. Gordon and William Nelson*, 6 Law & Hist. Rev. 139, 181–82 (1988).

39. Robert W. Gordon, *The Politics of Legal History and the Search for a Usable Past*, 4 Benchmark 269, 280 (1990).

40. Hendrik Hartog, *The Constitution of Aspiration and 'The Rights That Belong to Us All,'* 74 J. Amer. Hist. 1013, 1024, 1029 (1987).

41. Alfred H. Kelly, *Clio and the Court: An Illicit Love Affair*, 1965 Sup. Ct. Rev. 119, 122, 157.

42. Miller, *The Supreme Court and the Uses of History* at 195–96 (cited in note 2).

43. Nelson, 4 Benchmark at 284–91 (cited in note 33).

44. Michael Les Benedict, *Book Review*, 10 Law & Hist. Rev. 378, 379–80 (1992).

45. Id. at 380.

46. Robert Lowry Clinton, Marbury v. Madison *and Judicial Review* (U. Press of Kansas, 1989).

47. William M. Wiecek, *Liberty Under Law: The Supreme Court in American Life* 2, 190 (Johns Hopkins U. Press, 1988).

48. Goldstein, *In Defense of the Text* at 1 (cited in note 26).

49. Goldstein enumerates the following theories: intentionalism and textualism (often considered as a single theory under the name of originalism or interpretivism); extratextualism (also called fundamental values jurisprudence or noninterpretivism); indeterminacy; and Dworkinism. Id. at 2. Lief Carter identifies interpretivism (which he calls preservatism), and political and normative alternatives to interpretivism. Lief H. Carter, *Contemporary Constitutional Lawmaking: The Supreme Court and the Art of Politics* (Pergamon Press, 1985) (*"Contemporary Constitutional Lawmaking"*).

50. Dworkin, *Law's Empire* at 227 (cited in note 24).

51. Id. at 348, 350.

52. Id. at 369, 361.

53. David A. J. Richards, *Interpretation and Historiography*, 58 S. Cal. L. Rev. 490, 512, 505, 509 (1985).

54. Id. at 501.

55. Id. at 548.

56. Id. at 527. For a concise statement of the epistemological theory of radical historicism, see Gregory Leyh, *Toward a Constitutional Hermeneutics*, 32 Amer. J. Pol. Sci. 369 (1988).

57. Barber, *On What the Constitution Means* at 7 (cited in note 24).

58. Id. at 36.

59. Id. at 84–85.

60. Walter F. Murphy, *Constitutional Interpretation: The Art of the Historian, Magician, or Statesman?*, 87 Yale L.J. 1752, 1764 (1978).

61. Barber, 3 Stud. Amer. Pol. Dev. at 68 (cited in note 21).

62. Carter, *Contemporary Constitutional Lawmaking* at 123, 125–26 (cited in note 49). See Walter F. Murphy et al., *American Constitutional Interpretation* (Foundation Press, 1986).

63. Gary J. Jacobsohn, *The Supreme Court and the Decline of Constitutional Aspiration* 95 (Rowman & Littlefield, 1986).

64. Id. at 96. The quoted material and view criticized are those of Sotirios A. Barber.

65. Id.

66. Id. at 75.

67. The idea and the necessity of nonhistoricist historical inquiry is discussed in Leo Struass, *Natural Right and History* 33–34 (U. of Chi. Press, 1953).

68. Hadley Arkes, *Beyond the Constitution* 17–18 (Princeton U. Press, 1990).

69. Id. at 19–20.

70. For discussion of this outlook see Michael S. Moore, *Do We Have an Unwritten Constitution?*, 63 S. Cal. L. Rev. 107 (1989), Stanley C. Brubaker, *What Constitutes 'this Constitution'?* (unpublished paper presented at the 1990 Annual Meeting of the American Political Science Association), and *Conserving the Constitution*, 1987 Am. B. Found. Res. J. 261.

71. William M. Wiecek, *Clio As Hostage: The United States Supreme Court and the Uses of History*, 24 Cal. W. L. Rev. 227, 266 (1987).

72. Although this concept of historical method is held in intellectual disrepute among theorists of historiography, the practice of historians suggests there may be substantial truth in it.

73. Earl Maltz, *Foreword: The Appeal of Originalism*, 1987 Utah L. Rev. 773, 800, and *Some New Thoughts on an Old Problem—The Role of the Intent of the Framers in Constitutional Theory*, 63 B.U. L. Rev. 811 (1983).

74. John Phillip Reid, *Originalism and Subjectivism in the Bicentennial Year*, 68 Soc. Sci. Q. 687, 700 (1987).

75. Robert H. Bork, *The Tempting of America: The Political Seduction of the Law* (The Free Press, 1990).

76. Brubaker, *What Constitutes 'this Constitution'?* at 28 (cited in note 70).

77. Christopher Wolfe, *The Rise of Modern Judicial Review: From Constitutional Interpretation to Judge-Made Law* (Basic Books, 1986) (*"Rise of Modern Judicial Review"*).

78. Id. at 49–50.

79. Id. at 37, 71, 85, 88.

80. Brubaker, *What Constitutes 'this Constitution'?* at 37 (cited in note 70).

81. Wolfe, *Rise of Modern Judicial Review* at 14 (cited in note 77). Similar in methodology and in historiographical significance is Richard A. Maidment, *The Judicial Response to the New Deal: The US Supreme Court and Economic Regulation, 1934–1936* (Manchester U. Press, 1991).

82. Bruce Ackerman, *We The People: Foundations* 17, 22 (Belknap Press, 1991).

83. Id. at 22, 34–35.

84. Id. at 57. A similar goal is asserted in Sunstein, *The Partial Constitution* at 17–39 (cited in note 24).

85. Paul W. Kahn goes farther in arguing that American constitutional theory is centrally concerned with history for the reason that, after the founding generation, the state is a historical phenomenon. The task of constitutional theory is to explain how self-government is possible under the conditions of temporality in which the state exists. Kahn, *Legitimacy and History* (cited in note 29).

86. John Alvis, *Why a Proper Core Curriculum Is Political and Ought Not Be 'Politicized'*, 28 The Intercollegiate Rev. 28–29 (1993).

87. Ernst Breisach, *Historiography: Ancient, Medieval, & Modern* 409–10 (U. of Chi. Press, 1983); James W. Ceaser, *Liberal Democracy and Political Science* 20–24 (Johns Hopkins U. Press, 1990).

10

The Originalist Challenge to the Living Constitution

For most Americans, the Constitutional bicentennial of 1987 was an occasion for celebrating consensus and continuity in the American political tradition. In a study of cultural constitutionalism, historian Michael Kammen observed that the constitutive document written by the founders has "held up remarkably well and has thereby provided stability for the majority as well as shelter for aggrieved groups and individuals."[1] At the level of partisan politics, however, the bicentennial year was marked by two bitter constitutional controversies. In the Iran-Contra affair a major battle was waged between the president and Congress over the scope of executive power in foreign affairs. A second constitutional conflict arose when President Ronald Reagan nominated Judge Robert Bork to the Supreme Court.

Dramatic as it was, the constitutional politics of the Iran-Contra affair presented a familiar picture of confrontation between the president and Congress, based on the principle of the separation of powers that is inherent in the design of the Constitution. The fight over the Bork nomination was more significant constitutionally because it went beyond the problem of the scope of judicial review that had been the focus of controversy in Supreme Court appointments since the 1960s. Bork was a provocative nominee because he questioned the living constitutionalist consensus on which liberal jurisprudence and the structure of the regulatory-welfare state had been built since the New Deal. More than at any other time in the twentieth century, the nature of the Constitution and the meaning of constitutional government were at issue in the appointment of a Supreme Court Justice.

Bork's nomination was defeated. Contrary to the hopes and expectations of his opponents, however, the result was not an affirmation of judicial liberalism as a public philosophy.[2] In the following years, many liberal scholars perceived constitutional discontent not unlike that which inspired the original-intent jurisprudence that Bork represented. According to Morton J. Horwitz, for example, there was still a crisis of legitimacy in constitutional law caused by the destabilizing force of modernism. As before, American constitutionalism faced the problem of how to establish a system of legal fundamentality that would affirm the idea of continually changing constitutional meaning under the concept of the living constitution.[3] H. Jefferson Powell, a decade earlier acclaimed for his attack on originalism, lamented that fifty years of liberal jurisprudence had left American constitutionalism in a state of intellectual and moral confusion. Powell said contemporary constitutional theory was little more than "a veiled apology for rule by a liberal oligarchy."[4]

That judicial liberalism did not enjoy a restoration of public confidence does not mean that the defeat of Judge Bork, paradoxically, resulted in the vindication of originalist jurisprudence as a dominant philosophy of constitutional law. Conservatives disagreed among themselves over the importance of limiting judicial discretion, the main objective of originalist critics.[5] In general, therefore, the field of constitutional law in the 1990s was an ideological battleground. In contrast to the celebratory attitude of Constitutional bicentennialism, practitioners and critics of constitutional law talked past each other, able to agree neither on the nature and content of the Constitution nor on the principles and rules for interpreting and amending it. Although often described in "crisis language" by participants, from the standpoint of an external observer the constitutional debate was the product of normal historical change. What many observers saw as a crisis of legitimacy in the legal order resulted from the breakup of the liberal ideological consensus concerning the nature of government, law, and society in twentieth-century industrial capitalism.

This chapter examines original-intent jurisprudence as a challenge to the theory of the living Constitution that provided the normative framework for the post–New Deal liberal state. After considering the liberal response to originalism, it discusses the Bork nomination as a national referendum on originalism as a constitutional philosophy. The chapter then describes the development in the 1990s of neorepublican amendment theory and common-law constitutionalism as revised versions of unwritten living constitutionalism, and textualist-originalism as a variation on the founding project of written constitutionalism. The chapter concludes with an assessment of some recent Supreme Court decisions that reflect the tension between written and unwritten constitutionalism that has characterized American constitutional law in the twentieth century.

The principal finding is that the attempt to recover the founding project of written constitutionalism, while it has not gained many converts among liberal scholars and judges, has succeeded in revising the terms of debate in contemporary constitutional law. The main issue is no longer, as it was in the New Deal era, the proper scope of judicial review under the theory of the living Constitution. Increasingly, the focus of academic and judicial controversy is the fundamental question of the nature of the Constitution, in particular, whether the American people have a written or unwritten constitution. While admittedly a theoretical question, from the standpoint of citizens and actors within the constitutional order it raises the practical issue of whether the people of the United States are still capable of governing themselves under a normative fundamental law that limits politics and government. On this question ultimately depends the existence of liberal republican government: the end, purpose, and final cause of the project of written constitutionalism at the time the country was founded.

I

The historical context in which the crisis of legitimacy in living constitutionalism has occurred is the breakup of the ideological consensus of twentieth-century statist liberalism. Premised on the idea of market failure, modern liberal ideology assumed the necessity of state intervention to achieve social security, justice, and equality through the regulation of economic and social life. In the western democracies, statist liberalism resulted in the expansion of the discretionary authority of government and the relaxation, if not elimination, of constitutional and legal restraints on political action.[6] Constitutionalism, defined as limited government, individual rights, and private property, was repudiated in favor of unitary and activist government dedicated to securing liberty through promotion of the public interest based on recognition of class and group rights.

In the United States the New Deal state was rationalized under the theory of the living Constitution. In the 1960s living constitutionalism flourished in the constitutional jurisprudence of the Supreme Court and the programmatic liberalism of the modern presidency, supported by a compliant legislative branch. As it reached its apogee in the public policy and constitutional law of the "Great Society," however, living constitutionalism came under attack from conservative critics seeking a restoration of limited government based on written constitutionalism. Conservatives objected that legal liberalism reduced the written Constitution to a mere parchment barrier of no intrinsic value. In the hands of activist judges the document was only an empty symbol invoked to insulate judicial policy making against popular criticism. To understand the source of this criticism, it is necessary to consider the problem faced by liberal lawyers and judges since the 1930s of how to constitutionalize the New Deal.

Supporters and opponents alike agreed that the New Deal effected fundamental changes in constitutional meaning concerning the nature, purpose, and authority of the federal government. Liberal lawyers argued that the structural and policy changes effected by the New Deal were valid applications of executive and legislative authority, fulfilling principles and values embodied in the Constitution. Politically legitimate because they were approved by the people, New Deal changes were subsequently confirmed as constitutionally legitimate through the exercise of judicial review, resulting in a new deposit of constitutional law. If in practical terms the New Deal stood for sweeping and radical change in American government, in the eyes of its supporters it illustrated the uniquely American idea of a constitutional revolution: changes in the ends, powers, and procedures of government effected in a peaceful manner, consistent with the nation's fundamental law.

The public philosophy of the New Deal was democratic majoritarianism, expressed through executive control of legislation and administration. Judicial liberalism was defined with reference to the idea of judicial deference to policy making by the legislative and executive branches and was a subordinate theme in the New Deal constitutional revolution. Judicial liberalism was known principally by what it rejected—namely, the doctrines of laissez-faire constitutionalism under which conservative judges substituted their subjective policy preferences for those of democratically elected lawmakers. In the view of New Deal lawyers, Franklin D. Roosevelt's controversial plan of 1937 to pack the Supreme Court was intended to restore the division of responsibility whereby the political branches construed the Constitution for public policy purposes, while the judicial branch interpreted the Constitution where individual liberty and property rights were concerned.

Although characterized by the catch phrase "judicial self-restraint," judicial liberalism acquired greater policy-making significance as the Supreme Court's civil liberties and civil rights case load expanded in the 1940s and 1950s. *Brown v. Board of Education* (1954) was a milestone in this development.[7] The emergence of a new wave of liberal reformism outside the judicial branch, however, was the decisive factor stimulating the extraordinary line of judicial-activist decisions handed down by the Warren Court in the 1960s. The Court's unabashed policy making removed any lingering doubt about the character of judicial liberalism. By the end of the Warren era the debate within liberalism between advocates of judicial activism and judicial restraint, which preoccupied constitutional theorists in the 1950s, was resolved in favor of activism.

The earnest, straightforward, and persuasive appeal to "fairness" that marked Chief Justice Warren's most ambitious policy-making decisions disarmed critics of judicial activism. Warren's unaffected progressivism obscured the contradiction between judicial activism and the principle of judicial restraint that since the New Deal had served to reconcile the Court's policy-making role with the constitutional philosophy of democratic majoritarianism.[8] Even if Warren Court decisions did not achieve all that reformers hoped for, they pointed up a contradiction between judicial activism and the theory of judicial self-restraint that could no longer be denied. In fact, the Supreme Court's reformist activism looked for all the world like a resumption, at the opposite end of the political spectrum, of the substantive due process jurisprudence against which modern judicial liberalism originally defined itself in the New Deal era.[9]

After Chief Justice Warren left the Court in 1969, the revival of substantive due process jurisprudence continued in two landmark right-of-privacy cases. In *Eisenstadt v. Baird* (1972), the Supreme Court, in a 6–1 majority opinion written by Justice William J. Brennan, rejected a state's argument that a policy that differentiated between unmarried and married couples in the distribution of contraceptives was rationally related to the legitimate state purpose of drawing a moral distinction between sexual activity within and outside of marriage. The Court held that the state's moral choice was an unreasonable intrusion into the sphere of personal privacy concerning a matter that the Court deemed fundamental.[10] In the more widely publicized and controversial case of *Roe v. Wade* (1973), the Court held that a woman's right to an abortion was an attribute of an unenumerated right of privacy found in the due process clause of the Fourteenth Amendment.

The persistence of judicial activism under conservative judges in the 1970s led to efforts by liberal commentators to rationalize the revival of substantive due process jurisprudence. This reconsideration of constitutional theory was necessitated by the political opposition to liberalism that erupted in the late 1960s. In the legal academic community where it took place, theoretical revision was provoked by the emergence of a theory of constitutional interpretation known as original-intent jurisprudence. The driving force behind it was criticism of liberal jurisprudence for its disregard of democratic principle.

While approving the results of judicial activism, many judicial liberals were troubled by the apparent contradiction between policy making by nonelective judges and policy making by elected lawmakers. To

justify, explain, or otherwise resolve this contradiction, euphemisti-
cally referred to as "the countermajoritarian difficulty," was the burden of liberal legal scholarship in the 1970s. Proponents of original-
intent jurisprudence, interjecting a genuine conservative voice into constitutional debate for the first time since the New Deal, viewed this
effort as an attempt to evade the plain meaning and basic normative
principle of the constitutional order. This was the principle of republican self-government under a written fundamental law that limited the
authority of government, including the power of the judiciary.

The legal historian Raoul Berger, in his seminal study *Government by
Judiciary: The Transformation of the Fourteenth Amendment* (1977), almost
single-handedly revised the terms of debate in constitutional law. Berger was a former New Deal lawyer who a few years earlier had defended the institution of judicial review against the charge of judicial
usurpation.[11] Judicial review, he argued, was part of the original constitutional design. In *Government by Judiciary*, Berger attacked judicial-
activist living constitutionalism as a departure from the intent of the
Framers and called for a revival of the founding project of written constitutionalism.

Berger used the framing, ratification, and subsequent judicial interpretation of the Fourteenth Amendment as a case study of what both
critics and supporters of judicial liberalism referred to as the power of
the Supreme Court to amend the Constitution. The most famous recent
illustration of this de facto judicial amending power was *Brown v. Board
of Education* (1954), in which the Court held that the meaning of the
Fourteenth Amendment's equal protection clause could be determined
only by considering the importance of public education in contemporary society. According to Berger, the Court thus claimed "the power
to revise the Constitution to meet present needs."[12] He rejected the
idea, often asserted by judicial liberals, that the Supreme Court was
intended to act as a continuing constitutional convention. Berger contended, on the contrary, that "a democratic system requires adherence
to constitutional limits, by courts no less than presidents." The role
assigned to the judicial branch by the authors of the Constitution was
"to police the boundaries drawn in the Constitution."[13]

Although *Government by Judiciary* was promptly accepted as the bible
of original-intent jurisprudence, Berger gave relatively little attention
to the question of how to define or formulate the concept of original
intent—or "originalism," as it came to be called. To Berger, trained
in the older liberalism of judicial restraint, original intent was not a
problematic concept, but an obvious, if not self-evident, inference from
the fact that the United States had a written constitution. He noted that
the founders "were deeply committed to positivism," as reflected in

"their resort to written constitutions—positive law." Positivism in turn expressed their commitment to written limits on all power—the power of judges included—and rejection of the idea of a higher law beyond the Constitution to which judges and other government officials might appeal.[14]

Like a litany in the older judicial liberalism to which he would recall the legal profession, Berger recounted the story of conservative judicial activism from the 1890s to the 1930s. This was subjective, natural law jurisprudence under the pretense of interpreting "a constitutional catchphrase"—the due process clause of the Fourteenth Amendment. The conservative Court's due process jurisprudence, the basis of laissez-faire constitutionalism, disguised the judges' individual opinions and gave them " 'the sanction and prestige of a supreme fundamental law.' "[15] Berger argued that the equal protection jurisprudence of the Warren Court revived subjective, natural law judging. The Court, said Berger, believed that only its judicial intervention could serve the cause of justice and free the nation from the shackles of the Constitution—the Fourteenth Amendment as written, which permitted racial segregation.[16]

In Berger's theory of written constitutionalism, original intent was so logical, necessary, and inevitable as the correct method of interpreting the Constitution that it could be taken for granted. To dwell on it or explicitly underscore its practical value was to state the obvious. Nevertheless, it was necessary to restate the essentials of American constitutionalism.

The fundamental problem was limited government. Berger's key point, contrary to living constitutionalist orthodoxy, was that the Supreme Court could not amend the Constitution. The Court's duty was to police the boundaries in the Constitution. This was the "original intention" of the Framers, and it was binding on the Court because, in the words of Madison, "if 'the sense in which the Constitution was accepted and ratified by the Nation . . . be not the guide in expounding it, there can be no security for a consistent and stable [government], more than for a faithful exercise of its powers.' "[17] "On traditional canons of interpretation," Berger observed, "the intention of the framers being unmistakably expressed [as he believed it was in relation to the Fourteenth Amendment and school segregation], that intention is as good as written into the text."[18]

According to Berger, constitutional interpretation was a form of statutory interpretation in which effectuation of the drafter's intention was the controlling principle. Quoting James Wilson, he said, "The first and governing maxim in the interpretation of a statute is to discover the meaning of those who made it."[19] The whole point in having a written constitution was to establish the basic meaning and understanding of the principles, rules, forms, and procedures that were to limit and guide the exercise of government power posited by the document. In the absence of a commitment to adhere to the intention of the Framers, the written Constitution was not a real constitution.

Written in the spirit of a prophet calling the nation back to its founding principles, Berger's work had a clarifying and polarizing effect on constitutional law and theory. Liberal scholars scorned his constitutional fundamentalism, even as the passion of their attack betrayed fear of a formidable opponent. Among critics of judicial activism, Berger's study of the Fourteenth Amendment led to the articulation of a theory of original-intent jurisprudence as an alternative to living constitutionalism.

No criticism of conservative legal scholarship is implied in the observation that systematic elaboration of a jurisprudence of original intent did not go beyond the position outlined in *Government by Judiciary*. The strength of the originalist appeal lay in its correspondence to, if not identity with, the written Constitution. As a theory of constitutional interpretation and framework for judicial review, originalism was a logical inference to be drawn from the nature of the Constitution. The essential point, said originalists, was to insist on the textual character of the Constitution and the fixed meaning it embodies as a fundamental law limiting government and politics. Properly understood, constitutional interpretation seeks to elucidate and apply the original understanding of the authoritative text. Throughout most of American constitutional history, this understanding was readily acknowledged, if not taken for granted, in constitutional adjudication.[20] Following Berger's attack on judicial activism, scholars and commentators calling themselves "originalists" believed it was necessary to spell out this theory of the Constitution as a standard of political morality and public integrity.

The Tempting of America (1990) by Judge Robert H. Bork summarized a decade of scholarly and political controversy over original-intent jurisprudence. Written in the aftermath of his failed nomination to the Supreme Court, Bork's account supplanted Raoul Berger's landmark study as the bête noire of liberal living constitutionalists. A judicial restraint fundamentalist, Bork as a matter of intellectual argument chose to engage neither the deconstructionist hermeneutical theory nor the neo-Kantian moralism that were prominent in legal liberalism in the 1980s. The problem that he addressed was how to recover and reestablish the idea that the Constitution is law.

Bork stated the basic principle of originalism thus: "Either the Constitution and statutes are law, which means that their principles are known and control judges, or they are malleable texts that judges may rewrite to see that particular groups or political causes win."[21] According to Bork, to say that judges are bound by the law means that they are "bound by the only thing that can be called law, the principles of the text, whether Constitution or statute, as generally understood at the enactment." The judge is therefore "bound to apply the law as those who made the law wanted him to."[22]

In the view of Earl M. Maltz, a leading academic theorist of the movement, the appeal of originalism lies in a particular conception of law requiring the use of a specific judicial reasoning process. This is the idea of positive, written law that has an objective and real meaning. In the case of the Constitution, real and objective meaning is discoverable as a written source of authority by interpretation, using legal conventions analogous to those that govern the interpretation of other authoritative documents, especially statutes.[23] The theory of originalism—the theory of the Constitution, properly considered—holds that the framers of the Constitution had legitimate authority to create binding legal rules. The meaning of the Constitution was fixed in 1789 and does not evolve over time as circumstances change.[24]

Agreement on the nature and character of the Constitution would obviate the problem—in actuality a superficial one, in the view of originalists—of how to interpret the Constitution. As expressed by Gary L. McDowell, the basic point of the founders' constitutionalism was to establish the rule of law under a written document of clear and common language. To conceive of a nation's Constitution as a written document heralded a new age in political thinking and fundamentally altered the nature and extent of how political power was understood. Derived from and dependent on the written constitution, political power was to be limited in a new and effective way and recognized as legitimate only insofar as it conformed to the text that supplied the formal ground of its existence. A permanent body of written law, the Constitution did not include the unwritten English common law. McDowell said the founders thus rejected the idea of an unwritten constitution as fundamental law. In America, the fundamental law was to be the written Constitution. McDowell concluded that in the late twentieth century, as at the time of the founding, preservation of the literal provisions of the text Constitution was necessary to preserve the political and civil liberty that was the end of the constitutional order.[25]

As conceived by its proponents, the theory of original-intent jurisprudence was the common-sense practical result of having a written constitution. Essentially taken for granted since the Constitution's adoption, the idea required explicit elaboration in order to counter the effect of decades of judicial-activist policy making based on values derived neither from the text of the Constitution nor the structure created by it.[26]

Constitutional lawyer Henry Monaghan said it was clear that the Supreme Court in the 1960s was developing "a constitutional *lex non-scripta*."[27] The practical purpose of originalist criticism therefore was to question the legitimacy of modern judicial review as a substantive legislative activity. Monaghan observed that original intent was not simply an expository style in opinion writing. It was a way of thinking about constitutional meaning that followed from basic concepts that in the past had legitimated judicial review. The fundamental premise of originalist adjudication was that the Supreme Court was constrained by the written Constitution, just as the other branches of government were. The authoritative status of the written Constitution, Monaghan explained, was the incontestable first principle of American constitutional law. The written Constitution was the master "rule of recognition" in the legal system, that is, the rule that determined which of the many rules that might apply to a given situation were authoritative. That the constitutional text was binding and authoritative until changed by the procedure of formal amendment was a self-evident historical truth.[28]

Original-intent jurisprudence depended on and in practical terms was identified with textual interpretation of a written fundamental law. Yet, in the deepest sense, the significance of originalism transcended the model or method of linguistic analysis. It concerned the nature and tendency of republican government. The deeper foundation in political philosophy on which the originalist approach to constitutional interpretation rested appeared more clearly in relation to the eruption of postmodernist linguistic and hermeneutical theory in liberal jurisprudence in the 1980s. Referring to the postmodernist hijacking of constitutional law in the attempt to preserve liberal judicial activism, Earl Maltz stated that linguistic analysis was unpersuasive because constitutional theory ultimately concerned the role of courts in determining the powers of government and the relationship of governmental institutions to the citizenry and to each other. In Maltz's view, this was quintessentially a political task that made political theory the benchmark for evaluating methods of constitutional interpretation.[29] The significance of political philosophy as a normative framework for American constitutionalism, however, was a source of controversy among conservative scholars.

The main conservative objection to judicial liberalism was that activist judges used moral and political philosophy to deny the plain meaning of the constitutional text. In reaction to this alleged abuse of judicial authority, some critics argued that constitutional interpretation should abjure political philosophy and theory. Raoul Berger and Robert Bork, the most widely known proponents of original-intent jurisprudence, insisted that legal positivism was the only reliable basis on which to construct a jurisprudential alternative to unwritten living constitutionalism. Other commentators proposed an interpretive strategy based on philosophical realism, which aimed at discovering the "real meaning" of constitutional provisions rather than their historically validated original intent.[30]

It was exceedingly difficult, however, to extrude political theory or philosophy from constitutional law. To some extent, even positivists such as Bork found it necessary to appeal to political philosophy, as when they elevated legislative majoritarianism—the instrument and symbol of popular sovereignty as a public philosophy—to interpretive preeminence in constitutional adjudication.[31] Conservatives who appealed to moral realism were prepared, in their own words, to go "beyond the Constitution" to resolve problems of constitutional interpretation. In doing so they opened themselves to the charge of fusing law and morality, "evacuat[ing] the very notion of a constitution" and reducing the text Constitution to "a fiction of prudence."[32] Why not simply set the constitutional text aside, asked Graham Walker, and try to ensure that those who exercise power are virtuous and prudent?[33] Nevertheless, despite philosophical differences, originalists in both the positivist and moral realist camps agreed politically in opposing judicial activist policy making based on the theory of living constitutionalism.

II

Although dismissed as intellectually incoherent by liberal critics, original-intent jurisprudence had a decided impact on liberal constitutional theory. The doctrines and agenda of liberal jurisprudence were bound to change in any case as a result of the decline of liberalism and the ascendancy of conservatism in national politics in the 1980s. The originalist challenge to living constitutionalism had the effect, however, of forcing liberal theorists to develop arguments aimed at resolving the countermajoritarian difficulty exposed by the activism of the Warren Court.

The initial response of many legal liberals to originalist criticism was to argue that despite appearing to be procedurally nondemocratic, judicial policy making was democratic in purpose and effect and hence constitutionally legitimate. Some liberals contended openly for government by judiciary. Confident that original-intent jurisprudence had no professional or academic standing, they denied the existence of a countermajoritarian difficulty in constitutional law. Other liberals, responding more directly to the originalist account of American constitutionalism, argued that the Constitution was really a form of unwritten common law that courts necessarily revised in the course of fulfilling their policy-making role.

The continuation of activist policy making by the Supreme Court in the early 1970s had a polarizing effect on constitutional politics. While provoking conservative criticism, it stimulated more candid justification of judicial legislation on the part of liberal constitutionalists.

In a landmark article, Thomas C. Grey observed in 1975 that after a long period of consensus, the most fundamental issue in American constitutional law was again in dispute. This was the question whether judges, in the exercise of judicial review, should confine themselves to determining whether laws conflict with norms derived from the written Constitution. Could judges enforce principles of liberty and justice when the normative content of those principles was not found in the text of the Constitution? Grey asked. He attempted to show historically that the judiciary possessed such authority and that the framers of the Constitution believed that unwritten higher law principles, not codified in the written Constitution, were binding on the judiciary. From the outset, courts were authorized to enforce natural rights and expound doctrines not found in the written Constitution. It was accurate, therefore, to say that the United States had an unwritten constitution.[34]

Grey contended that contrary to official constitutional orthodoxy, the Supreme Court in actual practice did not decide cases by interpreting the text of the Constitution. Although the document occasionally provided a linguistic reference point, for the most part it was not the source of the values and principles that judges used to reach constitutional decisions. The text Constitution served only as a symbolic source of legitimacy for the development and explication of shared national values. The process of elucidating the changing meaning of basic conceptions of governmental structure and individual natural rights, Grey concluded, gave meaning to the metaphor of the "living Constitution."[35]

Liberal jurisprudence in the late 1970s and 1980s accepted the idea, paradoxical on its face, that interpretation of the text could be dispensed with in constitutional decision making. The formal Constitution was not the exclusive source of judicially enforceable constitutional law.[36] This theory was called noninterpretive judicial review, or "noninterpretivism." In an influential analysis of constitutional law, commentator John Hart Ely recognized it as an approach to constitutional decision making supported by many judicial liberals.

A former law clerk to Earl Warren, Ely defended the Warren Court against the charge that its activist policy making was based on the justices' subjective values rather than on the fundamental values of society and principles in the Constitution. Sensitive to the emerging orginalist criticism, Ely agreed that noninterpretivist judicial review was subversive of constitutional democracy.[37] He complained, however, that contemporary constitutional debate was dominated by a false dichotomy posing two undesirable alternatives. "Either . . . we must stick close to the thoughts of those who wrote our Constitution's critical phrases and outlaw only those practices they were outlawing, or there is simply no way for courts to review legislation other than by second-guessing the legislature's value choices."[38]

Ely argued for a third approach to constitutional interpretation— representation-reinforcing judicial review. This called for judicial intervention, but intervention based on the structural-procedural value of political representation that Ely said was integral to the Constitution. Explicated in the *Carolene Products* footnote, representation-reinforcing judicial review, according to Ely, was the operative principle used by the Warren Court. In Ely's opinion, this approach was distinguishable from noninterpretivist fundamental-values jurisprudence, which relied on sources outside the constitutional document and was increasingly recognized as willful and subjective policy making. In contrast, representation-reinforcing review was really a type of interpretivism. Its content was "derived from the general themes of the entire constitutional document," Ely claimed, "not from some source entirely beyond its four corners."[39] Yet, theoretically and politically, representation-reinforcing judicial review was far removed from the narrow, "clause-bound" interpretivism of original-intent jurisprudence.

Ely acknowledged that interpretivism had appeal because of its apparent consistency with democratic theory. In fact, it was undemocratic, he argued, because the written Constitution was the voice of the Framers, not the people. A second reason for rejecting clause-bound interpretivism was that it required judges to do what was really impossible under a written constitution, namely, decide cases exclusively on the basis of the text. Ely reasoned that the constitutional document "contains several provisions whose invitation to look beyond their four corners—whose invitation, if you will, to become at least to that extent a noninterpretivist—cannot be construed away."[40]

Ely's attempt to steer a middle course between text-bound interpretivism and text-liberated noninterpretivism was unsuccessful. Ely himself admitted that the distinction he tried to make—between Warren Court activism based on representation-reinforcing review and activism based on subjective, fundamental-values review—was "too fine for popular appreciation."[41] In contrast, there was nothing subtle about his conclusion that text-based interpretivism, or originalism, was intellectually impossible and therefore absurd. Although conceding that the dominant mode of noninterpretivist review, as seen in the activism of *Roe v. Wade*, was a "transparent failure," Ely placed himself on the liberal side of the constitutional debate.[42]

In expressing reservations about noninterpretivism Ely was an exceptional liberal scholar. The more characteristic reaction to originalist interpretivism was to justify judicial policy making on substantive moral grounds, rather than on the procedural basis used by Ely.[43] Michael J. Perry, for example, reviewing Raoul Berger's *Government by Judiciary*, denied that the commitment of American society to majoritarian policy making was a settled issue, as originalists assumed; it was an open question, Perry said, along with the definition of democracy itself. If, as a result of judicial intervention, public policy was more responsive to society's needs, then judicial activism was democratic. The crucial point in Perry's theory of constitutional adjudication was the moral content of government policy.[44]

In Perry's view the moral criteria for evaluating public policy were not fixed but were determined by each generation in the light of its political experience. The role of the Supreme Court was to represent society's ideals so government policy would be more responsive to them. Judges did not merely discern social ideals; they redefined them with greater precision, specifying the moral content required by the ideal. Standing in a dialectical relationship with the society, the judiciary "gives shape to morality." Courts in turn submit to the judgment of society about the "soundness" of judicial policy making, as indicated by the extent of public acceptance of the policy at issue. Perry offered this decision-making model as "a rigorous process of reasoned moral development" that promised a better political morality than would result from static originalist interpretivism, based on a simplistic definition of democracy.[45]

In 1980, in an article that achieved canonical status in liberal jurisprudence, Paul Brest summarized the mainstream academic response to originalism. With confidence and candor, Brest rejected fidelity to the text and original understanding of the Constitution as the touchstone of constitutional adjudication. Underscoring the central theme in twentieth-century progressive and liberal legalism, he appealed to the idea of a judicially fabricated unwritten constitution, unencumbered by any countermajoritarian difficulty.

Brest acknowledged the traditional appeal to the binding authority of the text of the Constitution and noted that it took two forms. The first was narrow originalism, consisting of text-based literalism and strict framer-intentionalism. A second type of appeal to textual authority was moderate originalism, which regarded key constitutional provisions as open textured. Brest said that in either form, originalism was inherently flawed because it rested on the false assumption that it was intellectually possible to acquire historical knowledge of constitutional original understanding and intent. Relying on the contextualist methodology employed by historians of political thought, he expressed doubt that professional historians themselves could ascertain the original intent and understanding of the author of a political text.[46] For a judge to try to discover original intent, translating framer and ratifier intention into contemporary policy choices, required counterfactual and imaginary projections that carried constitutional decision making into "a fantasy world" of the interpreter's making.[47]

Brest proposed "nonoriginalist adjudication" as the norm in constitutional theory. He claimed that it, rather than any form of originalism, was the principal source of constitutional meaning from the beginning of the government. Whatever legitimacy the written Constitution had as fundamental law, he said, came not from the authority of the Framers, but from the continuing acquiescence of subsequent generations of Americans in the decisions and practices of government institutions. Government actions constituted a tradition of "supplementing and derogating from the text and original understanding" of the Constitution, undermining the exclusivity of the written document as the source of constitutional legitimacy.[48] Nonoriginalism, Brest in effect argued, represented the original intent of the makers of the Constitution.

To say that the written Constitution was not the exclusive source of legitimacy in American government implied that the decisions and practices of government, including the judiciary, were intrinsically constitutional and capable of generating constitutional meaning. Brest did not expressly employ the concept of the unwritten constitution, but the fact that the country had such a constitution was the clear inference to be drawn from his analysis. Brest was explicit, however, in describing the basis on which nonoriginalist constitutional adjudication rested. It was not popular consent, as reflected in the operation of the forms and procedures of the written Constitution. Political and constitutional legitimacy depended, Brest reasoned, on the competence of government institutions in fulfilling the ends of constitutionalism or constitutional government, as seen in "the quality of our social life."[49]

According to Brest, history was important to theory because it showed that adjudication was the principal method of constitutional decision making and development. The originalist challenge made it necessary to elevate this historical phenomenon into the correct theory of the nature of constitutional decision making.[50] This involved the decisive step of denying that judges and other officials were bound by the text and original understanding of the Constitution.[51] Chastising the Supreme Court for its lack of candor in discussing the method of decision making actually employed in constitutional law, Brest urged the justices to abandon the expressions of moderate originalism that often justified their opinions. To conceal the nature of constitutional decision making, he concluded, was undemocratic.[52]

The original-intent controversy entered a new phase in 1985 when Attorney General Edwin Meese carried what had been largely an academic debate into the arena of national politics. Assuming that Brest was right about the failure of Supreme Court justices to come clean with the public, Meese provided an opportunity, if he did not provoke it, for liberal judges to speak with greater candor about the nature of constitutional adjudication. Justice William J. Brennan, the most renowned liberal jurist on the Court, accepted the attorney general's challenge. In an off-the-bench speech that attracted national attention, Brennan transmitted the substance of Brestian nonorginalism.

Justice Brennan did not go so far as to deny the final authority of the text of the Constitution or the idea of original understanding. More prudent than Brest, in a formal sense he accepted the constitutional document as the ground or framework of constitutional decision making. In reality, however, his interpretive theory dissolved the text into a warrant for judicial policy making by denying that it had fixed meaning and regulatory force.

According to Justice Brennan, interpretation of the Constitution as a written text was concerned primarily with two things: aspirations and fundamental principles. The Constitution, Brennan declared, "embodies the aspiration to social justice, brotherhood, and human dignity that brought this nation into being." As a result, the United States was committed to becoming a nation "where the dignity and rights of all persons were equal before all authority." The Constitution as a text also contained fundamental principles. Brennan asserted that the path of constitutional legitimacy lay in fidelity to fundamental principles and aspirations rather than to the intentions of the Framers, as the theory of originalism contended. In strong language, Brennan said that original-intent jurisprudence was a fraudulent and facile historicism that served as a pretext for denying claims of constitutional right.

Fidelity to the text qua fundamental principles did not, in Brennan's view, limit judicial decision making. Acceptance of constitutional principles did not bind judges, or later generations of Americans, to the precise contours that the principles assumed in the Framers' historical context, which were bound to become anachronistic. The genius of the text, said Brennan, lay in the adaptability of its content—the aspirations and principles it projected into the future to cope with current problems and needs. Constitutional adaptability took the form, therefore, of substantive value choices by which each generation of Americans could overrule or add to the principles adopted by the Framers.

Although the people could amend the Constitution under Article V, Brennan said the great effort required suggested as a practical alternative the method by which fundamental values were chosen by the judiciary on behalf of the people. Judicial interpretation of principles and aspirations in the text must therefore be defended as a way of remaining faithful to the content of the Constitution. In fact, it was the duty of Supreme Court judges, Brennan explained, to seek out "the community's interpretation of the Constitutional text," lest the document fall captive to the anachronistic views of earlier generations. In performing this role, judges read the Constitution in the only way they could: as twentieth-century Americans for whom the ultimate question was: "What do the words of the text mean in our time?"[53]

Justice Brennan's skillful summary of nonoriginalist jurisprudence set the stage for the dramatic confrontation that occurred when Judge Robert H. Bork was nominated for appointment to the Supreme Court in 1987. Bork believed the main issue in the Senate nomination hearing was the proper philosophy of constitutional interpretation and the role of the judiciary in a democracy.[54] He held that judges should apply the laws of the legislature and intepret the Constitution, not make laws themselves and amend the Constitution. Bork's liberal critics viewed originalism as a judicial philosophy that denied the legitimacy of changing constitutional meanings and rejected the idea of a living constitution.[55] Moreover, they attacked Bork as hostile to civil rights and civil liberties because he defined rights narrowly, either as enumerated in the Constitution or as intended by the Framers.[56]

Bork's nomination implicitly raised the question of the role of the executive and legislative branches in constitutional interpretation. The Senate's decision to focus on Bork's political ideology, rather than his professional legal qualifications, indicated the desire of lawmakers to influence the development of constitutional doctrine. Democratic opponents were determined to preserve the body of liberal jurisprudence that Bork, notwithstanding his avowed support of strict construction and judicial restraint, was perceived as threatening. In a broad sense, therefore, the Bork nomination served as a referendum on liberal jurisprudence as a constitutional philosophy and judicial activism as the proper theory of judicial review.

Bork later said that control of the legal culture was at issue in the nomination controversy, as part of a larger struggle for control of

American culture.[57] In his view, "The battle was ultimately about whether intellectual class values, which are far more egalitarian and socially permissive, were to continue to be enacted into law by the Supreme Court."[58] Although using different rhetoric, Bork's opponents agreed. Led by Senator Edward Kennedy, who treated the controversy as an opportunity to redeem his political reputation, they engaged in a desperate battle to preserve the political culture and programs of statist liberalism.[59]

Bork was rejected by the Senate in a 58–42 vote. Constitutional observers viewed the outcome as a vindication of the judicial liberalism that Bork so strenuously opposed. Conservative scholar Joseph D. Grano believed that the rejection of Bork reflected and brought to practical fruition the doctrine of constitutional indeterminacy that left judges free to give the text of the Constitution any meaning they chose.[60] At least in the short term, the liberal jurisprudence that was the object of originalist criticism would remain good law.[61] More broadly, liberal commentators interpreted the outcome of the nomination controversy as a confirmation of Justice Brennan's view of the Supreme Court as a policy-making institution authorized by the Constitution to make fundamental value choices for the American people.

In liberal opinion, Bork's rejection signified repudiation of original-intent jurisprudence, especially the claim that judicial activism was undemocratic. As a result of the Senate vote, declared Erwin Chemerinsky, it would be more clearly understood by the public at large that democracy did not depend mainly on the forms and procedures of majority rule, but on substantive values identified and defended by judges. Furthermore, liberal judicial activism was not a radical doctrine, as originalists charged, but in fact occupied a constitutional middle ground. The modern activist Court stood between legislative supremacy that threatened to overrule fundamental values embodied in the Constitution and the rule of a static and lifeless Constitution incapable of changing and evolving by interpretation.[62] Another liberal scholar stated that in view of the repudiation of Borkian originalism, the so-called countermajoritarian difficulty was no longer an issue. If it was not obvious before, there could now be no mistaking the fact that political ideology and moral philosophy, not theories about judicial methodology, controlled constitutional interpretation.[63] This was not a cause for alarm about the state of American constitutionalism, as originalists had long warned. Bork's defeat showed that the public knew and approved of the discretionary governing role of unelected judges.[64]

From the standpoint of constitutional history, perhaps the most important result of the Bork controversy was to politicize further the Supreme Court appointment process and expand the role of the Senate in determining the direction of constitutional interpretation. The desire of the legislative branch to influence constitutional law through nomination hearings was, if possible, even more evident a few years later, when Clarence Thomas, a black conservative Republican, was appointed to the Court. Even when less controversial appointments were made in the 1990s, the politicization of the nomination process was apparent. In the area of constitutional theory and judicial review, however, the defeat of Judge Bork appeared to have a less decisive impact than was thought at the time.

III

Contrary to liberal expectation, Bork's rejection did not undermine the appeal of original-intent jurisprudence or negate its influence on constitutional interpretation. In the 1990s Justice Antonin Scalia emerged as the outstanding exponent of originalist jurisprudence on the Supreme Court and was credited by judicial liberals with redefining the mainstream of constitutional discourse.[65] In the aftermath of the Bork controversy, moreover, many supporters of liberal constitutionalism were not content to reassert the judicial activist–fundamental values orthodoxy of Justice Brennan. Forced to come to grips with originalist fundamentalism, liberal theorists were obliged to take account of the Constitution's textuality and documentary character. They tried to demonstrate the fidelity of liberal jurisprudence to the Constitution as fundamental law. Most important, while avoiding, in their view, overt repudiation of the commitment to a written Constitution, some liberal commentators redefined the meaning of the constitutional amendment process in a way that makes the idea of the unwritten constitution the theoretical ground of the American polity.

In describing these developments in constitutional theory, it is important to note that the attachment to an activist judiciary that became liberal orthodoxy in the post–New Deal period has by no means been abandoned. In American law schools there seems to be an inexhaustible supply of partisans of judicial governance. Recently there has been an attempt to justify rule by courts under the concept of "public reason."[66] One theorist of reasoned adjudication explains it as a process in which the judge moves ever farther from the written Constitution, adding to the text a variety of materials including "principles, policies, theories, distinctions, syntheses, vocabulary, and historical evidence." As a form of constitutional interpretation, adjudication in this view is not required to conform to an independently existing rule of law. On the contrary, adjudication, based on and determined by moral and political considerations, *is* the rule of law. Adjudication is not a bulwark against the notion of an evolving perfect Constitution, as originalism holds, but is the means by which such a constitution comes into existence.[67]

Lawrence G. Sager offers a similar account of an "incorrigible Constitution" that is systematically opposed to popular self-government. In this view, constitutional government is "judgment-driven," meaning that it strives toward standards of justice that differ from the "preferences" that drive popular decision making. A society committed to "the ongoing project of constitutional justice," declares Sager, "is well served by a robust judiciary which sees its role as that of an active participant in that project." Courts are an asset in securing the ends of a just society because the judicial process is "an institutional projection of the method of reflective equilibrium," the philosphical method that is best suited for reasoning about normative matters.[68] In the view of still another theorist of adjudication, "the actual language of the Constitution serves as little more than a potential obstacle to judicial decisions reached independently by considerations of pure political philosophy." Constitutional adjudication, in other words, rests on "a judge's own normative beliefs about what the Constitution ideally ought to say."[69]

The writings of some commentators substantiate the assertion that constitutional theory is "a veiled apology for rule by a liberal oligarchy."[70] Yet this approach departs too radically from the constitutional tradition to gain acceptance among other liberal critics of originalism. A different method of preserving the post–New Deal liberal state claims, like originalist jurisprudence itself, to return to the political science of the founding. Based on the outpouring of scholarship on republican ideology in the fields of history and political science, neorepublican theory proposes to reconceptualize the American Constitution as an unwritten constitution. This constitution is made anew episodically through political actions of the people as the constituent power, which, though taken outside the formal Article V amending process, revise the legally binding Constitution. The theory of republican amendment expresses in the 1990s the attempt, evident in American legal theory since the late nineteenth century, of reform-minded critics to transform written constitutionalism into nonformal unwritten constitutionalism.

The writings of Bruce Ackerman, a political scientist, are a principal source of neorepublican constitutionalism. Ackerman describes the American constitutional order as a "dualist democracy" consisting of two types of political action: top-level (or higher law) constitution making and lower-level partisan political competition that includes statutory policy making. At the founding of the nation and at critical junctures thereafter, designated as "constitutional moments," the people of the United States have made, revised, transformed, or reconstructed their fundamental law. The theory, which is also a historical account, holds that in the intervals between constitutional moments the people attend to their own private affairs, while government officials and politicians manage the conduct of ordinary politics, preserving fundamental principles within the established constitutional framework.

Among many salient issues implicated in Ackerman's thesis, the most important concerns the nature of the Constitution. Unlike orthodox judicial liberals, Ackerman approaches this question not through the institution of judicial review, but through the problem of constitutional amendment. He observes that although there have been substantive changes in the original structure of the Constitution, the American people have not altered the process of constitutional revision.[71] Ackerman regards this as a defect in the constitutional system that his theory is intended to rectify.

Ackerman attempts to show through a historical narrative how on two epochal occasions—Reconstruction and the New Deal—American citizens engaged in self-conscious acts of constitutional creation. In these moments of higher-law constitution making they followed the model of constitutional change provided by the Federalist founders, who in the Constitutional Convention undertook a "solemn and authoritative act" that changed the established form of government. The making of the Constitution, Ackerman states, was one of the "great and extraordinary occasions," requiring application of the nation's revolutionary founding principles, for which the founders believed a constitutional road should always be open to the people.[72] Although not conforming to the legal rules for amending the existing constitution, the Articles of Confederation, this act of revolutionary reform was legitimate.[73]

What the founding Federalists did, Ackerman says, later generations of citizens did and can still do. They may change the Constitution through political action outside the requirements, forms, and structure of Article V of the Constitution. When they do so by means of legislative statutes and executive orders and proclamations, their amending action is as authoritative and legitimate as if done under the forms of Article V. According to Ackerman, this result obtains ultimately because "the Constitution . . . is an evolving historical practice, constituted by generations of Americans as they mobilized, argued, resolved their ongoing disputes over the nation's identity and destiny."[74]

Ackerman's project is the most ambitious in a long line of constitutional constructions that deny the primacy and ultimate authority of the written Constitution and seek to establish for the United States an unwritten constitution. It is not coincidental that the most serious previous attempt to establish unwritten constitutionalism in America occurred during the New Deal, the constitutional moment from which Ackerman takes his ideological and theoretical bearings. Ackerman admits that his practical purpose is to preserve the fruits of the New Deal constitutional revolution. The New Deal created the structure of the modern republic, but a price was paid, he says, for the informality with which New Deal liberals revised the Constitution. That price was the long-range impermanence and instability of the New Deal as a constitutional amendment, compared to constitutional revisions carried out under the Article V amendment process.[75]

While much of the New Deal constitution remains in the living Constitution of the 1990s, Ackerman laments that "the remorseless logic of generational passage is visible everywhere."[76] Evidence of constitutional erosion can be seen, for example, in *U.S. v. Lopez* (1995), in which, for the first time since the 1930s, the Supreme Court struck down an exercise of the federal police power under the commerce clause. Such tendencies in constitutional law lead Ackerman to assert that the main issue in contemporary constitutional law is the basis on which the continuing controversy over the reception of the New Deal should proceed. Will this issue be settled, Ackerman asks, on a "formalist understanding that the only constitutional achievements the present generation is bound to notice are those monumentalized through the processes of Article V?"[77] Or will a more realistic understanding prevail, based on the notion of an unwritten constitution, making it possible to see that the Constitution was in fact amended in the 1930s. The issue, in other words, is the nature of constitutional change and the Constitution itself.

Ackerman claims that his theory of generational constitutional transformation is not simply an attempt to protect the New Deal and liberal political philosophy against historical change. Yet his warning that refusal to accept the theory would be an "act of betrayal," inflicting "a terrible blindness" on the country, suggests that more is at stake in contemporary constitutional debate than the alleged desire of Ackerman and other neorepublican theorists to preserve popular self-government.[78]

Neorepublican constitutionalism is also represented in the theory of constitutional amendment advanced by Sanford Levinson.[79] In an earlier work, focusing on the uncertainty that exists in constitutional law concerning what counts as the Constitution, Levinson contemplated the "death of constitutionalism." Ambiguity about what the Constitution is, he wrote, was the result of conflicting traditions that defined it as the written text and also as the assumptions and practices of the American political tradition.[80] Recently, Levinson has discovered in Article V of the Constitution a text that authorizes the kind of political inventiveness that he believes can revive and sustain American constitutionalism.

Levinson's theory of amendment concedes that Article V of the Constitution expresses the Framers' thinking about how to amend the fundamental law when imperfections in it become apparent. Levinson contends, however, that the formal process stipulated in the text is not the only way to amend the Constitution. To reach this conclusion he defines an amendment as "a legal invention not immanent within or derivable from the existing body of accepted legal materials."[81] It is to be distinguished from "a numbered textual addition" to the written Constitution.[82] Throughout most of American constitutional history, Levinson says, the Article V process has been used to produce textual additions, not real constitutional amendments. An Article V outcome should not be referred to as an amendment, he contends, unless it effects a genuine change in the governmental order. To understand the practice of American constitutionalism, therefore, it is necessary to recognize—and assimilate in a "sophisticated theory"—"the extent to which the Constitution has been amended—been the subject of political inventiveness—by means other than the addition of explicit text."[83]

Levinson observes that despite constant conceptual revision resulting from " 'deconstructive' analysis," in political life there are "basic notions that we simply seem unable to leave behind."[84] The idea of "constitutional amendment" as something different from ordinary interpretation is one such notion; it continues to have great rhetorical force.[85] It is therefore necessary, says Levinson, "to discern the heretofore hidden alternative to Article V that fully legitimates" political action that changes the system of government in basic ways.[86] Levinson intends his theory to illuminate "one of the central mysteries of our operative constitutional practice," namely, "the radical transformation through time of central legal doctrines" without the necessity of formal amendment.[87]

What Levinson treats as "mystery" receives a rational explanation in the theory of constitutionalism advanced by Stephen M. Griffin, a political scientist writing in the constitutional realist tradition. Considered historically, the Constitution is both the fundamental law of a republican polity and the governing instrument of a sovereign nation-state. As such it requires application and construction in the distinct, though not entirely separate, modalities of law and politics. Griffin offers a descriptive-explanatory account that confirms this basic feature of the American constitutional order. He then transmutes the historical phenomenon of bimodal constitutional construction into a normative standard on the basis of which he posits an unwritten constitution of institutional and political practice.

In Griffin's view, the key to understanding American constitutionalism is the concept of constitutional change. Only through a consideration of how the Constitution has changed, he argues, can one observe what constitutionalism is and arrive at a valid definition of the Constitution itself. The decisive fact guiding Griffin's descriptive-explanatory account is the near consensus among constitutional scholars that fundamental constitutional changes have occurred without benefit or authorization of the Article V amendment process. This fact must mean, Griffin argues, that the theory of the Framers—that the Constitution is a rule of fundamental law controlling the state and alterable only through the procedure prescribed in Article V—is not valid. Historically undeniable constitutional change means further that the law versus politics distinction, on which the founders' theory of constitutionalism depends, breaks down. The conclusion follows that the Constitution is "primarily a political institution." More precisely, it is "political practice" or "text-based institutional practice."[88] An even more important conclusion can be reached: rule-of-law constitutionalism, which supplies the rationale of Article V as the means of constitutional change intended by the founders, is not valid. The founding project of written constitutionalism fails, Griffin argues, because it breeds reverence for the text Constitution that prevents rational constitutional reform from occurring.[89]

A partisan of the regulatory-welfare state, Griffin sees that the New Deal regime lacks the permanence that enactment by formal constitutional amendment might have provided. Assuming the persistence of written constitutionalism, the only way to protect the New Deal state against obliteration is to redefine the concept of constitutional amendment. More than other liberal theorists, however, Griffin seems to support the idea of the unwritten constitution as the normative basis of American government on intrinsic theoretical grounds. He implies that a constitution of text-based institutional practice, in which the political branches determine their own powers and departmental interactions determine the meaning of the Constitution, offers the promise of good government.[90] Nevertheless, his purpose is primarily critical. Seeking to disestablish the normative appeal of written constitutionalism, Griffin rejects the distinction between constitutional law and ordinary politics.[91] The nature of the constitutional document is accordingly altered. No longer constitutive of fundamental principles, it becomes—and has been from the outset, as Griffin sees it—a pretext for expedient political action and a symbol of civil-religious nationalism and patriotic sentimentalism.[92] In Griffin's view these habits and practices do not contribute to good government.

According to Griffin, reconceptualization of constitutional change in political-institutional terms is not incompatible with the traditional textual-documentary definition of the Constitution.[93] Unlike Ackerman and other proponents of the new amendment theory, Griffin denies that constitutional change as conceived of in his descriptive-explanatory account has legal meaning and effect equivalent to formal amendment under Article V.[94] His claim is that "norms not in the text are functionally equivalent to norms in the text."[95] From the standpoint of the founders' constitutionalism, however, this is an unacceptable and illegitimate claim. The point of having a written constitution was to identify the legitimate and authoritative norms of the political community. Norms not in the text are not constitutional norms. The claim of functional equivalency for norms not in the constitutional text ultimately undermines the authority of the written Constitution.

Griffin concludes that rule-of-law constitutionalism is self-defeating. Legally construed constitutional principles enforced by judges, he states, are incapable of controlling government officials, whose actions are driven by partisanship, ideology, and political expediency. The founders' constitutional theory may have been compatible with the eighteenth-century ideal of limited government, but it is not viable in the context of the twentieth-century activist state.[96] To cling to the constitutionalism of the founding may prevent structural reforms necessary for coping with policy challenges of the twenty-first century.[97] If reform is stifled and American constitutionalism cannot be renewed through theory, Griffin says with scholarly resignation, "then we should be candid that we are abandoning constitutionalism as a meaningful political ideal."[98]

IV

If neorepublican amendment theorists emphasize the political dimension of the constitutional tradition, other critics of written constitutionalism draw on its legal and juridical strand. Unwilling to surrender the aspiration to judicial governance, they seek to transform constitutional law into a type of common law constitutionalism that dispenses with the text as a limitation on government, although not for symbolic and rhetorical purposes. Like the new amendment theorists, common law constitutionalists propose to use the cultural authority of the text Constitution to legitimize the existence of an unwritten constitution in which judges and other government officials create constitutional meaning and norms.

Consideration of the Constitution in relation to the common law raises complex jurisprudential issues beyond the scope of this essay. For present purposes it is sufficient to say that the written Constitution as an embodiment of fundamental principles and prescriptive rules for government differed in essential respects from the English constitutional system based on unwritten common law. The authoritative textuality of the written Constitution, rationalized and applied through a deductive interpretive methodology, distinguished it from the customary, evolutionary, and inductive character of common law constitutionalism.

This is not to deny the possibility of coexistence and reciprocal recognition between text-based constitutionalism and unwritten, common law constitutionalism.[99] Judges in both legal systems were understood to discover law, rather than make it in a legislative manner. Moreover, the functional legalization of the Constitution that can be said to have occurred with the emergence of judicial review and the development of constitutional law caused constitutional adjudication to resemble common law adjudication.[100] In the twentieth century the elaboration of decisional rules not obviously deduced from the text of the Constitution—as in civil liberties, criminal procedure, and commercial regulation—could plausibly be viewed as a constitutional common law.[101] In the 1970s, it occurred to some scholars that the idea of the Constitution as the source of common law adjudication might bridge the gap between advocates of judicial activism and judicial restraint.[102] There was a risk, however, that activist judges, claiming to discover fundamental values in substantive constitutional guarantees, might be encouraged to create a body of federal law unrelated to the Constitution.[103]

In the 1990s common law constitutionalism appealed to judicial liberals who viewed original intent jurisprudence as a threat to the existing political order. The model of common law judging appeared as a moderate approach capable of resolving constitutional disputes that could not be settled by the deductive interpretation of written constitutionalism because of the uncertainty and opacity of the constitutional text.[104] While recognizing the relevance of constitutional text, structure, history, and tradition in settling constitutional disputes, common law judging permitted courts to look outside the written Constitution in order to interpret it and speak in its name.[105] In contrast to the judicial governance asserted by theorists of reasoned adjudication, the common law model, according to Cass R. Sunstein, called for a more limited judicial role in constitutional democracy. Using the common law tools of analogical reasoning and stare decisis, judges were seen to apply constitutional values consistent with the commitment to deliberative democracy that forms the basis of constitutional law.[106] Yet common law judging could revise constitutional meaning and understanding when social and political change required it.[107]

Common law constitutionalism refers in general to gradual, interpretive, and informal vehicles of change that since the New Deal are seen as characterizing American constitutional life.[108] Because it is more informal and more easily corrected as a method of constitutional revision, common law judging is considered preferable to the Article V amendment process. According to Sunstein, the formal amendment procedure elicits populist enthusiasm for short-sighted constitutional revision that is "essentially childish," as well as dangerous to the principle of deliberative democracy.[109]

The persistence of original-intent jurisprudence after the Bork nomination fight led liberal scholars to adopt a "big-tent" strategy of constitutional argumentation. Although differing in the emphasis they placed on the political and juridical strands of the constitutional tradition, they united in opposing originalist jurisprudence for the two "mortal sins of constitutional interpretation" it was guilty of. These sins are legal formalism and philosophic or normative foundationalism.[110] Yet liberal constitutional theorists did not succeed in dissociating themselves entirely from the constitutionalism of the founding. The new amendment theorists are unable or choose not to abandon the idea of "amendment." The common law constitutionalists feel obliged to engage the idea of constitutional fidelity, which since the publication of Raoul Berger's *Government by Judiciary* has been identified with the theory of originalism.

Liberal concern to break the monopoly on constitutional fidelity associated with originalist jurisprudence was a principal motive in organizing the 1997 symposium, "Fidelity in Constitutional Theory."[111] According to liberal critics, conservatives define constitutional fidelity narrowly to mean either adherence to the text as a body of legal rules or to specific understandings held by the framers and ratifiers of the Constitution. Liberals, in contrast, hold to a broad conception of fidelity in the form either of historical synthesis, as in Ackerman's descriptive-normative theory of constitutional amendment, or of constitutional interpretation based on moral and political philosophy. The jurisprudence of Ronald Dworkin illustrates the philosophical approach to constitutional fidelity.

Dworkin seeks to confound originalists by claiming that fidelity to the Constitution requires precisely what they most object to: reliance on moral philosophy.[112] According to Dworkin, fidelity takes into account the written text and structure of the Constitution, as well as past constitutional practice. Ultimately, however, constitutional fidelity requires broad judicial responsibility to hold legislation to moral standards. Such standards are abstract and are necessarily expressed in abstract constitutional language.[113] According to Dworkin, the Framers made a constitution "out of abstract moral principles, not coded references to their own opinions . . . about the best way to apply those principles."[114] Therefore, although it is proper to follow the Framers' "semantic intentions" in pursuing questions of moral judgment, such as the meaning of cruel and unusual punishment in the Eighth Amendment, Dworkin says it is wrong to consult the Framers' political intentions, that is, their assumptions and expectations about how a constitutional provision should be applied and enforced.[115] Constitutional fidelity thus insists on "fresh moral judgments" about issues that divide citizens, rendered by judges who read the Constitution "as a charter of principle" and who in individual cases give "the best interpretation of an abstract principle of constitutional morality."[116]

Neorepublican amendment theory and common law constitutionalism have been described as broad or "soft" originalism aimed at beating the originalists at their own game. According to one of the organizers of the 1997 fidelity symposium, it is a strategy dictated by the belief that the only hope of persuading Justice Antonin Scalia to accept liberal interpretations of the Constitution is to make originalist arguments.[117] If that is true, then Justice Scalia may have more effect on liberal opponents of originalism than on judicial colleagues, in relation to whom he appears to have no interest in coalition building. Despite a defiantly nonpolitical posture, however, Justice Scalia emerged as the leading advocate of originalist jurisprudence in the 1990s.

V

In the 1990s, original-intent jurisprudence earned a surprising measure of intellectual respect if, as appears to be the case, liberal constitutional theory was revised to take into account originalist claims. At the least, originalism was recognized as having rhetorical and symbolic value.[118] In constitutional politics it became possible, and perhaps strategically necessary, to distinguish between forms or variations of originalism.[119] In this theoretical context, Justice Scalia, in an academic lecture in 1996, presented a major statement of originalist jurisprudence that was text based rather than intent-seeking in the broader historical sense implied in Raoul Berger's theory of constitutional interpretation.[120]

The central theme in Scalia's analysis of the field of public law was the theory of the living constitution, which he believed was still dominant in the judicial and academic legal community.[121] He saw legal liberalism as the functional equivalent of common law judging. In noting that constitutional law is not mainly about the Constitution, he said that it is about previous cases that are adhered to as precedent or distinguished and evaded as not on point, in the manner of common law adjudication.[122] In substantive terms, constitutional law under the doctrine of living constitutionalism amounts to judges deciding cases on the basis of their personal, subjective view of what justice or good public policy requires.[123] Properly understood, neither the Constitution nor constitutional law warrants description as common law, defined as law developed by judges.[124] Yet in contemporary living constitutionalism the Constitution is treated as common law, and judicial policy making is protected and privileged by identification with the written Constitution. This symbolic association enables federal judges to trump policy making by legislative statute in an antidemocratic manner. For this reason Justice Scalia opposed common law, or living constitutionalism.[125]

In place of subjective common law judging, Scalia urged text-based originalism, or textualism. Every issue of law dealt with in federal courts, he said, involves interpretation of text, in the form of statute, administrative regulation, or constitutional clause or provision. In both statutory and constitutional interpretation, judges look for the "objectified" intent of the lawgiver in the text. This objectified textual intent, rather than what the original drafters intended, is "the original meaning of the text," according to Justice Scalia.[126] He concluded that in the American constitutional tradition the text is the law and must be observed. In democratic government, moreover, the popularly elected legislature writes the laws.

Justice Scalia offers little comment on the philosophy or art of interpreting texts. A text should be construed neither "strictly" nor "leniently," he says. Rather, "it should be construed reasonably, to contain all that it fairly means."[127] Elaborating, he notes that in textual interpretation, context is everything. The context of the Constitution tells the interpreter not to expect great detail, giving words and phrases an expansive rather than narrow interpretation, though not an interpretation that the language will not bear.[128] Scalia seems to be saying that if judges and lawyers can be brought to understand the fundamental character or nature of the Constitution, the problem of interpretation will take care of itself. The real problem is the "great divide" in constitutional interpretation between original meaning and current meaning.[129]

The current-meaning, or living-constitutionalist, school claims to provide the flexibility in public policy required by a changing society. Justice Scalia contends, however, that most of the "growing" cultivated by living constitutionalists has imposed greater restraints on democratic government. He states that in repudiating democratic government, devotees of the living constitution in reality seek to prevent, rather than facilitate, social change. At bottom, the doctrine of the living constitution is vacuous because there can be no agreement on the guiding principle of the constitutional evolution that the doctrine posits. Scalia asserts that evolutionism is simply not a practicable constitutional philosophy. Appealing to the written constitutionalism of the founding, he says that a constitution has an antievolutionary purpose. Although there can be disagreement over how the original meaning of the Constitution applies to a present problem, originalism can give many clear-cut answers. Living constitutionalism, however, makes every question an open question.[130]

The English scholar S. E. Finer observes that once the constitution of a country is written, thereafter it is always written. The constitution may be amended or an entirely new constitution adopted, but reversion to an unwritten or customary constitution does not occur.[131] Nevertheless, in the history of written constitutionalism, as Finer notes, a constitutional text may become a purely nominal or façade constitution.[132] Since the American Revolution, constitutions in the United States have assumed written, documentary form. In the theory of American constitutionalism, moreover, the forms of the Constitution are purposive. Properly understood, they are not simply a means to the end, but are united with the ends of the Constitution.[133] The form of the Constitution is intended to have substantive influence and effect. This is what is meant in saying that the Constitution has intrinsic, not merely instrumental, value. Constitutional government and written constitutionalism as the American project rest on the idea that law is an effort to constrain government with words inscribed in a text. It follows that when a legal text is made or becomes indeterminate, it serves as an invitation to exercise power by determining what the text shall mean.[134]

Liberal judicial interventionism as practiced by Chief Justice Warren and Justice Brennan, for all that it seemed to reach beyond the Constitution in seeking just outcomes of constitutional disputes, never simply dispensed with the text of the Constitution. In contrast, contemporary advocates of common law constitutionalism more readily and with greater candor admit to going outside the text of the Constitution in search of philosophical and historical grounds for constitutional decision making. To the extent that the constitutional text is retained in common-law constitutional theory, the retention is vestigial and practically inconsequential.

Despite an observable trend in this direction, it is doubtful that in the foreseeable future the constitutional text will be overtly repudiated or expunged from the language of American government and politics. It is not necessary for that to happen, however, in order to render the Constitution otiose, ineffectual, and of no account concerning the ends and purposes for which it was established. To be sure, the constitutional text has symbolic, rhetorical, and civil-religious significance that encourages, if it does not require, reference to it in political and legal discourse. There is a world of difference, however, between reference to the Constitution that describes and explains how acts of government conform to—hence, preserve and promote—principles, goods, and values embodied in the text; and constitutional allusion that treats the text as a justification, if not merely a pretext, for government actions based on partisan and ideological considerations unrelated to ends and principles embodied in the text. It is of course true that value judgments are involved in distinguishing between these different ways of recognizing or taking account of the Constitution. If values are not wholly subjective, however, then the judgment required in evaluating constitutionalism and constitutional government should not be categorically dismissed as personal and arbitrary.[135]

When the Constitution functions as a rhetorical pretext, the restraint on political power that is the principal reason for adopting a normative fundamental law is rendered illusory. Again, it is difficult to avoid the historical conclusion that in a practical sense the point of having a written constitution is to limit government. This is not to deny the obvious truth that a constitution grants, confers, or delegates power. Yet in the granting of power the constitution stipulates forms, procedures, and objects that define and limit governmental power. Limited government thus constitutes the logic, rationale, and end of written constitutionalism, if not the idea of constitutionalism itself.

Constitutional controversy in the United States still takes the form, ordinarily, of asking whether the Constitution permits, prohibits, or requires a particular act or policy of government that has been or may be called into question. In the deepest sense, however, the crisis that almost all commentators agree exists in contemporary constitutional law reflects uncertainty about the nature of the American Constitution. In this crisis the substantive issue goes beyond the role of the judiciary and whether judicial activism or judicial restraint is preferable. The real issue is the constitution of the American people. In essence, the controversy concerns the ends, principles, values, and institutions by which the people of the United States exist and govern themselves as a political community. With reference to the subject matter and specific materials considered in this book, the crisis concerns the relationship between the text of the U.S. Constitution and the nation's constitutive principles, institutions, and values.

These questions engage scholars.[136] They are of preeminent concern, however, to citizens and government officials, who are required to deal with constitutional controversy and have a practical interest in knowing what the Constitution is. Judges are by no means the only government officials who make constitutional decisions. Neverthless, preponderant authority to decide what the Constitution means has been acquired by the judicial branch or conceded to it by politically minded lawmakers and executive officers. This circumstance makes it pertinent to consider what justices of the Supreme Court have said in recent years about the nature of the Constitution.

VI

The constitutional jurisprudence of the Supreme Court rests on the assumption that decisions in this area of public law are based on the Constitution. Whatever the Court offers as the ground of decision in a particular case logically can be considered the Constitution, or a part of it. It comes as no surprise to discover, as even a small sampling of cases shows, that the justices disagree about what the Constitution is. More precisely, their opinions differ over what reference to the Constitution signifies and comprehends in political and legal discourse.

The justices frequently state that in constitutional cases sound adjudicative method requires consideration of the text, structure, principles, and history of the Constitution, as well as prior constitutional decisions of the Supreme Court and the federal judiciary. In practice, however, the political import of many cases, in addition to the adversarial nature of the litigation and adjudication process, requires the justices to select as decisive one feature of what to an outside observer might be described as an eclectic or pluralistic constitutional tradition, signified or represented in the written Constitution.

In *U.S. v. Lopez* (1995), for example, Chief Justice Rehnquist wrote a majority opinion striking down an act of Congress, purportedly based on the commerce clause of the Constitution, which prohibited possession of firearms in school zones. Beginning with what he regarded as "first principles" concerning the nature of the federal government as a government of enumerated powers, Rehnquist offered a text-based explanation of the constitutional impropriety of the congressional statute. He concluded that the possession of a gun in a local school zone was in no sense an economic activity affecting any sort of interstate commerce.[137] To uphold the act as constitutional, he reasoned, "would bid fair to convert congressional authority under the Commerce Clause to a general police power of the sort retained by the States." In Rehnquist's interpretive method, however, the constitutional text, enumerating specific legislative powers, embodied and signified a larger, abstract principle. This was the principle of divided sovereignty between the states and the federal government. To approve the act of Congress in question, he said, would be to conclude that there could never be a distinction between what is truly national and what is truly local.[138]

In *Seminole Tribe of Florida v. Florida* (1996), Chief Justice Rehnquist wrote an opinion that rested on a nontextualist foundation. In this case the Court held that the Eleventh Amendment, barring lawsuits against states by citizens of another state or a foreign state, prevents congressional authorization of suits by private parties, even when Congress acts under the exclusive power, conferred on it by the text of the commerce clause, to regulate commerce with the Indian tribes. Rehnquist said the decision was based on "the background principle of state sovereign immunity embodied in the Eleventh Amendment."[139] Viewed in this light, Rehnquist observed, the Eleventh Amendment prevents suits by private parties against unconsenting states even when Congress has exclusive authority in an area.[140]

In a dissenting opinion, Justice Souter accused the chief justice of importing the English common law into the Constitution, against the intention of the Framers. The common law was not received into federal constitutional law and cannot be considered an enforceable background principle, declared Justice Souter.[141] The Framers opposed transforming common law into constitutional law because they feared the exercise of judicial power over the substantive policy that common law jurisdiction conferred on courts.[142] Souter likened the majority decision to the judicial activist jurisprudence of the era of *Lochner v. New York* (1905), in which the Court subordinated the text of the Constitution to "judicially discoverable principles unfettered to any written provision."[143]

In *Printz v. U.S.* (1997), Justice Scalia wrote the majority opinion holding unconstitutional a provision in an act of Congress that utilized local law enforcement officers in a federal regulatory gun control policy. Scalia, noted for his textualist-originalist approach to constitutional interpretation, said that in this case no constitutional text spoke to the precise question at issue.[144] The Court must therefore seek the basis for its decision in historical understanding and practice, the structure of the Constitution, and the jurisprudence of the Supreme Court. The premise of Justice Scalia's opinion was the "incontestable" fact that the Constitution established a system of "dual sovereignty."[145] He documented this assertion with references to *The Federalist* and Madison's notes on the Constitutional Convention, which made clear that the division of governmental sovereignty into two separate spheres was "one of the Constitution's structural protections of liberty."[146] The most conclusive authority on which the decision rested, however, was prior Supreme Court decisions that said the federal government could not compel states to implement federal regulatory programs.[147]

In a dissenting opinion, Justice Stevens rebuked the Court for its display of text-disregarding judicial activism. He accused Justice Scalia of using historical sources, the structure of the Constitution, and prior Court decisions to establish the presumption "that it is the members of this Court, rather than the elected representatives of the people, who should determine whether the Constitution contains the unwritten rule that the Court announces today."[148] Justice Stevens declared: "There is not a clause, sentence, or paragraph in the entire text of the Constitution of the United States that supports the proposition" that a local police officer may ignore a congressional statutory command pursuant to an express delegation of power enumerated in Article I of the Constitution.[149] Challenging Scalia's textualist credentials, Justice Stevens charged him with the impropriety of fashioning a "judicially crafted constitutional rule" from a silent text, as well as a historical record that supported the federal regulatory scheme.[150]

A textualist interpreter in *Printz*, Justice Stevens employed the logic of "fundamental principles" in *U.S. Term Limits Inc. v. Thornton* (1995), the Arkansas term limits case. At issue was whether a state constitutional amendment prohibiting candidates for Congress from appearing on the ballot if they had served three terms in the House of Representatives or two terms in the Senate violated the federal Constitution. Justice Stevens, for the Court, declared the amendment "contrary to 'the fundamental principle of our representative democracy' embodied in the Constitution, that the 'people should choose whom they please to govern them.' " He said that to permit states to adopt qualifications for congressional service "would be inconsistent with the Framers' vision of a uniform National Legislature representing the people of the United States."[151]

In Stevens's opinion, it was not the text of the Constitution that was controlling, but principles believed to be embodied in the text. As so often in constitutional adjudication, the significance of the text in relation to fundamental constitutional principles was in dispute. In a dissenting opinion, Justice Thomas said textual provisions concerning qualifications of members of Congress did not necessarily embody the principles averred by Justice Stevens. Thomas believed the Arkansas constitutional amendment was consistent with the "notion of popular sovereignty that undergirds the Constitution." This principle, he declared, "does not erase state boundaries, but rather tracks them." To invalidate the Arkansas amendment, it was necessary "to point to something in the Federal Constitution that deprives the people of Arkansas of the power to enact such measures."[152]

Contemporary constitutional theory serves both descriptive-explanatory and normative functions. It accounts for existing governmental institutions while directing and prescribing constitutional decision making and governmental practice toward the ends and purposes of the regime.[153] The idea of an eclectic, pluralistic Constitution might be taken as an apt characterization of the choices in constitutional adjudication available to federal judges in the late twentieth century. Consistent with this view is the fact that the Supreme Court as an institution has not made a commitment to any one of the several methods of adjudication presently employed in constitutional law. No judge, including Justice Scalia—notwithstanding his proclivity toward textualist originalism—adheres with rigorous consistency to a single jurisprudential method.[154] The "analytical heart" of the Supreme Court in the 1990s, observes Cass R. Sunstein, consists of five justices who refuse to subscribe to a single approach. Thinking inductively rather than deductively, eschewing broad rules and abstract theories, they proceed on a case-by-case basis, focusing only on what is necessary to decide a particular case.[155]

Although supported by empirical observation, it is not clear that the idea of an electic-pluralistic Constitution has gained normative acceptance as an authoritative and legitimate account of the rule of law in American government and politics. For example, a theorist of the common law Constitution states that the terms of debate in constitutional jurisprudence continue to be set by the view that principles of constitutional law must ultimately be traced to the text of the Constitution. In this view, any alleged departure from the text is considered illegitimate.[156] The developments in constitutional theory surveyed in this book suggest, however, that this situation is changing. As further evidence of this trend, several Supreme Court justices in the 1990s appear to be engaged in an effort to shift the focus of constitutional adjudication away from the written Constitution. This would weaken, if not undermine, the textualist-originalist interpretive presumption that written constitutionalism introduces into American government.

A notable attempt to reconceptualize the nature of American constitutionalism appeared in *Planned Parenthood of Southeastern Pennsylvania v. Casey* (1992). Although upholding a Pennsylvania abortion regulation act against constitutional challenge, the Supreme Court in this case confirmed *Roe v. Wade* as the foundation of the right of abortion and national pro-choice policy. From the standpoint of constitutional theory, the significance of the decision lay in the attempt of Justices Kennedy, Souter, and O'Connor, in a plurality opinion, to provide a descriptive and normative account of the American polity in the late twentieth century.

The plurality opinion conceives of the Constitution as "a covenant" and "a coherent succession" running "from the first generation of Americans to us and then to future generations." Each generation, the justices admonish, must learn that the written terms of the Constitution embody ideas and aspirations that "must survive more ages than one." The Constitution is for the good of the people, but responsibility for the Constitution belongs to the Supreme Court. The Court's responsibility is explained in the assertion that the "root of American governmental power is revealed most clearly" in the power conferred by the Constitution on the federal judiciary—specifically, on the Supreme Court.[157] As a result of this revelation, it falls to the Supreme Court to decide intensely divisive national controversies. Not often is the Court asked to perform this duty; only twice in their lifetimes, the justices observe—in *Brown v. Board of Education* and *Roe v. Wade*—have they been called on to do so. On those occasions, however, or "whenever the Court's interpretation of the Constitution calls the contending sides of a national controversy to end their national division by accepting a common mandate rooted in the Constitution," the decision of the Supreme Court possesses a special dimension. It acquires "rare precedential force" to counter efforts that will inevitably be made to overturn the decision.[158] If the Court should yield to these political pressures— should it "overrule under fire in the absence of the most compelling reason to reexamine a watershed decision"—its legitimacy will be subverted.[159]

The question necessarily arises: What makes the decisions of the Supreme Court legitimate in ordinary cases, as well as on the extraordinary occasions when it is called on to settle national political controversy? Is there a particular manner or method of constitutional adjudication on which the legitimacy of a Supreme Court decision depends? In the view of the plurality justices, the answer to these questions is principled decision making, or the appearance thereof. Justices Kennedy, Souter, and O'Connor declare: "The Court must take care to speak and act in ways that allow people to accept its decisions on the terms the Court claims for them, as grounded truly in principle, not as compromises with social and political pressures having, as such, no bearing on the principled choices that the Court is obliged to make."[160] The opinion states further that "the Court's legitimacy depends on making legally principled decisions under circumstances in which their principled character is sufficiently plausible to be accepted by the Nation."[161]

The type of adjudication prescribed, and presumably practiced, by the *Casey* plurality is common law constitutional interpretation. Decisions are made and legal doctrines are developed incrementally, case by case. Decisions acquire precedential force and become authoritative not because they uphold fundamental law, in the sense of conforming to a fixed constitutional principle of unchanging meaning. Decisions are authoritative because they are "principled." In the view of the plurality justices, this means simply that a decision is not an expedient compromise between contending political forces.

The key point in constitutional common law judging is that there is a "promise of constancy" implicit in the Court's decision, especially a decision intended to settle a national political controversy. Once given, this promise "binds its maker for as long as the power to stand by the decision survives and the understanding of the issue has not changed so fundamentally as to render the commitment obsolete."[162] The plurality opinion thus identifies the doctrine of stare decisis, which in common law constitutional interpretation has much greater authority and effect than has traditionally been accorded it in constitutional law. Kennedy, Souter, and O'Connor hold that a decision-precedent is controlling until the Court determines that public opinion has changed to such an extent that the principle embodied in the decision no longer applies and the promise given no longer need be considered binding.[163]

The role envisioned for the Supreme Court by the *Casey* plurality, like the substantive-values activism it may be intended to supersede, raises the question of the countermajoritarian difficulty that has bedeviled liberal constitutional theory since the Warren Court. This impression is strengthened by the fact that *Casey* confirmed *Roe v. Wade*, perhaps the most activist Supreme Court decision of the twentieth century.

The members of the *Casey* plurality forfend against the charge of judicial imperialism by equating the legitimacy of Supreme Court decision making with the political well-being of the American people. They state that the Court's legitimacy is an achievement that has been earned over time. "So, indeed, must be the character of a Nation of people who aspire to live according to the rule of law." Americans' belief in themselves as a law-loving and -abiding people, the plurality justices immodestly aver, is inseparable from "their understanding of the Court invested with the authority to decide their constitutional cases and speak before all others for their constitutional ideals." Kennedy, Souter, and O'Connor warn, "If the Court's legitimacy should be undermined, so would the country be in its very ability to see itself through its constitutional ideals." This is not said for reasons of institutional self-interest, the justices explain, "but for the sake of the Nation to which [the Court] is responsible."[164]

Casey may signal a shift in the theory of constitutional adjudication used to justify the role of the Supreme Court in American government at the end of the twentieth century. Morton Horwitz, a liberal commentator, saw the decision as a repudiation of the originalist attempt to deny the legitimacy of changing constitutional meaning under the doctrine of the living constitution. According to Horwitz, the plurality opinion offered a theory explaining when and how fundamental constitutional change was legitimate and could be effected by the Supreme Court. Rejecting the notion of a timeless and unchanging fundamental law, the plurality gave promise of resolving the crisis of legitimacy in constitutional law by articulating a concept of "legal fundamentality" compatible with modernist philosophy. Horwitz believed the Court also avoided the appearance of a judicial imposition of values inconsistent with democratic theory.[165]

From a conservative perspective, too, the *Casey* decision appeared to mark a major shift in constitutional theory. Gerard V. Bradley treated the plurality opinion as promulgating a new constitution, the distinguishing feature of which is the power of the Supreme Court to create constitutional meaning. Bradley said the new constitution is related to the old one insofar as judicial opinions refer to provisions of the text and the justices believe they are being faithful to the original Constitution by addressing problems contemplated by the founders. In fact, this approach to interpretation perfects the judicial activism of the 1960s and rejects the written constitutionalism of the founding. It does so in the most significant sense, Bradley argued, by giving the Supreme Court authority to decide anything that it believes is controversial enough to require a uniform national policy.[166]

In *Cooper v. Aaron* (1958), the Little Rock school desegregation case, the Supreme Court claimed that its decisions interpreting the Constitution, no less than the Constitution itself, were the supreme law of the land. Instructed by liberal theorists, activist judges since then have with increasing candor treated constitutional law as a policy-making legislative endeavor. The *Casey* joint opinion, written by three Republican justices, suggests that the originalist challenge to judicial activism has forced judicial middle-of-the-roaders to associate themselves more openly with advocates of living constitutionalism. In *Casey* this willingness to break with written constitutionalism is seen in the decisive emphasis placed on stare decisis as a controlling principle in what in essence is conceived of as a common law constitution. This is the reason for affirming *Roe v. Wade,* a decision that some or all of the authors of the plurality opinion appear to believe erroneous under the original Constitution but which they accept under the new constitution posited in *Casey*.[167]

In public policy terms, the central feature of the *Casey* constitution is the right of abortion, redefined and relabeled as the right of personal liberty under the due process clause of the Fourteenth Amendment.[168] The substance of the new constitution in institutional terms is the sovereign, or ultimate, law-making authority of the Supreme Court. In Bradley's view, the joint opinion expresses the centrist Republican judges' appeal to public opinion for confirmation of the Court's authority as the ultimate maker of constitutional meaning. The question after *Casey* is whether the people will ratify the new constitution.[169]

It is perhaps surprising that Bradley's analysis of present constitutional tendencies, at a descriptive level, comports with the account of common law constitutional interpretation advanced by liberal theorists. Unless his argument is dictated by rhetorical strategy, Bradley seems prepared to recognize that the judicially fabricated constitution of the *Casey* decision may gain acceptance as the ground of legitimacy in American government.[170] Other conservative scholars, however, reject this description of the current situation and make a traditional textualist-originalist appeal for constitutional renewal.[171] Meanwhile, on the liberal side of the political spectrum, as we have seen, a variety of theories compete for ascendancy as the most persuasive account and justification of the contemporary liberal state.

VII

The symbols of American constitutionalism—the Constitutional document and ideas such as liberty, equality, popular sovereignty, and the rule of law—are so firmly embedded in the political culture that both sides in the contemporary debate are constrained to accept them. Consensus on the symbols exists at such a high level of generality, however, as to be practically meaningless. No one believes that it means very much for the actual decision of cases that a liberal like Ronald Dworkin should agree with Justice Scalia that constitutional interpretation properly takes into account the text, structure, past constitutional practice, and history of constitutional law.[172] Nor can it be encouraging to liberals that Scalia, the textualist-originalist, seems to adopt the outlook of a legal realist in rejecting the possibility of a neutral ground in the culture wars.[173]

There is, then, more perhaps than at any time in the twentieth century, disagreement, confusion, and uncertainty about what the Constitution of the United States is.[174] This does not prevent government officials from making constitutional decisions, especially if they believe there is no right answer to the question. In the absence of a federal constitutional convention, which though permitted by the text of the Constitution is politically inconceivable in the foreseeable future, the question—what is the Constitution?—will be decided pluralistically, at different levels of government and in various forums, including that of professional scholarship.[175] The Supreme Court will have a major voice in the constitutional debate, but it will not be the only voice.[176]

The deeper significance of the controversy over the nature of the Constitution concerns the character and condition of republican government in the United States. As in the founding period, the question is whether American citizens will govern themselves through limited constitutions, guaranteeing individual and local liberty under the rule of law. In constituting government it is still a practical consideration whether the ground of political legitimacy should be a written constitution or an unwritten constitution of custom, institutional practice, and common law adjudication. Written constitutions were conceived in the eighteenth century as an improvement in political science that could make fundamental law enforceable and effective. Establishing the ends, principles, and forms of republican government in a written constitution would not, by itself, be sufficient to limit government, but having a written constitution was seen as a necessary basis for placing limits on government.[177] A properly enforced constitutional document had a symbolic and civic-religious dimension that was integral to its effectiveness. Although recognizing the imprecision of language as a means of organizing and regulating government, the founders believed that "particular discussions and adjudications" of the Constitution, which were anticipated in its enforcement, would ascertain the meaning of the text.[178] Should adjudication and interpretation lead to trivialization and effective dismissal of the constitutional text, however, producing a situation where rhetorical symbolism was all that remained, the written Constitution would not be a real constitution, either of republican government or of fundamental law.

Written constitutionalism has declined in the twentieth-century United States, a corollary if not a consequence of the establishment of a national government of unlimited power. The desire to restore limited government is expressed in political opposition to the expansion of the regulatory-welfare state. It has been the main cause of the revival of written constitutionalism, as seen in the emergence of original-intent jurisprudence. As the federal government has extended its power ever farther into social and political life, more people have been led to ask: "What kind of government, and what kind of constitution, does the United States have, anyway?"

With the exception of the "imperial presidency" in the Johnson-Nixon era, debate on this question in constitutional law and theory since the 1960s has focused on the judicial branch and the counterma-joritarian difficulty. In the main, defenders of government by judiciary have argued that an activist Supreme Court promotes democracy by enacting public policies that promote democracy and are good for the people. More recently the claim is made that an activist Court pro-motes republican self-government by making its decisions through a deliberative process, thus demonstrating its consistency with demo-cratic rule and maintaining its political legitimacy.[179] Among liberals, however, the assertion of common law constitutionalism as a suppos-edly moderate alternative to more forthright judicial interventionism suggests that these arguments have lost much of their persuasiveness. Within the academic legal culture the idea that courts uniquely speak the voice of "public reason" is contradicted by the well-known anec-dotal account of Justice Brennan's reply to the question, what does it take to win a case in the Supreme Court? The answer, said Brennan, was five votes. It would be more accurate to say that when the judges engage in activist policy making, they illustrate the danger, perceived by the founders, that claims to protect minority rights may be a pretext for "introducing into the government a will not dependent on the [ma-jority], . . . a will independent of the society itself."[180]

As a practical matter, the Supreme Court for the foreseeable future will have the last word in constitutional interpretation. The elaborate depository of constitutional law, resulting from judicial review and le-galistic interpretation of the constitutional text, gives the Court the pre-sumptive upper hand in contests over constitutional meaning. All of the present justices, moreover, agree on the institutional value of main-taining the Court's authority as the ultimate interpreter of the Consti-tution.[181] Most of the time, moreover, members of Congress and officials in the executive branch are content to let the judges assume responsibility for resolving disputes over constitutional interpretation. Nevertheless, the tradition of written constitutionalism, which has been revived in original-intent jurisprudence, makes it possible to apply concepts and doctrines not recoverable, or more difficult to re-cover, under the doctrine of the unwritten living constitution. Under the originalist-textualist approach to constitutional interpretation, for example, doctrines of federalism and property rights have been revived that were long thought consigned to the dustbin of history. In contemporary constitutional politics these doctrines are regarded as conservative; but the originalist method and the tradition of written constitutionalism could also be used for liberal purposes, to defend the regulatory-welfare state on the basis of text-based doctrines of national supremacy, should that exigency arise.[182]

In conclusion, tension exists between the founding project of written constitutionalism and the twentieth-century project of unwritten living constitutionalism. As a matter of historical fact, the result of this tension may be said to be a pluralistic constitutional culture suitable to the needs of a pluralistic republican people.[183] Whether this perception will be elevated into a persuasive constitutional theory, providing a normative framework for limited republican government in the United States, remains to be seen.

Notes

1. Michael Kammen, *A Machine That Would Go of Itself: The Constitution in American Culture* (New York: Vintage Books, 1987), p. 399.

2. Describing Bork's defeat as a decisive "constitutional moment," an optimistic liberal commentator said it signified popular approval of judicial discretion exercised for the "protection of rights not specifically stated in the text or intended by the framers," and "public acceptance that the Constitution is a commitment that certain areas of public life should be governed by unelected judges with the authority to decide what values are so important that they should be protected from majority rule." Erwin Chemerinsky, "The Constitution Is Not 'Hard Law': The Bork Rejection and the Future of Constitutional Jurisprudence," *Constitutional Commentary* 6 (1989), 29–38, at p. 36.

3. Morton J. Horwitz, "Foreword: The Constitution of Change: Legal Fundamentality without Fundamentalism," *Harvard Law Review* 107 (1993), 33–34.

4. H. Jefferson Powell, *The Moral Tradition of American Constitutionalism: A Theological Interpretation* (Durham, N.C.: Duke University Press, 1993), p. 10.

5. David P. Bryden, "A Conservative Case for Judicial Activism," *The Public Interest* 111 (1993), 72–85.

6. Norman P. Barry, *The New Right* (London: Croom Helm, 1987), pp. 8–9.

7. But it may not have been the milestone that a generation of liberal constitutional scholars thought it was. For a revisionist view of the policy-making significance of *Brown v. Board of Education*, see Gerald N. Rosenberg, *The Hollow Hope: Can Courts Bring About Social Change?* (Chicago: University of Chicago Press, 1991).

8. G. Edward White, *Earl Warren: A Public Life* (New York: Oxford University Press, 1982).

9. H. Jefferson Powell, *The Moral Tradition of American Constitutionalism*, pp. 169–72.

10. Ibid., pp. 173–77.

11. Raoul Berger, *Congress v. The Supreme Court* (Cambridge, Mass.: Harvard University Press, 1969).

12. Ibid., p. 245.

13. Ibid., pp. 1–2.

14. Ibid., p. 252.

15. Ibid., pp. 252, 254.

16. Ibid., p. 282.

17. Ibid., p. 3.

18. Ibid., p. 7.

19. Ibid., p. 366.

20. Howard Gillman, "The Collapse of Constitutional Originalism and the Rise of the Notion of the 'Living Constitution' in the Course of American State-Building," *Studies in American Political Development* 11 (Fall 1997), 191–247, esp. 197–213.

21. Robert H. Bork, *The Tempting of America: The Political Seduction of the Law* (New York: Simon & Schuster, 1990), p. 2.

22. Ibid., p.5.

23. Earl M. Maltz, "The Failure of Attacks on Constitutional Originalism," *Constitutional Commentary* 4 (1987), 43–56, at 51, 55.

24. Earl M. Maltz, *Rethinking Constitutional Law: Originalism, Interventionism, and the Politics of Judicial Review* (Lawrence: University Press of Kansas, 1994), pp. 26–27.

25. Gary L. McDowell, "The Philosophic Dimension of Constitutional Interpretation," unpublished manuscript, pp. 1–4.

26. Henry P. Monaghan, "Our Perfect Constitution," *New York University Law Review* 56 (1981), 353–96, at 353.

27. Ibid., p. 354.

28. Ibid., pp. 375–76, 384.

29. Maltz, *Rethinking Constitutional Law*, pp. 15–16. See also Michael P. Zuckert, "Epistemology and Hermeneutics in the Constitutional Jurisprudence of John Marshall," in Thomas C. Shevory, ed., *John Marshall's Achievement: Law, Politics, and Constitutional Interpretations* (Westport, Conn.: Greenwood Press, 1989), pp. 193–216.

30. Michael S. Moore, "Do We Have an Unwritten Constitution?" *Southern California Law Review* 63 (1989), 107–39, and "The Constitution as Hard Law," *Constitutional Commentary* 6 (1989), 51–67; Stanley R. Brubaker, "Conserving the Constitution," *American Bar Foundation Research Journal* 1987, 261–80, and "What Constitutes the Constitution?" unpublished manuscript, 1990.

31. While insisting that the "principles of the actual Constitution make the judge's major moral choices for him," Bork acknowledged a role for moral philosophy in constitutional law. Observing that moral philosophy was valuable "at the retail level," he said that moral reasoning made judges aware of the complexities, likenesses, and dissimilarities of situations. Bork believed this

type of philosophical analysis was essential in applying the principles of the Constitution to new situations. There was a limit, however, on the use of moral philosophy: judges must not use it to create new constitutional principles. Bork, *The Tempting of America*, p. 254.

32. Graham Walker, *Moral Foundations of Constitutional Thought* (Princeton: Princeton University Press, 1990), pp. 62–63n.

33. Ibid., p. 63n.

34. Thomas C. Grey, "Do We Have an Unwritten Constitution?" *Stanford Law Review* 27 (1975), 703–18, at 703–09.

35. Ibid., p. 709.

36. Thomas C. Grey, "Origins of the Unwritten Constitution: Fundamental Law in American Revolutionary Thought," *Stanford Law Review* 30 (1978), 843–94.

37. Ely was the author of a stinging critique of *Roe v. Wade* as an example of unconstitutional judicial activism. While conceding that unlimited majority rule could be dangerous, he said it required a heroic inference to reach "the conclusion that enforcement by unelected officials of an 'unwritten constitution' is an appropriate response in a democratic republic." John Hart Ely, "Constitutional Interpretivism: Its Allure and Impossibility," *Indiana Law Journal* 53 (1978), 411; Ely, *Democracy and Distrust: A Theory of Judicial Review* (Cambridge, Mass. : Harvard University Press, 1980), p. 8.

38. Ely, *Democracy and Distrust*, p. vii.

39. Ibid., p. 12.

40. Ibid., p. 13.

41. John Hart Ely, "On Discovering Fundamental Values," *Harvard Law Review* 92 (1978), 21n.

42. Ely, *Democracy and Distrust*, p. 41.

43. Laurence H. Tribe, "The Puzzling Persistence of Process-Based Constitutional Theories," *Yale Law Journal* 89 (1980), 1063–80. Tribe criticized Ely's theory of constitutional review for trying to avoid substantive problems of moral philosophy.

44. Michael J. Perry, "Book Review," *Columbia Law Review* 78 (1978), 678–705, at 697.

45. Ibid., pp. 700–01.

46. Paul Brest, "The Misconceived Quest for the Original Understanding," *Boston University Law Review*, 60 (1980), 204–38, at 219. Citing the political philosopher Quentin Skinner, Brest said the historian brings to a text expectations and preconceptions that organize and determine her perceptions so as to preclude understanding an author as he understood himself.

47. Ibid., p. 221.

48. Ibid., pp. 225–26.

49. Ibid., pp. 205, 226.

50. Ibid., p. 234.

51. Ibid., p. 224.

52. Ibid., pp. 234–35.

53. Speech by Justice William J. Brennan, Jr., to the Text and Teaching Sym-

posium, Georgetown University, 12 October 1985, in *The Great Debate: Interpreting Our Written Constitution* (Washington, D.C.: The Federalist Society, 1987), pp. 11–25.

54. Bork, *The Tempting of America*, p. 300.

55. Morton Horwitz, "Foreword: The Constitution of Change," p. 117.

56. Chemerinsky, "The Constitution Is Not 'Hard Law,' " pp. 29–38, at 29.

57. Bork, *The Tempting of America*, pp. 271, 323.

58. Ibid., p. 337. A similar view is expressed in Joseph D. Grano, "Deconstructing the Constitution," *Academic Questions* 2 (Winter, 1988–89), 10–21.

59. Ethan Bronner, *Battle for Justice: How the Bork Nomination Shook America* (New York: W. W. Norton, 1989), pp. 98–104.

60. Grano, "Deconstructing the Constitution," p. 18.

61. Philip Bobbitt, "Constitutional Interpretation," in Kermit H. Hall, ed., *The Oxford Companion to the Supreme Court of the United States* (New York: Oxford University Press, 1992), p. 189.

62. Chemerinsky, "The Constitution Is Not 'Hard Law,' " 37–38.

63. Stephen M. Griffin, "What Is Constitutional Theory? The Newer Theory and the Decline of the Learned Tradition," *Southern California Law Review* 62 (1989), 493–538, at 495.

64. Chemerinsky, "The Constitution Is Not 'Hard Law,' " pp. 36–37.

65. Jeffrey Rosen, "Originalist Sin," *The New Republic*, 5 May 1997, p. 36.

66. Steven D. Smith, "The Constitution of Babel," *First Things* (January 1998), pp. 27–32, at 27. See Fred M. Frohock, "The Boundaries of Public Reason," *American Political Science Review* 91 (1997), 833–44.

67. J. M. Balkin, "The Rule of Law as a Source of Constitutional Change," *Constitutional Commentary* 6 (1989), 21–27, at 25.

68. Lawrence G. Sager, "The Incorrigible Constitution," *New York University Law Review* 65 (1990), 893–961, at 955, 958.

69. Edward B. Foley, "Interpretation and Philosophy: Dworkin's Constitution," *Constitutional Commentary* 14 (1997), 151–74.

70. H. Jefferson Powell, *The Moral Tradition of American Constitutionalism*, p. 10.

71. Bruce Ackerman, *We the People: Foundations* (Cambridge, Mass.: Harvard University Press, 1991), p. 43.

72. Ibid., p. 179, quoting *The Federalist*, No. 40.

73. Ibid., p. 195.

74. Ibid., p. 34.

75. Ackerman identifies three constitutional moments: the 1787 founding, the Reconstruction amendments, and the New Deal. The changes in the constitutional order that occurred on the first two occasions were in some sense irregular from the standpoint of the existing constitutional rules and forms. The Federalist Framers disregarded their commission to revise the Articles of Confederation and the requirement of unanimity in amending the Articles. In Reconstruction, the Thirteenth and Fourteenth amendments were irregular to the extent that the ex-Confederate states that ratified them did not participate in the deliberative process that formulated the amendments; the states were in

effect coerced into adopting them. The New Deal regime was not constitutionally irregular if conceived of as a series of institutional adaptations and policy
changes that were determined to be legitimate under existing constitutional
law by the federal judiciary and ultimately the electorate. The New Deal regime was constitutionally irregular, however, if conceived of, as in Ackerman's
account, as the establishment of a distinctive governmental order under new
constitutional principles, presumed to be as binding on courts, government
officials, and political actors as a constitutional revision effected under Article
V. The problem of constitutional amendment options and strategy in the New
Deal is discussed in David E. Kyvig, *Explicit and Authentic Acts: Amending the
U.S. Constitution 1776–1995* (Lawrence: University Press of Kansas, 1996), pp.
289–314.

76. Bruce Ackerman, "A Generation of Betrayal?" *Fordham Law Review* 65
(1997), 1519–36, at 1526.

77. Ibid., p. 1528.

78. Ibid., pp. 1528–29, 1535.

79. Sanford Levinson, ed., *Responding to Imperfection: The Theory and Practice
of Constitutional Amendment* (Princeton, N.J.: Princeton University Press, 1995),
pp. 3–36.

80. Sanford Levinson, *Constitutional Faith* (Princeton, N.J.: Princeton University Press, 1988), p. 36.

81. Levinson, ed., *Responding to Imperfection*, p. 21.

82. Ibid., p. 26.

83. Ibid., p. 26.

84. Ibid., p. 33.

85. Ibid.

86. Ibid., p. 34.

87. Ibid., p. 32.

88. Stephen M. Griffin, "Constitutionalism in the United States: From Theory to Politics," in Sanford Levinson, ed., *Responding to Imperfection*, p. 38; Stephen M. Griffin, *American Constitutionalism: From Theory to Politics* (Princeton,
N.J.: Princeton University Press, 1996), pp. 5, 28, 56.

89. Griffin, "Constitutionalism in the United States: From Theory to Politics," p. 53.

90. Griffin refrains from employing the terminology of the unwritten constitution because he says it simplifies issues that require more detailed explanation. It seems clear, however, that text-based institutional practice is
substantially the same thing as the unwritten constitution asserted in progressive and liberal legal thought in the twentieth century. Griffin, *American Constitutionalism*, p. 55n.

91. Griffin, "Constitutionalism in the United States: From Theory to Politics," p. 43.

92. Ibid.; Griffin, *American Constitutionalism*, p. 53.

93. Ibid., p. 55.

94. Ibid., p. 53.

95. Ibid., p. 55.

96. Ibid., p. 57.

97. Griffin, "Constitutionalism in the United States: From Theory to Politics," p. 61.

98. Griffin, *American Constitutionalism*, p. 211.

99. See James R. Stoner, Jr., *Common Law and Liberal Theory: Coke, Hobbes, and the Origins of American Constitutionalism* (Lawrence: University Press of Kansas, 1992); James E. Herget, *American Jurisprudence, 1870–1970: A History* (Houston: Rice University Press, 1990), pp. 126–29.

100. Sylvia Snowiss, *Judicial Review and the Law of the Constitution* (New Haven, Conn.: Yale University Press, 1990).

101. Henry Paul Monaghan, "Constitutional Common Law," *Harvard Law Review* 89 (1975), 1–45.

102. Ibid., p. 44.

103. Ibid., p. 45.

104. Henry P. Monaghan, "Stare Decisis and Constitutional Adjudication," *Columbia Law Review* 88 (1988), 723–73, at 727–31. In this article Monaghan aligns himself in opposition to original-intent jurisprudence, which he previously supported. See Henry P. Monaghan, "Our Perfect Constitution," *New York University Law Review* 56 (1981), pp. 353–96.

105. Cass R. Sunstein, *The Partial Constitution* (Cambridge, Mass.: Harvard University Press, 1993), pp. 94, 106, 116, 119–21.

106. Ibid., p. 123. In the view of its proponents, constitutional common law adjudication often does not change the Constitution but "translates" it in a contemporary context in a way that preserves the constitutional values contained in the text. Ibid., p. 121. For theoretical discussion of constitutional "translation" as a means of maintaining fidelity to the Constitution, see Lawrence Lessig, "Fidelity and Constraint," *Fordham Law Review* 65 (1997), 1365–1443. The key to constitutional translation is the proposition that the meaning of words depends on the context in which they are uttered. Ibid., p. 1370.

107. Cass R. Sunstein, "Making Amends," *The New Republic*, 3 March 1997, pp. 38–43, at 42.

108. Ibid., p. 43.

109. Ibid. In 1997 an organization, Citizens for the Constitution, was formed with the aim of protecting the Constitution against the threat posed by too frequent advocacy of formal constitutional amendment. In the view of this organization, constitutional amendments are routinely introduced by their supporters as "the favored first-step panacea for all societal ills." Proposing specific public policies, such amendments have "the potential to undermine an American culture that properly treasures and reveres our Constitution." Should they be adopted, they would turn "an effective and enforceable charter of government into a document of faddish aspirations." Citizens for the Constitution, "The Threat to Our Constitution" (Washington, D.C., 1997), p. 1. Sunstein is listed as a member of Citizens for the Constitution.

110. Cass R. Sunstein, "Against Tradition," *Social Philosophy and Policy* 13 (Winter 1996), pp. 207–28, at 208.

111. James E. Fleming, "Fidelity to Our Imperfect Constitution," *Fordham Law Review* 65 (1997), 1335–55, at 1336.

112. Ibid.

113. Ronald Dworkin, "The Arduous Virtue of Fidelity: Originalism, Scalia, Tribe, and Nerve," *Fordham Law Review* 65 (1997), 1249–68, at 1253.

114. Ibid.

115. Ibid., p. 1255.

116. Ibid., p. 1267.

117. Fleming, "Fidelity to Our Imperfect Constitution," pp. 1336, 1346.

118. Earl M. Maltz, *Rethinking Constitutional Law: Originalism, Interventionism, and the Politics of Judicial Review* (Lawrence: University Press of Kansas, 1994), pp. 46–73.

119. Jeffrey Rosen, "Originalist Sin," pp. 27, 36. In this article Rosen analyzed Justice Scalia in the context of the originalist revival. Rosen credited him with redefining the terms of constitutional debate and causing liberal theorists, such as Laurence Tribe and Ronald Dworkin, to talk like originalists. Rosen argued, however, that Scalia is not a true originalist, but a moral traditionalist who is guilty of interjecting his own values into his constitutional decisions. Rosen said Scalia is not the dispassionate guardian of the constitutional text that he professes to be.

120. Antonin Scalia, *A Matter of Interpretation: Federal Courts and the Law* (Princeton, N.J.: Princeton University Press, 1997).

121. Ibid., p. 38.

122. Ibid., p. 9.

123. Scalia recognizes that in earlier centuries, when the declaratory concept of law prevailed, common law judging did not have this character. It became subjective, willful, and politicized in the age of legal realism. Ibid., p. 10.

124. Ibid., p. 4.

125. Ibid., p. 38.

126. Ibid. Scalia says that to ask the intent of the legislative or constitution-writing body in practice becomes the question of what the legislature meant or what a reasonable and intelligent person should have meant. It follows that what the legislature meant is what the judge thinks the legislature meant or, what is the same thing, what the judge thinks is reasonable and intelligent. Ibid., p.18.

127. Ibid., p. 23.

128. Ibid., p. 37.

129. Ibid., p. 38.

130. Ibid., pp. 41–46.

131. S. E. Finer, "Notes towards a History of Constitutions," in Vernon Bogdanor, ed., *Constitutions in Democratic Politics* (Gower, England: Aldershot, 1988), pp. 17–32, at 21.

132. Ibid., p. 31.

133. Harvey C. Mansfield, Jr., *America's Constitutional Soul* (Baltimore, Md.: Johns Hopkins University Press, 1991), pp. 193–208.

134. Grano, "Deconstructing the Constitution," p. 18.

135. The problem of moral evaluation in the study of constitutionalism is discussed with insight by Carl J. Friedrich, *Constitutional Government and De-*

mocracy: Theory and Practice in Europe and America, 4th ed. (Waltham, Mass.: Blaisdell, 1968), pp. 125–28, and M. J. C. Vile, *Constitutionalism and the Separation of Powers* (Oxford: Oxford University Press, 1967), p. 308. In contemporary constitutional law there is abundant discussion of what appears to be an increasing tendency on the part of activist judges to protect controversial decisions by wrapping them in "the dictates of the Constitution's fine garb." Grano, "Deconstructing the Constitution," p. 11. Lino Graglia, a conservative scholar, states that judicial activists protect the judiciary from popular control by obfuscation and mystification, by appealing to the Constitution as "a quasi-sacred document, a mysterious compendium of commands and limitations on the popular will." Lino Graglia, "Judicial Activism: Even on the Right, It's Wrong," *The Public Interest* 95 (1989), 57–74, at 60. On the left, the Critical Legal Studies group has long been known for its reductionist view of legal reasoning as a form of political ideology used by the ruling class to maintain hegemonic control.

136. The relationship between constitutional scholarship and constitutional government is in a general sense the subject of this book. Professional and academic legal scholarship both reflects and influences doctrinal and philosophical tendencies in constitutional practice. In the crisis situation that is seen to exist in late twentieth-century American constitutionalism, some commentators may exaggerate the significance of their critical function. For a candid statement of scholarly ambition in shaping the direction of constitutional law, see Sanford Levinson, "Authorizing Constitutional Text: On the Purported Twenty-Seventh Amendment," *Constitutional Commentary* 11 (1994), 101–14. Levinson states that in their role as textbook and treatise writers, legal academics have power, influence, and authority as "legal decision makers." As theorists and critics, they have the ability to create meaning and act as legitimators and delegitimators. Ibid., pp. 108, 112.

137. 131 L Ed 2d 626, at 642.

138. Ibid., p. 643. In a dissenting opinion, Justice Breyer said the case should be decided by adherence to the Court's historical development of commerce clause jurisprudence. This led Breyer to regard the text of the commerce clause not as a legal conception, but as referring to practical relationships in society. 115 S. Ct. 1624 (1995) at 1659.

139. 116 S. Ct. 1114 (1996) at 1131.

140. Ibid.

141. Ibid., p. 1165.

142. Ibid., p. 1169.

143. Ibid., p. 1177. Although the common law was not received into constitutional law at the founding, Justice Souter recognized that the Supreme Court adopted a doctrine of federal common law under the Eleventh Amendment in *Hans v. Louisiana* (1890). Souter accepted *Hans* because it formed a historic strand in the federal-state relationship that warranted protection under the doctrine of stare decisis. Ibid., p. 1184.

144. 117 S. Ct. 2356 (1997) at 2370.

145. Ibid., p. 2376.

146. Ibid., p. 2378. Justice Scalia also enumerated the separation of powers and the unity of the executive branch as structural principles in the Constitution.

147. Ibid., p. 2379.

148. Ibid., p. 2387.

149. Ibid., p. 2389.

150. Ibid., pp. 2393–94.

151. *U.S. Term Limits Inc. v. Ray Thornton et al.* 1995 WL 306517 *2 (U.S.), 3.

152. Ibid., p. 38.

153. Stephen M. Griffin, "What Is Constitutional Theory? The Newer Theory and the Decline of the Learned Tradition," *Southern California Law Review* 62 (1989), 493–538.

154. Cass R. Sunstein, "Foreword: Leaving Things Undecided," *Harvard Law Review* 110 (1996), 6–101, at 13–14. In the spectrum of adjudicative theories, substantive-values activism and textualist-originalism are at the extremes, and middle-ground positions are based on constitutional history, structure, tradition, case law, and doctrinal development.

155. Ibid., p. 14.

156. David A. Strauss, "Common Law Constitutional Interpretation," *University of Chicago Law Review* 63 (1996), 877–936, at 878.

157. *Planned Parenthood of Southeastern Pennsylvania v. Casey*, 112 S. Ct. 2791 (1992), at 2814.

158. Ibid., p. 2815.

159. Ibid.

160. Ibid., p. 2814.

161. Ibid.

162. Ibid., p. 2815.

163. In a dissenting opinion, Chief Justice Rehnquist described the plurality's view of stare decisis as "truly novel." He said it meant that "when the Court has ruled on a divisive issue, it is apparently prevented from overruling that decision for the sole reason that it was incorrect, *unless opposition to the original decision has died away.*" Ibid., p. 2863.

164. Ibid., p. 2816.

165. Horwitz, "Foreword: The Constitution of Change," pp. 116–17.

166. Gerard V. Bradley, "Shall We Ratify the New Constitution? The Judicial Manifesto in *Casey* and *Lee*," in Terry Eastland, ed., *Benchmarks: Great Constitutional Controversies in the Supreme Court* (Grand Rapids, Mich.: Wm. B. Werdman's, 1994), pp. 117–140, at 125–27.

167. Ibid., pp. 125–26.

168. Referred to by Bradley as the "megaright" in the new constitution, the definition of this right is worth noting as a reflection of the ambitious scope of the plurality justices' theoretical project. The opinion states: "At the heart of liberty is the right to define one's concept of existence, of meaning, the universe, and of the mystery of human life. Beliefs about these matters could not define the attributes of personhood were they formed under the compulsion of the State." 112 S. Ct. 2807.

169. Bradley, "Shall We Ratify the New Constitution?" pp. 130–31.

170. Bradley says: "The sheer fact of effectiveness—that a given body's pronouncement can and will be taken as authoritative—may be taken to engender obligation *if* in truth the authority secures and advances the common good." Ibid., p. 129. He opposes ratification of the new Constitution asserted in *Casey*, but not because it rests on a false interpretation of the 1787 Constitution. He says that "now that we are clearheaded," that kind of error is beside the point. "We are asking about an original act of constitution-making, not interpretation of settled authorities." Ibid., p. 132.

171. Steven G. Calabresi, "The Tradition of the Written Constitution: A Comment on Professor Lessig's Theory of Translation," *Fordham Law Review* 65 (1997), 1435–56; Michael W. McConnell, "The Importance of Humility in Judicial Review: A Comment on Ronald Dworkin's 'Moral Reading' of the Constitution," *Fordham Law Review* 65 (1997), 1269–93; Stephen B. Presser, *Recapturing the Constitution: Race, Religion, and Abortion Reconsidered* (Washington: Regnery, 1994).

172. Ronald Dworkin, "The Arduous Virtue of Fidelity," p. 1250.

173. Louis Michael Seidman, "*Romer*'s Radicalism: The Unexpected Revival of Warren Court Activism," *1996 Supreme Court Review*, 67–121, at 105–06.

174. Although indirectly more than directly, this view is confirmed in a study by Mark A. Graber of how contemporary constitutional theorists use the *Dred Scott* case to show the superiority of their approach to constitutional interpretation and the fallacy of other approaches. Arguing that the superiority of any theory cannot be demonstrated, Graber says: "No contemporary approach to the judicial function in constitutional cases is immune to proslavery results in the particular fact situation presented by *Dred Scott* or, for that matter, in the broader context provided by the American law of slavery." Mark A. Graber, "Desperately Ducking Slavery: *Dred Scott* and Contemporary Constitutional Theory," *Constitutional Commentary* 14 (1997), 271–318, at 280.

175. See the discussion in Walter F. Murphy, James E. Fleming, and William F. Harris, *American Constitutional Interpretation* (Mineola, N.Y.: The Foundation Press, 1986), Part 2: "*What Is the Constitution?*" pp. 81–183.

176. See Louis Fisher, "Constitutional Interpretation by Members of Congress," *North Carolina Law Review* 63 (1985), 707–47, and Louis Fisher, "The Curious Belief in Judicial Supremacy," *Suffolk University Law Review* 25 (1991), 85–116.

177. Matthew J. Franck, *Against the Imperial Judiciary: The Supreme Court vs. the Sovereignty of the People* (Lawrence: University Press of Kansas, 1996), pp. 208–14.

178. *The Federalist Papers*, intro. by Clinton Rossiter (New York: New American Library, 1961), p. 229.

179. Kevin M. Stack, "The Practice of Dissent in the Supreme Court," *Yale Law Journal* 105 (1996), 2235–59, at 2246.

180. *The Federalist Papers*, p. 325.

181. In *City of Boerne v. Flores* (1997), although split on the substantive question of church-state separation, the Court was unanimous in its view that the

Court's "exposition of the Constitution" is controlling and determinative throughout the federal government. 138 L Ed 2d 624, at 638. While stating that Congress has an obligation to draw its own conclusions regarding the Constitution's meaning, Justice O'Connor, in a dissenting opinion, said: "when it enacts legislation in furtherance of its delegated powers, Congress must make its judgments consistent with this Court's exposition of the Constitution and with the limits placed on its legislative authority by provisions such as the Fourteenth Amendment." 117 S. Ct. 2157, at 2176.

182. See the dissenting opinion of Justice Breyer in *U.S. v. Lopez*, 115 S. Ct. 1624, at 1659.

183. In my view there is reason to question Justice Scalia's statement, apparently offered as historical description: "The American people have been converted to belief in The Living Constitution, a 'morphing' document that means, from age to age, what it ought to mean." *A Matter of Interpretation: Federal Courts and the Law*, p. 47. A more accurate description of the eclectic-pluralistic constitutional outlook of the late twentieth century is found in Michael Kammen, *A Machine That Would Go of Itself: The Constitution in American Culture* (New York: Random House, 1986).

Index

About the Author

Herman Belz is professor of history at the University of Maryland at College Park and academic advisor to the James Madison Memorial Fellowship Foundation, Washington, D.C. He is the author of *Abraham Lincoln, Constitutionalism, and Equal Rights in the Civil War Era* (1998), *Equality Transformed: A Quarter Century of Affirmative Action* (1991), and several works on the Civil War and Reconstruction including *Reconstructing the Union: Theory and Policy during the Civil War* (1969). He is coauthor of *The American Constitution: Its Origins and Development* (7th ed., 1991). He has been the recipient of numerous awards including fellowships from the John Simon Guggenheim Memorial Fellowship Foundation, the American Bar Foundation, the Earhart Foundation, the Social Philosophy and Policy Center at Bowling Green State University, and the American Historical Association and American Political Science Association. In 1966 he received the Albert J. Beveridge Award of the American Historical Association.